Political Economy
of
Public Distribution System in India

ABOUT THE AUTHOR

Bhaskar Majumder is a Senior Faculty in Economics in G.B. Pant Social Science Institute, University of Allahabad, Allahabad. He is also a Visiting Faculty at the Malaviya Centre for Peace Research, Banaras Hindu University, Varanasi. He did his M. Phil. and D. Phil. from the University of Calcutta. Dr. Majumder has so far published more than sixty papers in journals of national and international repute. He has authored seven books and contributed several chapters in books edited by eminent scholars. He has completed a number of research projects supported by Planning Commission, Government of India, ICSSR, World Bank, etc.

Political Economy of Public Distribution System in India

BHASKAR MAJUMDER
G.B. Pant Social Science Institute,
Allahabad

CONCEPT PUBLISHING COMPANY, NEW DELHI-110059

ISBN-13: 978-81-8069-641-1 **ISBN-10: 81-8069-641-3**

First Published 2009

Published and Printed by

Concept
Since 1974

Concept Publishing Company
Regd. Office:
A/15-16, Commercial Block, Mohan Garden
New Delhi-110059 (India)
Phones : 25351460, 25351794, *Fax* : 091-11-25357109
Email : publishing@conceptpub.com,
website: www.conceptpub.com

Editorial Office:
H-13, Bali Nagar, New Delhi-110 015, India.

Cataloging in Publication Data--*Courtesy:* D.K. Agencies (P) Ltd. <docinfo@dkagencies.com>

Majumder, Bhaskar, 1956-
Political economy of public distribution system in India / Bhaskar Majumder.
p. cm.
Study conducted in Uttar Pradesh, India.
Includes bibliographical references (p.).
Includes index.
ISBN 13: 9788180696411 ISBN 10: 8180696413

1. Food supply--Government policy--India--Uttar Pradesh. 2. Rationing--India--Uttar Pradesh. 3. Poor--India--Uttar Pradesh. 4. Household surveys--India--Uttar Pradesh--Statistics. I. Title.

DDC 338.19542 22

For My Mother

Preface

National food self-sufficiency by production and presence of food in the economy, or in the market, does not automatically ensure food security. Even the ability to buy may not guarantee food security of the poor unless it is accompanied by a functioning distribution system. The public distribution system as a social safety net can be appreciated by the fact that aggregate availability of foodgrains *per se* is not enough to ensure the ability of people at the bottom to buy foodgrains.

This book examines the extent to which the Public Distribution System (PDS) in India has succeeded in providing essential commodities to the people living below poverty line (BPL). Keeping in mind this purpose, it examines the functioning of the delivery system beginning from the procurement of food grains by the government till their distribution to the beneficiaries of the Public Distribution System. The role of the Panchayati Raj Institutions (PRIs) in ensuring the smooth delivery system for food security of the poor has also been examined in addition to analyzing the constraints faced by Fair Price Shops (FPSs) meant to deliver essential commodities to the households. The success of the system is understood by the extent of fulfilment of consumption requirements of essential commodities of the households particularly at the bottom of the economic ladder. The book examines why the poor fail to have access to life-support commodities from the FPSs. Do the factors like absence of purchasing power, non-information about distribution of items, absence of the household while items are distributed, short period of distribution, long distance of the shop from the residence and cardlessness explain the deprivation, if it is there, of the target poor or is it ignorance of the poor that obstructs them from having access to the system? In addition to the deprived households, the book also looks into the reasons for exclusion of the eligible non-beneficiaries. Do the people consider PDS related benefits as 'benevolence of the government (*sarkar*)' or do they consider it as a component of their 'right to food'? Are the included and excluded people aware of the system? Do the Panchayats and Government machinery work for the success of the system and suggest for its rectification as and when warranted? These are some of the questions dealt with in this book. In addition to these questions the book also examines if the existing distributive set up is efficient to run the PDS.

As a case study we have examined the PDS in Uttar Pradesh, which is alleged to have remained defective because of non-transparency and lack of coordination between the Supply Department, Gram Panchayats and Block Offices. The local power structure characterized by the village Pradhan-FPS dealer nexus in a state of ignorance and fear of the downtrodden are alleged to go against the poor. The role of the Supply inspector is alleged to oil the corrupt machinery by receiving 'speed money' on behalf of the whole system. From the first step of getting dealership to the final consumption point, the political-administrative intervention complicates the system and 'loot' is carried out in the name of 'vigilance' by the competent authority.

Since the FPS dealers, the polity and the local administration in the shape of the Gram Pradhan are the bottommost rung of the PDS, the local power structure in the context of PDS is often explained by the relations between them. In the book we will examine the kind of relationship existing between these three vertices of the triangle. As a corollary we will examine our apprehension that the 'fear' of the local power structure obstructs the deprived poor people from complaining against the FPS dealers. The fear may be because of the prevailing or perceived strong nexus between the FPS dealers and the powerful people of their village. Ignorance of the deprived majority may be another reason for them to keep silent. In spite of being aware of the connivance they may abstain from lodging their complaints because of 'voicelessness of the poor' and inability to miss a day's wage-labour. Social insecurity at the local level and desire to avoid conflict may be other reasons for not lodging complaints against the corrupt system. Expressing their voice may also cause them to be penalized by being excluded from the existing meagre entitlement. Poor people also act based on past experience and in case of no expected outcome in response to complaints lodged earlier future complaints may be nipped in the bud.

Some other allegations regarding the system like leakage of foodgrains from godowns, purchase of foodgrains from open market, subsidy grabbed by the non-poor, purchase of foodgrains by private corporate firms from the field, bribing and other types of corruption in the system emanate from the weaknesses built-in and/or inserted in the system are examined in this book. The book explores these questions and apprehensions for the less than optimum functioning of the system in India and tries to find their answers within the political economy frame of food security in India.

The book is an offshoot of a research project that I completed for the Planning Commission, Government of India in 2006. I wholeheartedly thank Sri A.S. Ahluwalia, Adviser in the Commission, Sri Harminder Singh, Deputy Secretary to the Government of India, Sri Anil Malhotra, Deputy Secretary to the Government of India and Mr. S.A. Rahim, Under Secretary to the Government of India for providing support for the research. I take the opportunity to thank the Secretary, Food and Civil Supplies, Government of UP, all the DMs, CDOs, DSOs and Supply Inspectors for providing support in the field. I thank the Gram Pradhans and other representatives of the Panchayats, the FPS dealers, the in-charge of Godowns and Depot-in-charge for cooperating in our efforts to collect data. I cannot forget to thank the households without whose support we could not have collected necessary data.

I take the opportunity to thank Jean Dreze, Ravi Srivastava, Kripa Shankar, Ajit Singh and D.M. Diwakar for providing me adequate inputs on the theme. I must mention the names of my project team without whom the endeavour would have remained incomplete. They are M. G. Gupta and J.N. Jha, the research officers, S. Jaiswal, the computer assistant, and Divanath Mishra, the research assistant. Ms Mousumi Majumder provided me love's labour by translating the whole field diary from Hindi to English. I cannot forget my family at Allahabad and Kolkata who are always with me with their love and blessings in my academic efforts.

I believe the book will be useful for not only the decision-makers in the Government but also for the students, civil society organizations and concerned citizens of the country.

Contents

List of Tables

List of Boxes

1

Public Distribution System in India: An Overview

1.1 PDS in India: The History

The Bengal Famine of 1943 and food scarcity during the Second World War (1939-45) were the starting points of the post-independence agricultural policy and the public distribution system of India. An official government report conservatively estimated that by 1944 one and a half million lives had been lost in the 1943 famine. Public intervention in Indian agriculture after independence became the compulsion of the government to counteract the food scarcity that had occurred in the colonial period. By 1947, about 54 million people in urban India were covered by statutory rationing and an additional 19 million by other forms of public distribution (Dantwala, 1993, p. 182). At present, as reported by the 10th Five Year Plan, Planning Commission, Government of India, 'with a network of more than 4.62 lakh fair price shops (FPSs) distributing commodities worth more than Rs. 30,000 crore annually to about 160 million families, the PDS in India is perhaps the largest distribution network of its kind in the world (Planning Commission, 2002-07, Vol. II, p. 367).

The root of food security through PDS goes to Kautilyan '*Arthashastra*'. In his analysis on the methods of counteracting the effects of famine, Kautilya suggests the following:

- Distribute to the public, on concessional terms, seeds and food from the royal stores;
- Undertake food-for-work programmes such as building forts or irrigation works;
- Share out the royal food stocks;

- Commander, for public distribution, private stocks of food;
- Seek the help of friendly kings;
- Shift the affected population to a different region;
- Encourage (temporary) migration to another country;
- Move the entire population (with the King and Court) to a region or country with abundant harvest or near the sea, lakes or rivers; and
- Supplement the harvest with additional cultivation of grain, vegetables, roots and fruits, by fishing and by hunting deer, cattle, birds and wild animals (Rangarajan, 1987, p. 130).

According to Kautilya, 'social security was both a private and a state matter. The primary responsibility for maintaining the family—wife, children, parents, minor brothers and unmarried or widowed sisters—lay with the head of the family; no one could become an ascetic without first providing for his wife and children. ...However, the state had the obligation to provide a safety net and maintain children, the aged, childless women and the helpless' (Rangarajan, 1987, p. 92).

The history behind introduction of the PDS in India is rooted in famines and food scarcities during the entire period of British colonial rule in India. The first one was the Bengal famine of 1770. An estimated ten million people died in this famine that was essentially the consequence of plunder by the colonists of the East India Company. Between 1860 and 1910, there occurred twenty major famines and scarcities. The last famine in British India was the Bengal famine of 1943 (Ghose, 1999, p. 355).

Table 1.1: Pre-Independence Famines in British (Colonial) India, 1770-1943

Year	*Event*
1770	Formidable famine in Bengal
1770-1858	Frequent and severe famines
1861-80	Frequent and severe famines
1880-96	Very few famines
1896-97	Large-scale famine affecting large parts of India
1899-1900	Large-scale famine
1901-43	Very few famines
1943	Bengal famine

Source: Structured from Dreze, Jean, 1990, 'Famine Prevention in India', in *The Political Economy of Hunger*, Ed. by Dreze, Jean and Sen, Amartya, Vol. 2, p. 16.

During the colonial period a number of committees were formed to study the famines that had occurred in the country at various times in

British India, which submitted their reports from time-to-time. These included the Report of Baird Smith on the 1860-61 famine, the 1880 Famine Commission Report, the Famine Commission Report on the 1896-97 famine, Famine Commission Report on the 1899-1900 famine, 1945 Famine Commission Report on the Bengal Famine (Dreze, 1990, p. 16). The 1880 Famine Commission Report was followed by the Famine Codes which embodied a number of famine relief strategies whose backbone was the organization of massive public works (Dreze, 1990, p. 26).

In 1943 the first Foodgrains Policy Committee was formed which recommended only informal rationing in rural areas. By implication, free or open market in foodgrains was permitted in the rural areas, that is, the producing areas (Dandekar, 1994, p. 209). After independence in 1947 the government was expected to do away with controls on production, distribution, and prices of foodgrains. The Foodgrains Policy Committee set up in that year suggested progressive decontrol in the foodgrains sector following which a policy of gradual decontrol was announced by the government in November 1947 (GOI, 1976, Part I, p. 145). 'However, the expectation that decontrol would lead to dishoarding of stocks, increase in procurement and stability in prices did not materialize and prices began rising fast... A reversion to controls was, therefore, decided upon in September 1948. With the return of controls, procurement of adequate stocks for public distribution assumed crucial importance' (GOI, 1976, Part I, p. 145). By August 1949 the Government of India started receiving complaints on quality of foodgrains distributed and appointed the Foodgrains Investigation Committee that submitted its report on April 30, 1950 confirming the complaints (Dandekar, 1994, p. 212). In view of the persisting gap between the commitments of public distribution and the procurement, a Foodgrains Procurement Committee was appointed on February 8, 1950, in pursuance of the recommendations of the All India Food Ministers' Conference held in August 1949. The Foodgrains Procurement Committee of 1950 recommended 'monopoly procurement of foodgrains, abolition of the free market, imposition of complete statutory rationing in towns with a population of 50,000 and above and informal rationing elsewhere' (GOI, 1976, Part I, p. 145). Since it was admitted by the Government of India that any scheme of decontrol would involve risks, hence on 8th July, 1952, the Government issued the Foodgrains (Licensing and Procurement) Order, 1952. This Order prohibited any individual from engaging in any business which involved purchase, sale or storage for sale of any foodgrains except under and in accordance with a licence issued by the state governments (Dandekar, 1994, p. 216). The Essential Commodities Act, 1955, entrusted the government with taking steps for regulation of 'production, supply, distribution and trade in essential commodities for securing equitable distribution' (GOI, 1976, Part I, p. 167). Following the recommendations of the Foodgrains Prices Committee set up in 1964, there came an Agricultural Price Commission in January 1965. The important point is that the floor or support prices for major foodgrains recommended by the Committee for 1964-65 were 'generally higher than the average post-harvest prices during the preceding three seasons' (GOI, 1976, Part I, p. 167). It is thus not an automatic fact that the public distribution will depress the price against the producers-sellers. The National Commission on Agriculture in fact recognized that 'the minimum support price should be fair to the farmer and should cover his cost of production and leave him a reasonable margin of profit' (GOI, 1976, Part II, p. 83).

Table 1.2: Committees Formed by Government of India, Pre-Green Revolution Period

Year	*Committees*
1943	Foodgrains Policy Committee
1947	Foodgrains Policy Committee
1949	Foodgrains Investigation Committee
1950	Foodgrains Procurement Committee
1964	Foodgrains Prices Committee
1965	Agricultural Price Commission

Source: Available literature.

The Essential Commodities (EC) Act that came into force in 1955 was meant to facilitate government regulation of trade and commerce. The EC Act, 1955 empowered the public officials in enforcing the public distribution system. The 1955 Act was not the first one for imposition of controls on trade and distribution but it was the first one in independent India. The British Colonial Government under the Defence of India Rules had implemented some control measures. Since 1946, there came legislation in the form of the Essential Supplies (Temporary Powers) Act, which was replaced by the EC Act of 1955 (Mooij, 1999, p. 193). The number of commodities declared essential under this Act was 10 items.

The PDS soon assumed the status of being the centerpiece in the anti-poverty programme. The plentiful supplies of foodgrains generated by the Green Revolution were matched by the ambitious target of extending the PDS to cover the entire population—both rural and urban (Rao, 2001, p. 82). In 1992 the number of items too rapidly increased to 60. In August of that year it was decided to extend the EC (Special Provisions) Act by another five years. Under this system, the price at which government procures foodgrains determines the price at which consumers receive foodgrains through the PDS. From the beginning, the Government of India has made it clear that remunerative prices are to be a central feature of its policy towards agriculture. The concept of state trading was revived in January 1965 when, by an Act of Parliament, the Government of India set up the Food Corporation of India (FCI). For procurement and price setting respectively, there came the FCI and the Agricultural Prices Commission (now Commission for Agricultural Costs and Prices) in 1965. The post-1965 period thus brought about institutionalized arrangements and procedure for procurement, stocks, pricing, and distribution of foodgrains.

The procurement of foodgrains for distribution through PDS is maintained through domestic procurement rather than through imports. Probably this was facilitated by the Green Revolution of the late 1960s. The availability of foodgrains that are distributed through the PDS is ensured through a network of Fair Price Shops (FPSs) licensed by the State/UT administrations where each such shop is envisaged to serve a population of 2000. From over 4 lakhs in March 1992, the number of FPSs rose to over 4.33 lakhs as on 31 March, 1995. Most of these FPSs are in rural areas. In 1995, the rural areas had three times the number of FPSs in the urban areas.

1.2 Public Distribution System: The Rationale

The objective of the Government of India's Food Security Policy is to ensure availability of foodgrains to the public at an affordable price. The objectives are thus (i) ensuring adequacy or sufficiency in supply of foodgrains, and (ii) distributing foodgrains at an affordable price. The Public Distribution System (PDS), which continues to exist in the country since the Second World War, attempts to meet these twin objectives (GOI, 1995-96, p. 88). In view of the Government of India, 'the PDS aims at insulating the consumer from the impact of rising prices of these commodities and maintaining the minimum nutritional status of our population. The PDS supplies have a stabilizing effect on open market prices by increasing availability, removing scarcity psychosis and deterring speculative tendencies' (GOI, 1991-92, Part II, p. 53).

The public distribution system as a social safety net can be appreciated by the fact that aggregate availability of foodgrains *per se* is not enough to ensure the ability to acquire foodgrains. Production does not automatically guarantee consumption. The beginning of initial production is an unknown world explorable to man. The urge for survival or initial material existence compels him to transform nature (observable and accessible to him) by application of his labour power. Initial output is produced by man independent of his own choice and independent of the question of any consensus. It is the individual compulsion which becomes a social phenomenon because of (i) the inability of the individual to produce all the commodities he needs; (ii) the choice-neutrality of any particular individual in the sense that if (i) holds good, he will have to produce in excess for others and hence exchange. At the same time, it is a fact that location of individuals in the production map shows the location of the same individuals in the consumption map. The latter, namely, the relative command of individuals over commodities produced may not satisfy all individuals equally. Thus, there comes command-differential over commodities produced. The command differential is derived from resource differential: unequal resources owned and transformed by the resource owners in the domain of production of commodities (Majumder, 1998, pp. 635-36). Concentrating on production of food, the corollary is that the mere presence of food in the economy, or in the market, does not entitle a person to consume it (Dreze and Sen, 1989, p. 9). The rural poor in developing (income-poor) countries and the urban poor with inadequate purchasing power, neither of the categories having regular employment (paid work) or unemployment benefits, are often denied the right to food. For such poor, the exercise of the right to food and being free from hunger are synonymous (Zhou and Gandhi, 2002, p. 533). Even the ability to buy may not guarantee food security, unless there is an efficient distribution system (Suryanarayana, 2000, p. 80). Food security may be viewed from a number of angles like spatial (regional, national, international) and cross-sectional. This book deals with cross-sectional (of the poor section in society) security. As opined by the 10th Five Year Plan, Planning Commission, Government of India, 'the availability of food grains is not a sufficient condition to ensure food security to the poor. It is also necessary that the poor have sufficient means to purchase food. The capacity of the poor to purchase food can be ensured in two ways—by raising the incomes or supplying food grains at subsidized prices. While employment generation programmes attempt the first solution, the PDS is the mechanism for the second option' (Planning Commission, 2002-07, Vol. II, p. 367). Colonial history of India also confirms that 'the major famines and scarcities occurred during a period when India was a food surplus country and was in fact exporting large quantities of foodgrains'. At the national level at least, famines in British India 'were not precipitated by absolute shortages of food caused by uncontrollable vagaries of nature' (Ghose, 1999, p. 359). The command over food of different economic cross-sections of population in an economy depends on many legal-institutional factors including governance, political will and competence, target setting, ownership and control over food etc. 'The overall availability of food is thus a very poor guide to the fortunes of different socio-economic groups' (Dreze and Sen, 1989, p. 26). The Bangladesh food famine of 1974 was delinked from reduced food availability as was the case of 1973 Ethiopian food famine (Dreze and Sen, 1989, pp. 27-28). Historically, we find no one-to-one causal relation between per capita availability of food and deprivation of a section of population in terms of food consumption.

Food security and self-sufficiency in food are two different issues, though linked in a national economy in the context of size of population, with different cross-sections with and without purchasing power. Macro self-sufficiency in food (taking food economy as the single unit) is no guarantee of food security. Many of the countries in Asia, Africa and Latin America have large and increasing size of population. Many of this increased size remain hungry and malnourished. For example, in 1985 about 100 million people or about one-fourth of the settled population in Africa, were estimated to have remained chronically hungry and malnourished. In the mid-1980s, expenditure on food import came to be around 20.0 per cent of the total export earnings of Africa, compared to 16.0 per cent in 1980 and much less in 1970 (Platteau, 1990, p. 280). An economy needs to import food whenever domestic supply falls short of demand at the macro level, while hunger and malnutrition may be because of absence of purchasing power of the bottom sections of the population in the same economy (Platteau, 1990, p. 279). The task is to ensure food security of the vulnerable sections of the economy, even if it is at the cost of food imports. However, for a large economy like India with a population more than 1000 millions now the ability to import food is limited. For example, in 1989 India's rice production was five times world trade in rice and India's wheat production was half of world trade in wheat. In 1989 India produced 21.2 per cent of world output of rice and 10.0 per cent of world output of wheat (Kashyap, 2002, p. 474). The better solution for a large economy like India is not to depend on imports of food to ensure food security because of the absolute consumption requirements of food which may exceed what is exported by the rest of the world. This is because the advanced countries have shifted away from production of food while the developing countries produce food basically to ensure food-feed equilibrium within the national economy. Hence, the rationale of intervention by the Government in the food production-distribution frame comes.

At the all-India level, between 1972-73 and 1993-94, according to National Sample Survey Organization (NSSO) data, per capita consumption of cereals declined from 15.3 to 13.4 kg per month over the two decades. During these two decades ending 1993-94, there occurred a steady decline in the food share from about 73 per cent to 55 per cent at the all-India level. This decrease occurred in all regions. As informed by the NSSO, food shares declined for all income groups, including the first (poorest) quartile (Meenakshi, 2000, pp. 34-35). This is in spite of the fact that the poor people continue to spend most of their budget on food and much higher than the percentage spent by the non-poor on food. This seems to confirm Engel's Law, which says that economic development is accompanied by declining food shares. However, the converse is not necessarily true, namely that declined and declining food share implies economic development. Even if it implies economic development then the social base of that development is weak, so that it becomes unsustainable. The flexibility in the consumption habit of the vulnerable sections of the society may conceal the real reasons of reductions in food consumption, sometimes occasionally. For example, 'the reduction of food consumption may be an early response to the threat of entitlement failure, apparently motivated, at least partly, by the preservation of productive assets' (Dreze and Sen, 1989, p. 77). The decline in per capita consumption of food per period may, however, be attributable to the changed inner composition of food. Bennett's Law argues that consumers gradually switch to a more expensive diet, substituting quality for quantity. This is confirmed in the Indian context by the NSSO data. During the period from 1972-73 to 1993-94, the decline in per capita consumption of cereals is wholly attributable to a decline in coarse cereal consumption, down from 4.8 kg to 2 kg per capita per month. An increase in wheat consumption from 3.9 kg to 4.4 kg per capita per month was not enough to compensate for the decline in total cereal consumption. The consumption of rice remained virtually unchanged during this period (Meenakshi, 2000, p. 35). Following NSSO data, the substitution away from coarse cereals into rice was prominent in the lower income groups and the non-poor sections experienced almost no change in the consumption of rice and wheat. The reason is likely to be that the non-poor section already has enough quantities of high quality cereals to the extent of their satiety. The fact remains that before the income-poor population shift from cereals to non-cereals, they shift from less expensive cereals to more expensive cereals. In the Indian context, this implies a switch away from the coarse cereals to either wheat or rice, or both.

The PDS has remained a major instrument to execute the Government of India's economic policy to protect the poor. Public intervention in the foodgrains market aims at procurement of foodgrains for public distribution and maintenance of buffer stocks to ensure not only short-term but also long-term stability of prices of essential commodities and protect the interest of the consumers. Procurement of foodgrains also ensures remunerative returns to the farmers and provides them incentives to invest more on agriculture and to ensure that in the event of any glut or due to any other reason, the market prices do not fall below the support prices (GOI, 1991-92, p. 55).

The purpose of the Government of India, since the early 1970s when it started following the policy of Minimum Support Price (MSP), was 'to ensure that farmers get remunerative prices for their produce and there is no distress sale particularly during the harvesting season' (GOI, 1998-99, p. 73). As declared by the government, 'procurement prices are based on support prices announced by the government. The procurement operations of wheat, paddy and coarse grains are totally voluntary. The producers have the option to sell their produce to FCI/ State agencies at support prices or in the open market whichever is advantageous to them' (GOI, 1998-99, p. 70). The PDS aims at ensuring stability in the foodgrains market when open market prices of foodgrains fluctuate less because of steady availability in the hands of the government. This removes scarcity psychosis and checks speculative tendencies. The disadvantaged and vulnerable sections of the society are the targets of this PDS. The government also pledges to pay attention to distress areas like drought prone areas, desert areas, tribal areas, urban slum areas and selected hilly areas. From June 1992, a special scheme to strengthen the PDS was introduced by inclusion of additional items like tea, soap, iodized salt and pulses to serve the tribal and hilly population in the backward and remote areas (GOI, 1994-95, p. 78). The reasons of this special scheme seem to be both poor infrastructure and income-poverty. The Integrated Tribal Development Project (ITDP) is an example of the concern of the Government of India to provide foodgrains (wheat and rice) at special subsidized rates (below PDS rates) for tribal people (Government of India, 1991-92, p. 54). On June 1, 1997, the GOI introduced a revised scheme of distribution known as Targeted Public Distribution System (TPDS). This showed a deviation from the earlier ones in the sense that since 1997 the distribution of foodgrains would be operated under two-tier system of delivery to households, those below poverty line (BPL) and those above poverty line (APL). The BPL families were planned to receive foodgrains at heavily subsidized prices (Government of India, 1998-99, p. 69). To execute PDS and TPDS the government had to procure foodgrains at the prices declared by the government. The government believed that the procurement of foodgrains would serve the objective of providing price security to the farmers, which would induce them to sustain production levels. This was in addition to PDS working as 'an instrument to protect the vulnerable sections against price volatility' (GOI, 1998-99, p. 70).

1.3 Revamped Public Distribution System: Some Features

In 1991 the Government initiated, in consultation with the State Governments and the Union Territory (UT) administrations, steps to revamp the PDS to improve its reach based on an area approach (GOI, 1991-92, Part II, p. 53). Preference was planned to be given in this revamped system to the population living in the most difficult areas of the country. This included areas such as the drought prone areas, desert areas, tribal areas, certain designated hilly areas and the urban slum areas (*ibid.*). In June 1992 a Revamped Public Distribution System (RPDS) was thus launched in 1,700 blocks of the country. For the tribal, hill and arid area populations remotely located and having poor infrastructure, additional items like tea, soap, pulses and iodized salt were made available under the RPDS. It was decided by the Government of India during mid-1990s that the geographical coverage of RPDS would be extended to the entire 2,446 Employment Assurance Scheme (EAS) Blocks (GOI, 1995-96, p. 84). Under the scheme of RPDS, foodgrains (rice and wheat) are allocated to states and union territories for RPDS blocks at lower prices; Rs. 50 per quintal lower than Central issue prices (CIPs) for normal PDS blocks. The State Governments are required to ensure that the retail prices of these commodities in these blocks are not higher than CIPs by more than 25 paise per kg. Sugar is also distributed at lower prices (GOI, 1992-93, p. 90). The CIPs (ex-FCI godowns) are fixed by the Central Government for PDS as well as RPDS. The retail end prices for PDS and

RPDS are fixed by the State Governments, taking into account the transportation cost and the dealer's commission (GOI, 1995-96, p. 87). The difference between the PDS and the RPDS in terms of retail end prices is that for RPDS, a maximum ceiling of Rs. 25 per quintal has been fixed by Central Government on account of transportation cost etc., which can be built up by State Government in fixing retail prices for RPDS (GOI, 1995-96, p. 87).

The Programme Evaluation Organization of the Planning Commission identified four major weaknesses of the RPDS. These were (i) proliferation of bogus cards, (ii) inadequate storage arrangements, (iii) ineffective functioning of vigilance committee, and (iv) failure to issue ration cards to all eligible households (Dev and Ranade, 1997, p. 67).

1.4 Targeted Public Distribution System: Features

Following the recommendations of the Chief Ministers' Conference held in July 1996, an effort was made to further streamline the PDS. Thus, the Targeted Public Distribution System (TPDS) was launched in June 1997. This also coincided with the celebration of completion of fifty years of India's independence. The PDS, as it was being implemented earlier, had been criticized for its urban bias and its failure to serve effectively the poorer sections of the population. It was also criticized for its negligible coverage in the states with the highest concentration of the rural poor and lack of transparent and accountable arrangements for delivery (Planning Commission, 2002-2007, Vol. II, p. 368). The latent problem was that a sizeable number of marginalized people, in the absence of cash income that can be transformed into purchasing power are excluded from the planning process because they do not constitute effective demand. This is true irrespective of the technological (green) revolution after the mid-1960s in India. Thus, the TPDS came to replace the erstwhile PDS from June 1997. This system divided the potential beneficiaries into families Below Poverty Line (BPL) and those Above Poverty Line (APL). Under TPDS the Government was committed to distribute 10 kgs of foodgrains per month per BPL family at a price equal to half of the economic cost of FCI. Quantity of foodgrains earmarked to meet BPL requirements was 72 lakh tonnes per annum benefiting an estimated 6 crores population (GOI, 1999-2000, pp. 79-80). The Lakdawala Committee of the Planning Commission calculated the number of poor in each state. The identification of the poor was to be done by the states. The emphasis was on inclusion of only the poor and vulnerable sections of the society such as landless agricultural labourers, marginal farmers, artisans/craftsmen in the rural areas and slum dwellers and daily wage earners in the informal sector in the urban areas (Planning Commission, 2002-07, Vol. II, p. 368). The State Governments were assigned the task to streamline the PDS by issuing special cards to BPL families and distributing essential items under TPDS to them at specially subsidized prices, with better monitoring of the delivery system. The bifurcation of BPL and APL quotas of foodgrains into rice and wheat had been left to the states. In case of those states, which had not indicated the bifurcation, the average lifting of rice and wheat over the last 10 years had been adopted on provisional basis. Following the TPDS guidelines, any requirement from states over and above TPDS quotas could be met subject to availability of foodgrains in the Central Pool and at the rates equal to FCI's average economic cost (GOI, 1997-98, p. 72).

Box 1.1: Features of TPDS in India

States to identify families Below Poverty Line (BPL) who would be issued 10 kgs of foodgrains per month per family at prices less than the Central Issue Price (CIP).

Population above the poverty line (non-poor) now under PDS would continue to receive normal entitlement at the full CIP.

The Centre should guarantee supply of foodgrains for the BPL at 10 kgs per month per family to states. Additional quantities required by states would depend on the availability of stocks in the Central Pool.

States will be free to add to the quantum, coverage and the subsidy from their own resources.

Subsidized foodgrains will also be issued to all beneficiaries under the EAS/Jawahar Rojgar Yojana as per guidelines at the rate of 1 kg per man-day for which food coupons would be issued to beneficiaries for exchanging at FPS.

Source: GOI, Ministry of Finance, *Economic Survey*, 1996-97, p. 77.

No one denies that 'the safest and most obvious way of guaranteeing the universal protection of entitlements is to provide direct and unconditional support to everyone without distinction... it does have the advantage of altogether bypassing the various difficulties which any form of selectivity in the provision of relief is bound to entail. ...Universal support can be a simple expression of ...right to food' (Dreze and Sen, 1989, p. 104). The fact is that the strategy of universal support has several disadvantages. It involves an administrative and logistic burden. In addition, 'universal support may require a commitment of resources that can be hard to obtain' (*ibid.*). The PDS, as it was planned to be carried on in post-independence India, cannot today encompass all and offer benefits to all in terms of all essential commodities. 'The need for reducing government expenditure under the stabilization programme calls for a discriminatory approach in providing PDS benefits and hence should be targeted only to the vulnerable groups, since malnutrition is caused by an unequal distribution of food and misplaced consumer choices rather than inadequate supply' (Suryanarayana, 2000, p. 80). So the targeted system comes. The targeted system has the advantage that it can ensure the greatest economy of resources by withholding public support from less vulnerable groups. In addition, the targeted system can promote the redistribution of resources by concentrating public support exclusively on the most deprived groups. In India, targeting should take care of not only exclusion of the non-poor but also covering all the poor excluded so far from the PDS network.

1.5 Public Intervention in the Foodgrains Market

Agricultural production is land-centred. We use the term 'land' in the loose sense to include 'physical soil area' covered by agricultural crops. The physical soil input is privately owned, in addition to some other complementary inputs like fertilizers, pump sets, tractors etc. Water, as the most important ingredient to keep 'physical soil input' cultivable, is provided as input by the government through medium and major irrigation systems. This is supported by private initiatives through minor irrigation systems. The point we would like to make clear here is that agricultural production by its nature remains primarily in private hands. The physical volume of output per period, thus, remains in private hands. How does the government then intervene in the domain of agriculture?

One answer is since the government allows the individuals to own and use physical soil which is a free gift of nature, and in turn allows the individuals to derive benefits from universal nature by its transformation, hence the government can claim a share out of it. Privatization, sanctioned by the government, allows the government to have a share out of it. The second answer is activity-specific. Since the government helps the production system through irrigation etc., water being universal gift of nature, the government can intervene to get a return on it. Hence, the government intervenes. The third answer is distribution of specific benefits. Some individuals are producers of crops who are at the same time owners of physical soil. Hence, some individuals who are not owners of soil, and hence do not have the scope to transform it into crops after appropriate use of other inputs including labour, have to get a share of that crop. This establishes not only production by social cooperation but also consumption of crops by individuals who do not produce crops but produce some other commodities. Production of crops by sale of labour power, or by owning and using marginal landholdings, may fetch little earnings for the agricultural labourers and marginal farmers. This earning is likely to be insufficient for them to buy foodgrains required for physical survival in the free market. The question of price protection for the income-poor, thus, comes in when it centres on meeting their food needs. This poor, vulnerable, and left-out sections of the society provide the base for the PDS.

It is often argued that the government should not intervene in agriculture. The arguments against government intervention in agriculture seem to be synonymous with liberalization of agriculture. The disapproval of government intervention in agricultural markets 'is part of a larger critique of development strategies that promoted domestic industrialization behind trade barriers, which were financed through the taxation of agriculture *via* pricing policies that depressed food and agricultural commodity prices so that wages could be kept low... Not surprisingly, the major policy implication is that to foster sustained growth of agricultural productivity, output and exports the terms of trade should improve for farmers through a reduction in the discrimination against agriculture. The major way of getting the prices right for agriculture is by means of a thorough liberalization of the foreign trade regime, reducing the tariff and quota protection of industry, eliminating the real exchange rate misalignment and removing the anti-export bias in agriculture' (Storm, 1997, p. 68). We concentrate on the arguments restricted to government intervention in Indian agriculture through procurement and distribution. It is a fact that the government does not directly control agricultural production other than creating storage facilities to take care of bumper production and hence holding stocks, or offering support price in the post-harvest period when price has a tendency to fall below unit cost level. The addition to stocks by the government in case of bumper production is also a measure against abrupt fall in price. These exceptions show that the government is the ultimate protector of home producer, quantitatively through checking downward flexibility in foodgrains prices. The questions come when the government intervention restricts the freedom of the producers-*cum*-sellers through imposition of restrictions on movement of goods and marketing. Such restrictions keep the benefits of the products localized and price of the final product faces a downward flexibility. Such 'restrictions are usually defended on the ground that they are not aimed at producers but at unscrupulous traders' (Ahluwalia, 1996, p. 421). One example is the Essential Commodities Act of 1955 that restricts stocks held by traders. The other is the Maharashtra Cotton Monopoly Procurement Scheme that ensures institutional arrangement for government procurement of cotton.

In 1991 the Government of India adopted the New Economic Policy (NEP), a major component of which was liberalization of initiatives and enterprises in production-investment-trade. It pledges for reducing role of the government in the context of opening the economy in favour of a competitive regime. The NEP aims a 'domestic price reforms that free agriculture from internal controls and raise prices of agricultural output (that) are expected to have positive impact on agricultural growth' (Bhalla, 1995, p. 8). It is known that since 1990s 'there are no quotas of procurement in surplus states for delivery to the central pool. The strictly centrally imposed zonal restrictions on inter-state movement of commodities no longer exist' (Dantwala, 1993, p. 176). One argument against public intervention in the foodgrains market is that the groups whose interests are served include mainly the non-poor. This includes richer farmers from 'Green Revolution' areas, government and public bureaucracy, urban consumers and foodgrain traders and millers (Rao, 1996, p. 138). Hence, subsidized sale of foodgrains through Fair Price Shops (FPSs) benefits mainly the already benefited socio-economic categories.

It is argued that the supplies through PDS 'have contained the vigour of inflation but part of their impact has been offset by monetization of budgetary deficit to meet food subsidies. Maintaining supplies to PDS involves continuation of food procurement, grant of subsidies and reintroduction and perpetuation of some controls. But several weaknesses have emerged in the distribution system, which have diluted the essence of the system of benefit for the vulnerable sections. The financial liabilities of the State Governments in maintaining this system have increased. Leakage and blackmarketing in PDS items have also reduced the full impact of PDS in containing inflation' (GOI, 1992-93, p. 92). The policy of the government, to keep both input and output prices low, leads to subsidized provision of inputs like water, electricity, and fertilizer, and subsidy to consumers. It is argued that most of this subsidy is realized by the final consumers of foodgrains. The distribution of procured foodgrains through the PDS involves a consumer subsidy to make good the losses incurred by the Food Corporation of India (FCI) (Rao, 1996, p. 138).

The PDS thus is argued to be too expensive. The budgeted estimate to food subsidy for 1995-96 was Rs. 5,250 crore, which was more than the total estimated budget deficit of the Centre in the same year. The fixed cost component, in particular, the operational cost of the FCI, is considered too high (Mooij, 1999, p. 241). The huge subsidy explains a part of the fiscal deficit of the government of surrendering the scope to save income earned elsewhere. It is also argued that were the farmers given international prices for the inputs, farm income would go up (Parikh, 1999, p. 5). Meeting demand for food in national economy depends on food production and supply on a world scale.

There is a realization that the PDS serves only a limited proportion of the poor and that there are large variations in the coverage between the states. Thus, the target setting and subsidy question should receive attention for solution. In view of the Government of India, two major aspects of PDS that need a national consensus are: (i) the norms of excluding the non-poor, and (ii) limiting the open-ended subsidy because of FCI operations (GOI, 1993-99, p. 66).

1.6 Family Budget and the Poor: Arguments for PDS

We consider a general budget equation of the households where total household income is spent on food and non-food. In Fig. 1.1 the budget line with fixed income is shown in quadrant IV. The inverse relation between demand for food and price per unit of food is shown in quadrant I and the inverse relation between demand for non-food and price of non-food is shown in quadrant III. We ignore here the relation between price of non-food and demand of food. Similarly, we ignore the relation between price of food and demand for non-food. This implies that we ignore cross-elasticities. Hence, we derive the relation between the price of food and the price of non-food. This shows terms of trade between agriculture and non-agriculture, which we find to be inverse. This is presented in quadrant II.

In Fig 1.2, we repeat the same in quadrant I. In quadrant IV we have the relation between demand for food (actual by market/ distribution access) and number of poor population in an economy. Food being at the bottom of the consumption ladder, and assuming that the price elasticity of demand for food being low and probably less than one, we derive that a higher/lower demand for foodgrains means a lower/higher number of the poor population included in the market for foodgrains.

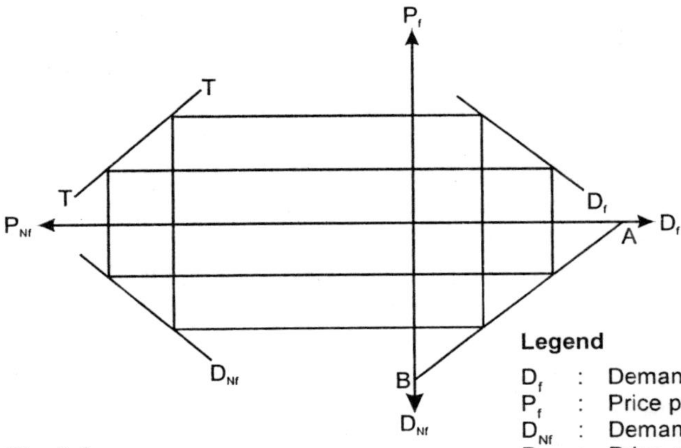

Fig. 1.1

Legend

D_f	:	Demand for food
P_f	:	Price per unit of food
D_{Nf}	:	Demand for non-food
P_{Nf}	:	Price per unit of non-food
AB	:	Budjet line of the household as consumer
TT	:	Derived relation between P_f and P_{Nf}
N_p	:	Number of poor population in an economy
I_f	:	Income of the poor.

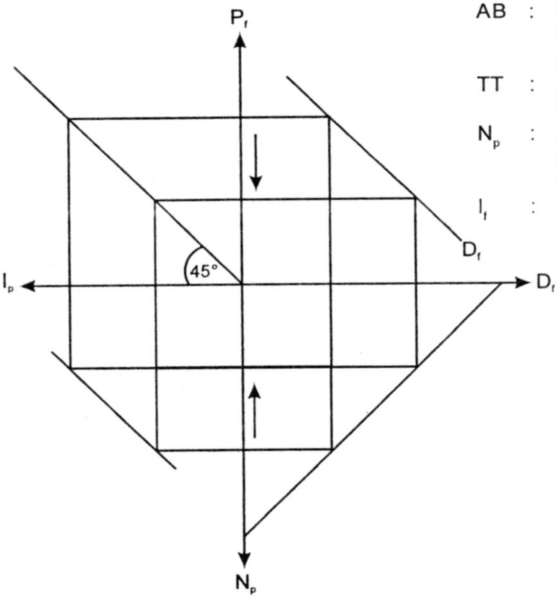

Fig. 1.2

The total household income that we talked about in Fig 1.1 now can be seen as total (national) income distributed as income of the poor and income of the non-poor. If the poor are suppòsed to be the sellers of foodgrains, then low price of foodgrains will imply low income (absolute and relative) of the poor. While low price of foodgrains shows the possibility for the poor to buy food, low income of the poor (derived from sale of low-priced food) shows less access to food for them. Demand for non-food remains a rare possibility when demand for food remains unfulfilled. We take an identity between price of food and income of the poor. Hence, we derive the relation between income of the poor and the number of the poor population in quadrant III.

The price-income method left to itself cannot solve this dilemma, i.e., whether the price of food is to be kept low or high. There may also be diversion/black marketeering of food whereby the poor may be deprived of the produced food. Food-processing and better marketing of food-converted higher-order good meant for the income-rich may deprive the poor of the food that was available in the market. Hence, the Government should intervene in the market for food.

1.7 Prices, Poverty and Public Distribution System

Price per unit of a single commodity has a double face, one who pays and the other who receives. The person who is in a position to produce/sell the product at a positive price earns income, while the person who buys the same product spends from her family budget. Food being an inescapable commodity-mix, any individual will have to consume it on a day-to-day basis and hence either will have to produce it for consumption-*cum*-sale or will have to buy it. In case she produces non-food items, the relative price has to enable her to buy food on a regular basis at least for minimum necessity based survival. This is where the question of control over the food producers comes in. However, it is not necessarily true that the food-producers will be able to buy non-food items. The fact is that while non-food producers are generally assured of consumption of food in any economy, food producers may be deprived of even the food that they produce. Government intervention in the foodgrains market, thus, has a double face/edge. On the one hand it has to ensure the elimination of vulnerability of the food producers by price-related measures (minimum support price, procurement price etc.), while on the other it will have to ensure the interests of the consumers at large. The level of food prices is one of the crucial variables mediating the relationship between aggregate food availability and individual entitlements. Generally, the successful containment of increases in food prices helps in protecting the entitlements of vulnerable groups (Dreze and Sen, 1989, p. 88).

The specific command over food is not necessarily linked with absolute and relative prices of food. In case of landlessness of the people settled in rural regions, in case of marginalized and cardless urban slum dwellers, age-*cum*-ill health of the individuals not being able to sell labour power, particularly in case of assetlessness, the individuals may be deprived of food. Breakdown of the joint family system also may lead to failure to food entitlement. Historically or through government policy, poverty may be imposed on a region or a section of population, particularly if it is colonized, leading to failure of sections of population to have access to food. In many such cases, often the failure is not questioned. The state authority or the government policy is also often not questioned. For example, '... in the disastrous Irish famines of the 1840s (in which about one-eighth of the population died, and which led to the emigration of a comparable number to North America), the law and order situation was, in many respects, apparently "excellent" ....In many famines people starve and die in front of food shops, without attempting to seize law and order by the collar. It would be particularly a mistake to relate the causation of famines to violations of legality' (Dreze and Sen, 1989, p. 22).

In India, the population in general and vulnerable population in particular feels the prolonged impact of natural disasters, as and when they occur. If price increases following deficits in output and supply of essential commodities, it is the landless people, the land-poor farmers, the urban unemployed and the rural underemployed, and the urban slum dwellers that will bear the brunt of it. In famines the victims typically come from the bottom layers of the society (Dreze and Sen *op cit.*, p. 48). The social objective of sharing the regional deficit in food output on a national basis remains absent. The PDS aims at protecting the vulnerable sections of the society by encompassing them in the distribution network. One of the objectives of PDS, namely, ensuring price stabilization of foodgrains, is executed through buffer stock operations as an instrument. It is a fact that in an underdeveloped agricultural production system, agricultural production varies not only between one year and another but also within a year. This may lead to income destabilization if prices are rigidly fixed. For example, in case of a fall in agricultural output, a fall in income is not compensated if the prices of agricultural products are not allowed to rise. Price changes, thus, are expected to provide a compensatory effect to changes in output (Khusro, 1973, p. 13). This output variation is not only inter-temporal but also spatial. In terms of production, seasonal and annual, some of the states in India may show surplus, while some other states may show deficit. This surplus or deficit is to be understood in terms of consumption requirements per period *vis-à-vis* production. Surplus states will have a tendency to exhibit lower prices relative to the deficit states. If surplus foodgrain is transferred from the surplus states to the deficit states, prices will have a tendency to equalize. Public intervention in the foodgrains market, thus, attempts to ensure dynamic equilibrium in the foodgrains market (*ibid.*, p. 9). A direct link between food prices and income-poverty becomes an important issue sometimes. It is argued that high foodgrains prices may accentuate poverty. From the buyers' point of view, 'when there is limited amount of food, with the market dividing it among the population according to their respective purchasing power and market pulls, a worsening of the relative position of some groups in the scale of money incomes can lead to an absolute decline in their ability to command food' (Dreze and Sen, 1989, p. 49). From a seller's point of view, a high or a rise in foodgrain prices will have different implications. For example, for the marginal farmers it will have very little impact by revenue gain while for the big farmers it leads to a big surplus. The fact remains that the big farmer, by ownership over big plot of land, produces marketable surplus much more than that of the marginal farmer.

In the Indian context, however, the problem is less acute because of continuous monitoring in prices of foodgrains by government. In addition, the positive aspect of the scenario in the Indian context is that producer and consumer price interventions by government are determined somewhat independently. This relieves the dilemma of foodgrain prices affecting different sections of population differently. These dual interventions, however, occur at a high cost to the public exchequer. That is the question of subsidy. In the next chapter we will discuss the Public Distribution System in India in terms of the availability of foodgrains in the different states of the country, their procurement by the government, their storage in government godowns, the modes of distribution and the policy of the government regarding ensuring food security to the poor including the subsidy provided for food security.

2

Public Distribution System in India: The Strength and the Weaknesses

2.1 India's Agriculture: Growth of Output, Availability, and Imports

The year 1966 marked a turning point in the history of agriculture in post-independent India. While pre-1966 growth of agricultural output (all crops) is explained more by area expansion, post-1966 growth is explained more by productivity (yield). However the decade following the emergence of a new input package in Indian agriculture (1966-1976) witnessed growth rates in output of all crops that were marginally lower than that witnessed during the pre-1966 period. Obviously post-1966 growth in productivity per unit of land could not compensate limited area expansion that could otherwise have accelerated total agricultural output at a much faster pace. The rate of area expansion in agriculture showed a monotonic decline for all crops and separately for foodgrains and non-foodgrains, and yield growth maintained a steady acceleration for each during the successive medium-term periods. There was in fact a reduction in area under foodgrains by 0.26 per cent during 1999-90 and 2006-07 while during the same period the growth in yield was 1.43 per cent (GOI, ES, 2007-08, p. 161). The effect had been a moderately accelerating growth of output for all crops during the forward-moving time-horizons. While foodgrains maintained accelerating growth trend in production, non-foodgrains marginally decelerated afterwards (Ghose, 1988, p. 17).

Net availability of foodgrains per period equals net production plus net imports. The percentage of net availability per year remained below 10.0 during the decade 1953-1963 and above 10.0 during 1964-1998 with a few years of exception. Five years post-1998, the percentage declined a little below 10.0. The net availability of foodgrains experienced monotonic increase from a low base at 52.4 million tonnes in 1951 to reach one and a half times in 1964 (pre-Green Revolution era) and became twice in availability in 1994 relative to what it was in 1964.

Table 2.1: Net Availability, Procurement and Public Distribution of Foodgrains in India, 1951-2005

Year	*Net Production*	*Net Imports*	*Net Availability @*	*Procurement*	*Public Distribution #*	*Col. 3 as per cent of col. 4*	*Col. 5 as per cent of col. 2*	*Col. 6 as per cent of col. 4*
(1)	(2)	(3)	(4)	(5)	(6)	(7)	(8)	(9)
1951	48.1	4.8	52.4	3.8	8.0	9.2	7.9	15.3
1951-55	55.2	2.4	57.6	2.4	4.6	4.2	4.3	7.9
1956	60.7	1.4	62.6	Negligible	2.1	2.2	Negligible	3.4
1956-60	63.8	3.4	66.8	0.6	3.8	5.1	0.9	5.9
1961	72.0	3.5	75.7	0.5	4.0	4.6	0.7	5.3
1961-65	72.6	5.0	77.8	1.4	6.5	6.4	1.9	8.3
1966	63.3	10.3	73.5	4.0	14.1	14.0	6.3	19.2
1966-70	76.2	6.4	81.8	5.7	11.1	7.8	7.5	13.6
1971	94.9	2.0	94.3	8.9	7.8	2.1	9.3	8.3
1971-75	90.2	3.6	93.1	8.0	10.4	3.8	8.9	11.2
1976	105.9	0.7	95.8	12.8	9.2	0.7	12.1	9.6
1976-80	105.0	(-)0.06	104.3	11.7	11.6	0.1	11.1	11.1
1981	113.4	0.7	114.3	13.0	13.0	0.6	11.4	11.4
1981-85	120.8	1.7	119.7	16.6	14.6	1.4	13.7	12.2
1986	131.6	0.5	133.8	19.7	17.3	0.4	15.0	12.9
1986-90	135.6	1.3	138.3	18.5	1.4	0.9	13.6	1.0
1991	154.3	(-) 0.1	158.6	19.6	20.8	Negligible	12.7	13.1
1991-95	157.6	0.2	155.	22.8	1.9	Negligible	14.5	1.2
1996	157.9	(-) 3.1	163.3	19.8	18.3	(-) 1.9	12.5	11.2
1996-00	183.6	(-) 1.4	168.3	35.6	17.1	0.8	19.4	10.2
2001	172.2	(-) 2.9	157.0	42.6	13.2	(-) 1.8	24.7	8.4
2001-05	174.3	(-)5.5	174.1	31.7*	10.7**	(-)3.2	18.2	6.1

(P) Provisional; @ Net availability = Net production + Net imports – changes in Government stocks; # Includes quantities released under the Food for Work Programme during the year 1978 to 1990; * Based on four years, 2001-04; ** Based on three years, 2001-03.

Notes: Production figures relate to agricultural year: 1951 figures correspond to 1950-51 and so on. Figures for procurement and public distribution relate to calendar years. Net imports from 1981 to 1994 are only on Government account and from 1995 onwards the Net Imports are total Imports and Export of the Country.

Source: Government of India, Ministry of Finance, *Economic Survey*, 2004-05, p. S-22; — 2007-08, p. A-23.

In the following decade (1994-2004), net availability increased at a slower rate. This increasing net availability of foodgrains was explained by increasing internal production of foodgrains and not by net imports. For example, excepting a few years between 1960 and 1967, net imports as percentage of net availability remained low and often negative (implying net exports). Net production of foodgrains during 2000-2003 reached three and a half times on average of what it was in the beginning of India's planning (Table 2.1). Procurement and public distribution are the components of government intervention in foodgrains market that depend on net availability.

Relative to the rate of growth of population in India's economy neither internal production of foodgrains nor its availability imposed any threat on the 'food-based living' of the population with the assumption of unchanged per capita consumption requirement of foodgrains. If availability had been a problem, it would have surfaced in the beginning, which was not a fact recorded by data on hunger in India's economy.

Let us look at the production conditions of distributable items, with a focus on major regions in India (Table 2.2).

Table 2.2: Production of Rice and Wheat in Major States in India, 2003-2004

(Production Million Tonnes)

Foodgrains	*States*	*Production*	*Per cent Share of Production to all-India*	*Cumulative per cent of Production*
Rice	West Bengal	14.71	16.91	16.91
	Uttar Pradesh	13.01	14.96	31.87
	Punjab	9.66	11.10	42.97
Wheat	Uttar Pradesh	25.57	35.48	35.48
	Punjab	14.42	20.00	55.48
	Haryana	9.13	12.68	68.16
Total	Uttar Pradesh	44.18	20.83	20.83
Foodgrains*	Punjab	24.66	11.63	32.46
	Rajasthan	18.05	8.51	40.97

Note: *Include rice, wheat, maize, coarse cereals, pulses.

Source: Government of India, Ministry of Finance, *Economic Survey*, 2004-05, p. S-19.

The major rice producing states in India are West Bengal, UP and Punjab. In 2003-04 these states contributed 42.97 per cent of total rice production in India. The major wheat producing states in India are UP, Punjab and Haryana, which together contributed 68.16 per cent of total wheat production in India in 2003-04. Most of the states (and people settled therein) are thus non-producing but consuming states so far as rice and wheat are concerned. If other food items are included like maize, coarse cereals and pulses, then the major producing states are UP, Punjab and Rajasthan.

Before the mid-1960s, the food security system in India was in an embryonic stage. At that time the government policies and measures aimed at solving localized scarcity in the face of crop failure, famine and drought. 'Until the mid-sixties access to concessional imports of foodgrains (mainly wheat) was available under US Public Law 480. Further, the domestic price of wheat was considerably higher than the landed cost of imports. It is not surprising that the government as the sole legal importer of foodgrains, used imports as a major source of supply for the public distribution system. Indeed, until the late sixties, imports constituted over 60 per cent of the grains distributed during thirteen of the seventeen years, 1951 to 1967' (Narayana, Parikh and Srinivasan, 1991, p. 151). The situation changed radically with the phenomenal growth in wheat output that was associated with Green Revolution.

Till the early 1960s India resembled a big 'vulnerable spot' with low level of foodgrains output and stagnating yield. The economy of India experienced two successive droughts in 1965-66 and 1966-67 along with the Indo-Pak War of 1965. A famine was predicted, forcing the Government of India to bow down to the US for import of wheat under the US PL (Public Law) 480 programme. Along with this, the Government of India introduced internal 'zoning' to facilitate procurement from surplus zones and supposedly transfer this surplus to deficit zones (Dreze, 1990, p. 49).

The economy of India started exporting foodgrains (rice) since the 1970s which accelerated subsequently (Table 2.3).

Table 2.3: Exports of Rice from India, 1970-2004

Year	*Value (Rs. in crores)*	*% of Total Exports*
1970-71	5	0.32
1980-81	224	3.34
1990-91	462	1.42
1995-96	4568	4.29
2000-01	2943	1.44
2001-02	3174	1.52
2002-03	5831	2.28
2003-04	4708	1.60

Source: 'Government of India Ministry of Finance, *Economic Survey*, 2004-05, pp. S-84 to S-86.

During pre-1966 post-independence period, India did not export rice. In 1970-71, export of rice came to be only 0.32 per cent of the total exports from India, which jumped to 3.34 per cent in 1980-81 and reached the peak in 1995-96 at 4.29 per cent. In other years of the recent past, exports of rice as per cent of total exports from India remained between 1.0 and 2.5. In value terms the decade 1995-2004 showed significant exports of rice as percentage of total exports from India. For the highly populated rice consumption-dependent potential consumers, the exports of rice in a state of monotonically increasing total imports by the economy of India showed a shift in the mindset of the Government of India from its earlier vulnerability since 1989. India had become a major producer in the world economy of rice, wheat and sugar, the three distributable items in her PDS (Table 2.4).

Table 2.4: India's Output of Rice, Wheat and Sugar, 1970-89

(*Selected Years*)

Crops	*As Percentage of World Output*			*World Trade (As % of World Output)*	*India's Output (As % of World Trade)*
	1970	*1980*	*1989*	*1989*	*1989*
Rice	20.0	20.1	21.2	4.1	512.5
Wheat	6.3	7.1	10.0	19.8	50.7
Sugar	6.4	5.0	9.7	10.2	94.7

Source: Kashyap, 2002, p. 474.

The very volume of India's output that is a response to internal requirement, particularly of rice, shows that India cannot invite failure on the internal production of rice to ultimately rely on imports. Her trade in rice is an insignificant part of world output of rice so far. Similar is the case for sugar and wheat, where India cannot rely on import. The international trade of each of rice, wheat and sugar is also dominated by foreign-originated major multinationals implying not only market control by dominant share but also price control. However, the TWCs like India cannot rely on these MNCs for trade-related benefits (Table 2.5).

Table 2.5: Control of MNCs over Rice, Wheat and Sugar, 1983

Commodity	*World Exports ($ million)*	*% Marketed by 3-6 Largest MNCs*
Rice	3613	70
Wheat	17851	85-90
Sugar	10636	60

Source: Kashyap, 2002, p. 476.

A shift away from relying on production of cereals to production of cash crops may not help such countries much because these are dominated more by the MNCs in the domain of international trade relative to the cereals (Kashyap, 2002, p. 476). Hence, for large (highly populated) countries like India there is no escape from relying on internal production-*cum*-consumption of cereals. Trade cannot be relied upon in cereals much unless the consumption pattern changes radically in favour of non-cereals.

2.2 Availability, Consumption and Procurement of Foodgrains in India

Production of foodgrains in 2000-01 was two and a half times what it was in 1960-61. The corresponding multiples were more than six for wheat, two and a half for rice, and more than two and a half for cereals over the forty-year span. The possibility of acceleration in production and its realization was manifest more during 1960-61 to 1990-91 after which it slowed down. For example, wheat production in 1990-91 was five-times what it was in 1960-61, rice production more than twice, cereals more than twice, and all foodgrains more than twice. During the last decade, 1990-91 to 2000-01, production of foodgrains increased by 0.12 per cent, cereals 0.14 per cent, wheat 0.26 per cent and rice 0.14 per cent. The growth calculations are based on variables in real terms (Table 2.6).

Table 2.6: Production of Foodgrains in India, 1960-2004

(Qty. in Million Tonnes)

Years	*Wheat*		*Rice*		*Cereals*		*All Foodgrains*	
	Quantity	*Annual Growth (%)*	*Quantity*	*Annual Growth (%)*	*Quantity*	*Annual Growth (%)*	*Quantity*	*Annual Growth (%)*
1960-61	11.0	—	34.6	—	69.3	—	82.0	—
1970-71	23.8	116.4	42.2	22.0	96.6	39.4	108.4	32.2
1980-81	36.3	52.5	53.6	27.0	119.0	23.2	129.6	19.6
1990-91	55.1	51.8	74.3	38.6	162.1	36.2	176.4	36.1
2000-01	69.7	-8.8	85.0	-5.2	185.7	-5.4	196.8	-6.2
2001-02	72.8	4.4	93.3	9.8	198.5	6.9	211.9	7.7
2002-03	65.1	-10.6	72.7	-22.1	163.0	-17.9	174.2	-17.8
2003-04	72.1	10.8	87.0	19.7	196.8	20.7	212.0	21.7

Source: Government of India, Ministry of Finance, *Economic Survey*, 2004-05, p. S-16.

Per capita net availability of cereals, based on a five-yearly moving average, reached its peak during 1991-95 compared to what it was during 1981-85 and 1986-90. These moving averages also show monotonic increase, not only for cereals as a whole but also for rice. Though the average for cereals, and separately for rice, was lower during 1996-2000, the reduction was insignificant. For wheat the peak average was attained during 1996-2000, that showed monotonic increase. The overall mean (trend average) on a time span of twenty years (1981-01) for cereals showed steady and stable availability compared to what it was during earlier medium (five year) periods. The same is true item-wise by rice and wheat. The mean deviation in availability of cereals, what was actual availability minus grand mean, remained positive for most of the years in 1990s, while it remained negative for most of the years in 1980s. The same was true for rice and wheat separately, but not true for other cereals. As opposed to steady and stable availability of rice and wheat, other cereals showed a declining trend in availability (Table 2.7).

Table 2.7: Per Capita Net Availability of Foodgrains in India: 1981-2001

(*kg/annum*)

Years	Rice		Wheat		Others		Total	
	Avail.	Mean Deviation	Avail.	Mean Deviation	Avail.	Mean Deviation	Avail.	Mean Deviation
1981	72.2	–2.3	47.3	–8.1	32.8	5.5	152.3	–4.9
Mean (81-85)	69.16	–5.34	49.74	–5.66	33.2	5.9	152.1	–5.1
1986	77.4	2.9	55.1	–0.3	25.8	–1.5	158.3	1.1
Mean (86-90)	75.24	0.74	54.88	–0.52	27.56	0.26	157.68	0.48
1991	80.9	6.4	60.0	4.6	29.2	1.9	170.1	12.9
Mean (91-95)	77.9	3.4	58.06	2.66	26.1	–1.2	162.06	4.86
1996	74.8	0.3	64.4	9.0	22.7	–4.6	161.9	4.7
Mean (96-2000)	75.46	0.96	60.8	5.4	23.52	–3.78	159.78	2.58
2001	75.9	1.4	45.3	–10.1	21.3	–6.0	142.5	–14.7

Note: Mean Deviation = Actual Value – Overall Mean.

Source: Directorate of Economics and Statistics, Ministry of Agriculture, Government of India.

Per capita net consumption of cereals in India declined a little during 1990s relative to what it was during 1980s. Considered over the whole period (1983-2000) following several NSS rounds, the mean deviation (from mean) of per capita net consumption of cereals remained positive during 1983-1992 and became negative afterwards. Considered over the whole period (1983-2000), the peak per capita net consumption of cereals (169.9) was in 1983 and the minimum was 144.9, implying the average variation at 25.0, which was 15.9 per cent of the grand mean. Per capita net consumption of rice experienced oscillation during the whole period (1983-2000), with peak and higher consumption during the earlier decade relative to the latter one. The range of variation in rice consumption was 4.7 (Maximum-Minimum). The mean deviation in rice consumption varied between 2.8 in 1997 and 1.9 in 1992. Per capita net consumption of wheat recorded its peak in 1988 and the minimum in 1996, with the grand average (mean) around which the mean deviations are calculated, did not show much oscillations. Average (per capita) net consumption of wheat, however, declined a little during 1990s relative to what it was during 1980s. Per capita net consumption of other cereals remained much lower than rice and wheat. This type of consumption also experienced sharp decline during late 1990s. All the calculations are in real terms (Table 2.8).

Table 2.8: Per Capita Net Consumption of Cereals in India: 1983-2000

(kg/annum)

Years	NSS Rounds	Rice		Wheat		Others		Total	
		Cons.	Mean Deviation	Cons.	Mean Deviation	Cons.	Mean Deviation	Cons.	Mean Deviation
1983	38	76.9	-2.5	55.3	-0.7	37.7	16.3	169.9	13.1
1987	42	81.2	1.8	58.2	2.2	24.3	2.9	163.7	6.9
1988	43	80.5	1.1	60.2	4.2	25.3	3.9	166.0	9.2
1989	44	81.2	1.8	57.5	1.5	28.2	6.8	166.9	10.1
1990	45	79.6	0.2	57.5	1.5	23.9	2.5	161.0	4.2
Mean (1983-90)		80.6	1.2	58.4	2.4	25.4	4.0	164.4	7.6
1991	47	80.4	1.0	56.9	0.9	20.8	-0.6	158.1	1.3
1992	48	81.3	1.9	56.0	0.0	20.8	-0.6	158.1	1.3
1994	50	79.8	0.4	54.6	-1.4	19.8	-1.6	154.2	-2.6
1995	51	79.4	0.0	54.3	-1.7	18.1	-3.3	151.8	-5.0
Mean (1991-95)		80.2	0.8	55.5	-0.5	19.9	-1.5	155.6	-1.2
1996	52	79.7	0.3	53.0	-3.0	16.6	-4.8	149.3	-7.5
1997	53	76.6	-2.8	55.5	-0.5	15.5	-5.9	147.6	-9.2
1998	54	78.0	-1.4	53.4	-2.6	13.5	-7.9	144.9	-11.9
2000	55	77.3	-2.1	56.1	0.1	13.7	-7.7	147.1	-9.7
Mean (1996-2000)		77.9	-1.5	54.5	-1.5	14.8	-6.6	147.2	-9.6
Overall Mean (1983-2000)		79.4	0.0	56.0	0.0	21.4	0.0	156.8	0.0

Note: Mean Deviation = Actual Value – Overall Mean.

Source: Directorate of Economic and Statistics, Ministry of Agriculture, Government of India.

Table 2.9: Per Capita Availability and Consumption of Foodgrains: The Gap

(*kg/annum*)

Years	*NSS Rounds*	*Rice*			*Wheat*			*Others*			*Total Foodgrains*		
		Avail.	*Cons.*	*Gap**	*Avail.*	*Cons.*	*Gap**	*Avail.*	*Cons.*	*Gap**	*Avail.*	*Cons.*	*Gap**
1983	38	62.0	76.9	-14.9	52.7	55.3	-2.6	30.4	37.7	-7.3	145.1	169.9	-24.8
1987	42	75.2	81.2	-6.0	57.6	58.2	-0.6	25.9	24.3	1.6	158.7	163.7	-5.0
1988	43	67.7	80.5	-12.8	56.3	60.2	-3.9	25.1	25.3	-0.2	149.1	166	-16.9
1989	44	78.5	81.2	-2.7	57.0	57.5	-0.5	29.3	28.2	1.1	164.8	166.9	-2.1
1990	45	77.4	79.6	-2.2	48.4	57.5	-9.1	31.7	23.9	7.8	157.5	161	-3.5
Mean (83-90)		74.7	80.6	-5.9	54.8	58.4	-3.5	28.0	25.4	2.6	157.5	164.4	-6.9
1991	47	80.9	80.4	0.5	60.0	56.9	3.1	29.2	20.8	8.4	170.1	158.1	12.0
1992	48	79.2	81.3	-2.1	57.9	56.0	1.9	21.5	20.8	0.7	158.6	158.1	0.5
1994	50	75.7	79.8	-4.1	58.2	54.6	3.6	24.5	19.8	4.7	158.4	154.2	4.2
1995	51	80.3	79.4	0.9	63.0	54.3	8.7	23.7	18.1	5.6	167.0	151.8	15.2
1996	52	74.8	79.7	-4.9	64.4	53.0	11.4	22.7	16.6	6.1	161.9	149.3	12.6
Mean (91-96)		79.0	80.2	-1.2	59.8	55.5	4.3	24.7	19.9	4.9	163.5	155.6	8.0
1997	53	78.5	76.6	1.9	65.7	55.5	10.2	26.7	15.5	11.2	170.9	147.6	23.3
1998	54	73.7	78.0	-4.3	55.7	53.4	2.3	22.9	13.5	9.4	152.3	144.9	7.4
2000	55	75.3	77.3	-2.0	58.4	56.1	2.3	21.9	13.7	8.2	155.6	147.1	8.5
Mean (97-2000)		75.6	77.9	-2.3	61.1	54.5	6.6	23.6	14.8	8.7	160.2	147.2	13.0
Total Mean		75.3	79.4	-4.1	58.1	56.0	2.1	25.8	21.4	4.4	159.2	156.8	2.4

Note:* (Gap = Availability – Consumption). Only those years have been taken for which consumption data are available.

Source: Directorate of Economics and Statistics, Ministry of Agriculture, Government of India.

Following several rounds of NSS data on per capita availability and consumption of foodgrains, we got the gap between the two. Availability of foodgrains fell short of consumption during 1983-1990, and came to exceed consumption during 1991-2000, in a state of reducing consumption of all foodgrains that include rice, wheat and others. The same was true separately for wheat, but here the decline in consumption, if at all, was not significant, and availability maintained a steady and stable level. We found no significant decline in mean consumption of each of rice and wheat. While the mean availability of wheat showed accelerating trend, for rice it showed highly decelerating trend. We found a sharp decline in mean consumption of foodgrains other than rice and wheat (Table 2.9).

2.3 Procurement of Wheat and Rice from Selected States

The states on which the Government of India (GOI) relies for procurement of wheat are Punjab, Haryana and Uttar Pradesh, all the three contributing around 95.0 per cent of total procurement of wheat, considered over last three years (2002-05). The states the GOI relies on for procurement of rice are Punjab, Andhra Pradesh, Uttar Pradesh and Chhattisgarh, which together accounted for around 80.0 per cent of total procurement of rice during 2002-05. We don't find much year-wise variation in percentage contribution of wheat by each of the major states during this period. By implication, those states have remained a major buffer (surplus) zone so far as planned procurement of wheat is concerned. Punjab remains the major contributor of wheat and rice for procurement by GOI, contributing more than 50.0 per cent in wheat and more than one-third in rice. We find year-wise variations in procurement of rice from states, the magnitude of variation remaining very high for the major two contributors, Punjab and Andhra Pradesh. Wheat procurement (all-India total) varied between years, as did rice procurement. A similar variation is true for major contributing states over the years (Table 2.10).

For all-India, the allocation of wheat oscillated around 10 million tonnes during 1991-2000, while during the same period the allocation of rice varied between 10 and 15 million tonnes. Off-take of wheat as a percentage of allocation came to be below 50 per cent during 1994-95 and 1995-96 and again in 1999-2000. For the remaining years of the 1990s, this ratio per year was around three-fourths. For rice also, off-take as a ratio of allocation declined during 1994-95 and 1995-96 to around three-fifths and for 1999-2000 to around half. For the rest of the 1990s, the ratio was more than three-fourths (Table 2.11).

Table 2.10: Procurement of Wheat and Rice from Major States in India, 2002-05

(Quantity in lakh tonnes)

Food-grains	*States*	*2002-03*	*2003-04*	*2004-05*
		Quantity % Share	*Quantity % Share*	*Quantity % Share*
Wheat	Haryana	30.95	32.42	30.46
	Punjab	51.85	56.57	55.02
	Uttar Pradesh	11.07	7.68	10.37
	Total Share	93.83	96.67	95.85
	All-India	(190.54)	(158.01)	(167.95)
		100.00	100.00	100.00
Rice	Andhra Pradesh	29.04	16.04	18.53
	Chhattisgarh	8.68	7.86	10.40
	Haryana	6.71	8.06	5.84
	Punjab	32.91	48.35	37.94
	Uttar Pradesh	8.75	8.28	11.19
	Total Share	86.09	88.59	83.90
	All-India	(221.29)	(164.23)	(228.28)
		100.00	100.00	100.00

Note: Figures in brackets show total quantity.

Source: *Economic Survey*, 2004-05, Government of India, Ministry of Finance, 99, 100.

Table 2.11: Procurement of Wheat and Rice, 1980-2005 (Central Pool Stocks)

(in Million Tonnes)

Year/Average	*Rice*	*Wheat*	*Total (Rice+Wheat)*
1980	8.58	8.15	16.73
Average of 1981-1985	5.48	8.38	13.86
Average of 1986-1990	6.64	9.25	15.89
Average of 1991-1995	10.88	8.30	19.18
Average of 1995-2000	13.11	11.31	24.42
Average of 2000-2005*	19.40	17.72	37.12

Note: Data for procurement of rice refer to October-September and that for wheat April-March, for 1995-2005.

* As on January 14, 2005.

Source: Government of India, Ministry of Agriculture, Bulletin of Food Statistics (Several Years).

Government of India, Ministry of Finance, 1999-2000, *Economic Survey*, p. 82.

———, 2000-01, *Economic Survey*, p. 93.

———, 2001-02, *Economic Survey*, p. 120.

———, 2004-05, *Economic Survey*, p. 99.

2.4 Allocation and Off-take of Foodgrains

Of total allocation of wheat and rice considered over three years (2003-06), at the level of U.P., percentage of wheat (by quantity) remained higher, which subsequently declined to be more or less equal with allocation of rice. For all-India, wheat allocation was ahead of that of rice though the gap was not that significant as in case of U.P. For 2005-06 for all-India, allocation of rice was much ahead of that of wheat. Of total allocation of wheat and rice under BPL, the percentage of wheat was much higher for 2003-04 and 2004-05 to decline in 2005-06, while that of rice remained low for the first two years to reach high percentage in 2005-06. Allocation of wheat under APL remained high (above that of rice) for all the three years at the level of U.P. The same was true for all-India, excepting in 2005-06 when it declined but remained above that of rice. Thus the allocation of wheat by percentage was higher at both the levels, U.P. and India, under both BPL and APL categories. The other scheme where rice and wheat were allocated was Annapurna Anna Yojana (AAY), where the percentage of wheat was higher at the U.P. level while rice had higher percentage at the all-India level (Table 2.12).

Table 2.12: Allocation and Off-take of Foodgrains in India under PDS, 1991-2002

(in Million Tonnes)

Year	Wheat		Rice	
	Allocation	*Off-take as % of Allocation*	Allocation	*Off-take as % of Allocation*
1991-92	10.36	85.23	11.36	89.52
1992-93	9.25	84.86	11.48	84.40
1993-94	9.56	61.82	12.41	71.47
1994-95	10.80	44.72	13.32	60.28
1995-96	11.31	46.77	14.62	64.70
1996-97	10.72	79.47	15.16	73.48
1997-98	10.11	70.02	12.81	77.16
1998-99	10.11	78.63	12.93	83.06
1999-00*	10.37	48.21	13.84	79.12
2000-01	7.51	36.21	10.96	52.46
2001-02**	9.08	34.69	11.48	45.55

Note: *April-December 2000. ** Up to December.

Source: Government of India, 1996-1997, *Economic Survey*, p. 79.
Government of India, 1999-2000, *Economic Survey*, p. 81.
Government of India, 2000-2001, *Economic Survey*, p. 92.
Government of India, 2001-02, *Economic Survey*, p. 123.

Off-take of foodgrains (rice and wheat) in U.P. in 2003-04 under BPL was 72.18 per cent of total off-take, the rest covered by off-take under APL (0.36%) and Annapurna (AAY) (27.45%). Off-take of and foodgrains (rice and wheat) under BPL in 2004-05 was 71.0 per cent; in 2005-06 it was 63.39 per cent for U.P. The off-take of foodgrains under BPL at the all-India level was 66.03 in 2003-04, which reached 59.45 in 2004-05 and 50.28 in 2005-06. Off-take of each of wheat and rice at both the levels, U.P. and all-India, under BPL was much ahead of not only off-take under APL but both APL and AAY combined. By implication, TPDS aimed mainly at BPL households.

The off-take of foodgrains (rice and wheat) as a percentage of allocation under TPDS for U.P. and all India remained low during 2003-06. The low off-take was because of low off-take under APL that remained less than 1.0 per cent for each of these years in U.P. and remained less than 20.0 per cent for all India. The off-take under Antyodaya Anna Yojana (AAY) was more than 90.0 per cent during these years for U.P. for all foodgrains. Off-take under BPL category in U.P. for all foodgrains accelerated over years. For all-India, off-take of wheat under BPL increased over years while for rice it remained steady. Off-take of each of rice and wheat for both U.P. and all-India under APL category showed failure. This may raise questions on dual system (Pricing etc.) in distribution of foodgrains (Table 2.13).

Table 2.13: Off-take of Foodgrains as Percentage of Allocation under TPDS, 2003-06 *(in %)*

Cereals	*Category of HHs.*	*UP*			*India*		
		2003-04	*2004-05*	*2005-06*	*2003-04*	*2004-05*	*2005-06*
Wheat	BPL	61.77	78.15	86.72	68.34	79.42	81.67
	APL	0.23	0.16	1.05	8.43	12.68	15.79
	AAY	91.16	83.36	92.08	86.98	86.00	88.52
	Total	27.41	31.45	30.01	28.87	34.61	38.08
Rice	BPL	50.96	93.21	87.07	71.34	84.10	81.35
	APL	0.04	0.03	0.08	9.69	16.91	20.19
	AAY	108.51	117.57	94.27	95.06	93.58	9.44
	Total	25.52	43.32	43.31	38.66	47.79	22.43
Total	BPL	58.06	83.75	86.93	70.02	82.04	81.47
	APL	0.16	0.12	0.62	8.98	14.50	18.08
	AAY	97.11	96.32	93.41	91.43	90.29	14.02
	Total	26.77	35.62	36.79	33.59	40.94	26.67

Source: Ministry of Food and Consumer Affairs, Department of Food and Public Distribution, Government of India.

In 2005-06, off-take as percentage of allocation in U.P. for wheat was 93.4 under Annapurna Yojana while for rice the off-take was 600 tonnes with no allocation for the specific year. For Mid-day Meal (MDM), off-take as percentage of allocation for wheat in U.P. was 86.2, which was 84.6 for rice. The off-take of wheat at the level of all-India under Annapurna Yojana was 91.1 per cent which was 77.1 for rice. The corresponding percentages under MDM for wheat and rice were respectively 76.9 and 76.7 (Ministry of Food and Consumer Affairs, Department of Food and Public Distribution, Government of India).

2.5 Off-take of Foodgrains from Central Pool under Different Schemes

Of total off-take of foodgrains (wheat and rice) from central pool under TPDS, the percentage under BPL category remained high (above 60.0%) since 2000-01 up to 2003-04. On a span of five years (1999-2004), the percentage of off-take under APL from total foodgrains under TPDS was high (59.04%). The off-take under Antyodaya Yojana, that got launched in 2000-01, came to be significant over the subsequent years. Total off-take from central pool covered TPDS plus open market sale, welfare schemes and exports. TPDS, covering all schemes, was the major scheme during 1999-2004. Open market sale, as percentage of total off-take, oscillated over the years. Off-take under welfare schemes increased monotonically over years. Exports as percentage of off-take had oscillations over years (Table 2.14).

2.6 Food Stocks, Allocation, and Off-take: Purpose and Position

In agriculture while production is generally seasonal, consumption is continuous throughout the year. The gap between production as a stock in agriculture and consumption as a flow in agricultural commodities is bridged by storage or carrying forward the output (Balakrishnan and Ramaswami, 2000, p. 118). The main plank of Central Government's food security operations lies in building up public stocks of foodgrains and its release each month for distribution to the State Governments for supply through the PDS (Government of India, 1994-95, p. 78). Conceptually, foodgrains stocks can be regarded as divisible into three — pipeline stocks, buffer stocks, and reserve stocks.

Table 2.14: Off-take of Foodgrains (Wheat +Rice) from Central Pool, 1999-2004

(*Quantity in Lakh Tonnes*)

Schemes/ Areas	1999-2000		2000-01		2001-02		2002-03		2003-04	
	Qty.	%	Qty.	%	Qty.	%	Qty.	%	Qty.	%
BPL*	69.95	40.96	96.53	80.16	100.52	72.65	135.13	67.13	147.51	60.97
APL*	100.82	59.04	23.65	19.64	21.06	15.22	30.78	15.29	42.17	17.43
Antyodaya*	0	0.00	16.78	13.93	35.39	25.58	38.24	19.00	27.1	11.20
TPDS	170.76	74.07	120.42	64.03	138.36	42.01	201.3	40.56	241.94	49.21
Welfare Schemes	14.26	6.19	31.93	16.98	71.84	21.81	113.8	22.93	135	27.46
Open Market Sale	45.51	19.74	14.88	7.91	55.98	17.00	56.61	11.41	13.3	2.71
Exports	—	0.00	20.85	11.09	63.15	19.18	124.64	25.11	101.4	20.62
Total Off-take	230.53	100.00	188.08	100.00	329.33	100.00	496.35	100.00	491.64	100.00

Note: * The percentage calculated on TPDS.

Source: *Economic Survey*, 2004-05, Government of India, Ministry of Finance, pp. 99 & 100.

Box 2.1: Public Stocks of Foodgrains as Food Security Measures

Categories	*Purpose*	*Functions*
Pipeline Stocks	Current Consumption	Maintaining Operational Stocks
Buffer Stocks	Counter Speculative	Price Fixing, Allocation and Off-take
Reserve Stocks	Bridging Gap between Normal Consumption and Low Production	Tackling Bad Contingency Year (Support against War, Drought etc.)

Source: Structured from Khusro, 1973, p. 4.

Public procurement of foodgrains is the first pre-condition of food security. It provides the producers the price security and scope for sale on a voluntary basis by the producers. There is thus no fixed procurement over years. Procurement prices of foodgrains are based on support prices announced by the Department of Agriculture and Co-operation. The chances of distress sale are thus reduced. Minimum support prices are the prices at which the government is willing to buy any amount offered to ensure that the open market price does not fall to un-remunerative levels in years of surplus. Procurement prices are the prices at which the government secures a limited quantity for the distribution system. Both procurement and support prices are policy-determined. The Government's procurement operations, as an instrument of agricultural price policy, is intended to provide a benchmark remunerative return to the farmer, and prevent a sharp fall in prices at harvest time. In other words, procurement prices serve as a protective shield against price uncertainty, which, in turn, provides a sustained incentive for the farmer to improve productivity and rationally re-allocate resources between various crops. Minimum Support Prices (MSPs) thus ensure stability of market supply (Government of India, 1994-95, pp. 80-81). Food stocks are maintained by the Central Government (i) to meet the prescribed Minimum Buffer Stock norms for food security, (ii) for monthly release of foodgrains for supply through the PDS, and (iii) for market intervention to augment supply so as to help moderate the open market prices (Government of India, 1996-97, p. 78; Government of India, 1997-98, p. 73; Government of India, 1999-2000, p. 81). Stocks are released each month for distribution to the State Governments for supply through the PDS. Each state is allocated a prescribed quantity based on past demand, off-take trends, relative need and other related factors. Stocks are also released for open sale to augment supplies and help moderate the open market prices (Government of India, 1995-96, p. 85).

Under PDS, the Central Government shoulders the responsibility for the procurement and supply of five commodities, viz., rice, wheat, sugar, imported edible oils, and kerosene to the States and UTs. Some states distribute a few more commodities under PDS (Government of India, 1998-99, p. 69). In the early 1990s, the Government was supplying six essential commodities through the PDS, namely, wheat, rice, sugar, edible oils, kerosene, and soft-coke (Government of India, 1991-92, Part II, p. 53). These commodities were supplied at reasonable (below market) prices, the access to the system being universal. Given the occasional variation in commodity coverage, rice and wheat constitute the bedrock of India's food security through the PDS. At any given point of time, a minimum stock of rice and wheat is maintained as a central buffer stock for meeting food security needs. In case there is a shortfall, the stock is replenished through imports. If there is an excess of stocks, they are released for open sale to improve supplies and moderate prices in the open market (Government of India, 1994-95, p. 78). Wheat and rice are the two major foodgrains used by the Central Government for market price stabilization and for ensuring food security through the PDS. Rice is mainly procured for the Central Pool from a levy imposed on the rice millers/traders under the Essential Commodities Act, 1955 and the levy orders issued by the State Governments. The foodgrains stock maintained in the Central Pool by the government is utilized for distribution to states for the PDS. In the years when public stocks fall below the minimum buffer stock norms or when production shortfalls are anticipated, the government takes recourse to imports for augmenting the buffer stocks. However, depending on the behaviour of the open market prices and the stock position in the Central Pool, the public stock of foodgrains is also utilized for market intervention as an instrument of supply management policy (Government of India, 1996-97, p. 81).

The steady availability of foodgrains to the targeted population constitutes food security for them. Among the steps initiated by the Government of India, the setting up of the Food Corporation of India (FCI) in 1965 was a big step forward in the direction of food distribution and maintenance of quality (Government of India, 1976, Part II, p. 154). The FCI is assigned the responsibilities of sale, purchase and distribution of foodgrains, maintain adequate buffer stock and quality of stored materials, installation and modernization of rice and flourmills, manufacture and distribution of processed food. We are concerned with public sector stocks and storage only, which are held by FCI, the Central and State Governments and the State Warehousing Corporations both on an ownership basis and on a rental basis (Khusro, 1973, p. 3).

The average procurement of each of rice and wheat per year increased over years. The procurement of foodgrains by the FCI is largely concentrated in a few Green Revolution states like Punjab and Haryana. These two states accounted for more than 80.0 per cent of the procurement of wheat by the FCI in the years 2002-2005. The states Punjab, Haryana, Uttar Pradesh and Andhra Pradesh accounted for around 80.0 per cent of the rice procured by the FCI in the years 2001-03.

2.7 Release of Surplus Stocks through Non-FPS Measures

During 1992-95, the actual off-take of wheat and rice by the States was poor, leading to accumulation of stocks. Consequently, the Government of India in August 1994 announced new schemes for utilization of surplus public stocks of foodgrains. This included Supply of Subsidized Foodgrains to SC/ST/OBC Hostels, Mid-Day Meal Scheme, release of Subsidized Wheat to Modern Food Industries India Ltd. (MFIL), release of surplus foodgrains (wheat and rice) for Employment Generation Scheme, and Open Market Sale of Foodgrains by FCI (Government of India, 1995-96, p. 85-86). The Employment Generation Scheme was meant for manufacture of food products by families living below poverty line. The Mid-Day Meal Scheme was initially meant for the benefit of the students enrolled in primary schools in 2,368 RPDS/EAS blocks. During 1996-97, this scheme was proposed to be extended to 2006 Low Female Literacy (LFL) blocks. During 1997-98, the scheme was planned to all primary schools in the country (828 blocks and 3,000 Nagar Palikas). "FCI was authorised to sell wheat and rice in the open market to serve the twin objectives of disposing of some of its surplus stock and to check the rise in their market prices as a part of its market intervention function to moderate supply side effects on inflation" (Government of India, 1995-96, p. 86).

2.8 Economic Cost and PDS Issue Price of Foodgrains

Procurement incidental cost of wheat per quintal increased monotonically over years, while that of rice varied over years (1999-2005). Procurement cost of wheat per quintal year-wise always remained higher than that of rice. Distribution cost of wheat per quintal varied over years, as it did for rice. Excepting for wheat for 2001-02, distribution cost for each of wheat and rice remained above procurement cost. The economic cost of foodgrains to FCI was on the rise over years (1999-2005). Procurement cost equals Minimum Support Price (MSP) plus state-level levies. Economic cost equals procurement cost (including incidentals) and distribution cost. The economic cost of foodgrains to FCI influences not only the food subsidy bill but also the country's competitiveness in international markets for foodgrains (Government of India, 2004-05, p. 102). APL issue price for each of wheat and rice as multiple of BPL issue price declined during 2001-03 (Table 2.15).

Table 2.15: Economic Cost and PDS Issue Price of Wheat and Rice, 1999-2005

(Rs./Quintal)

Food-grains	Years	Procurement Incidentals (Cost)	Distribution Cost	Economic Cost#	PDS Issue Price		
					BPL	APL	APL as multiple of BPL
Wheat	1999-00	117.1	202.0	887.5	250	682	2.73
	2000-01	128.2	166.15	883.78	415	830	2.00
	2001-02	134.7	126.7	852.9	415	610	1.47
	2002-03	137.6	145.6	884.0	415*	610*	1.47
	2003-04 (P)	156.3	156.3	952.5	—	—	—
	2004-05 (P)	156.8	156.8	924.8	—	—	—
Rice	1999-00	56.1	187.5	1074.8	350	905	2.58
	2000-01	69.89	189.94	1137.07	565	1130	2.00
	2001-02	66.8	119.6	1098.0	565	830	1.46
	2002-03	61.7	157.7	1165.0	565*	830*	1.46
	2003-04 (P)	74.9	207.5	1253.0	—	—	—
	2004-05 (P)	76.4	192.9	1262.5	—	—	—

Note: * As on July 2002-03, # Weighted average of common and grade-A rice taken together.

PC = MSP + Levies (state level)

EC = PC + DC

So, EC = MSP + Levies + DC, where PC is Procurement cost, DC is distribution cost and MSP is minimum support price.

Source: *Economic Survey*, 2004-05, Government of India, Ministry of Finance, p. 103.

2.9 Subsidy on Foodgrains: A Trend

The total subsidy released on foodgrains (FCI & States) monotonically increased over years. Subsidy to FCI explains almost the whole of total subsidy released by the Government of India operating the decentralized procurement schemes. FCI accounted for 94.79 per cent the total (cumulative) subsidy during 1997-2005. The rate of growth (percentage change per annum) of subsidy remained positive over the years for each of FCI and states, excepting that for states for 2003-04 (Table 2.16).

Table 2.16: Subsidy Released on Food-grains to FCI and States for Operating the Decentralized Procurement Schemes, 1997-2005

(*Rs. in Crore*)

Year	FCI			States			Total			Subsidy to FCI as % of Total Subsidy (xi=ii/viii)
	Subsidy	Cumulative Value	% Annual Growth	Subsidy	Cumulative Value	% Annual Growth	Subsidy	Cumulative Value	% Annual Growth	
(i)	(ii)	(iii)	(iv)	(v)	(vi)	(vii)	(viii)	(ix)	(x)	(xi)
1997-98	7,472	7,472	—	28	28	—	7,500	7500	—	99.62
1998-99	8,646	16,118	15.7	54	82	92.9	8,700	16,200	16.0	99.37
1999-2000	8,857	24,975	2.4	343	425	535.2	9,200	25,400	5.7	96.27
2000-01	11,462	36,437	29.4	548	973	59.8	12,010	37,410	30.5	95.43
2001-02	16,724	53,161	45.9	770	1743	40.5	17,494	54,904	45.7	95.59
2002-03	22,764	75,925	36.1	1,502	3245	95.1	24,176	79,080	38.2	94.15
2003-04	23,874	99,799	4.9	1,286	4531	-14.4	25,160	1,04,240	4.1	94.88
2004-05*	19,987	1,19,786	NC	2,143	6,674	66.6	22,130	1,26,370	NC	90.31

Note: * As on February 10, 2005, NC—Not calculated.

Source: *Annual Report*, 2004-05, Ministry of Food and Civil Supply, Government of India.

Food subsidy in India as a percentage of GDP rose over time though not monotonically. The percentage reached the peak at 0.98 in 2002-03. Mean food subsidy, on a five-year basis, increased from Rs. 3747.4 crores during 1990-95 to be more than double during 1995-2000. The mean food subsidy for 2001-03 came to be nearly five times what it was during 1990-95 and more than twice what it was during 1995-2000. The cumulative food subsidy accelerated over time to reach Rs. 92,850 crores in 2002-03. Taking 1990-91 as base year (Index=100), food subsidy index reached 986.8 in 2002-03, that is nearly ten times the base. Excepting 1992-93 and 1994-95, the rate of change of food subsidy per annum was always positive (Table 2.17).

Table 2.17: Growth of Food Subsidy in India, 1990-2003

Years	Food Subsidy (In Crores)	Growth of Subsidy from base Year 1990-1991 (In %)	Cumulative Food Subsidy (In Crores)	Annual Growth of Food Subsidy (In %)	Food Subsidy as % of GDP
1990-91	2450	100.0	2450	—	0.43
1991-92	2850	116.3	5300	16.33	0.44
1992-93	2800	114.3	8100	-1.75	0.37
1993-94	5537	226.0	13637	97.75	0.64
1994-95	5100	208.2	18737	-7.89	0.50
Mean (90-95)	3747.4	153.0	—	—	—
1995-96	5377	219.5	24114	5.43	0.45
1996-97	6066	247.6	30180	12.81	0.44
1997-98	7900	322.4	38080	30.23	0.52
1998-99	9100	371.4	47180	15.19	0.52
1999-2000	9434	385.1	56614	3.67	0.49
Mean (95-2000)	7575.4	309.2	—	—	—
2000-01	12060	492.2	68674	27.84	0.58
2001-02	17499	714.2	86173	45.10	0.77
2002-03	24176	986.8	92850	38.16	0.98
2003-04	25160	1026.9	118010	4.07	—
2004-05	257746	1050.8	143756	2.32	—
Mean (2000-05)	20928.2	854.2	—	—	—
2005-06	23071	941.6	166827	-10.38	—
2006-07	23828	972.5	190655	3.28	—
Overall Mean (1990-2007)	4655.8	190.0	—	—	—

Source: PEO report No. 189, Planning Commission, Government of India, 2005.

Government of India, Ministry of Finance, *Economic Survey*, 2007-08, pp. 178-179.

2.10 Subsidy on Essential Commodities Distributed through the PDS

In view of the Food and Agriculture Organization (FAO) of the UN, food subsidy schemes are oriented towards urban people partly because urban people can use political system to subsidize food prices. In its view, the use of food subsidies for the benefit of rural poor is a feasible policy option only when there is a large number of rural landless who must buy their food, as in South Asia (FAO, 1987, p. 79). While food subsidies in general can have beneficial effects, their costs can become extremely high to the income-poor countries. For example, food subsidy as a percentage of government expenditure was 4 in India in 1978 as opposed to 1.6 for Indonesia, 0.2 for Brazil, 2.2 for Mexico. For the countries in South Asia, like Pakistan and Bangladesh, this percentage was high at around 5 during 1978-80. For China also, this percentage was very high during the mid-1970s (*Ibid.*, p. 81). Food subsidy as percentage of Central Government expenditure in India remained low and varied between 2 and 4 per cent during the whole of 1990s (Meenakshisundaram, 2001, p. 445). All the countries mentioned are the large economies by size of population and are in the income-poor Third World.

In India, around 10.0 per cent of total output of selected essential commodities is supplied through the PDS per year. As PDS supplies are made at concessional rates, and the Central Government had to spend over Rs. 2,000 crores on subsidizing distribution of wheat and rice alone in the early 1990s (Government of India, 1991-92, Part II, p. 53). 'The gap between the economic cost incurred by the FCI towards procurement, storage, distribution and wastage of foodgrains and its average realization based on the issue prices under PDS has been widening over the years. This gap is filled by the Central Government through consumer subsidy' (Government of India, 1999-2000, p. 82). Although the minimum support prices of wheat and paddy have been raised each year and the procurement prices of levy rice have also been revised upward consequent to the revision of the minimum support price, there has been no corresponding revision in the CIP of rice and wheat since February 1994. Before that, during the 1980s, the issue price of wheat was revised upward from Rs. 160 per quintal in August 1982 to Rs. 234 in May 1990, that is an increase of 46.25 per cent over eight years. For rice, the issue price was revised upward from Rs. 188 in October 1982 to Rs. 289 in June 1990, that is, an increase of 53.72 per cent. This upward revision was monotonic over years (Government of India, 1996-97, p. 79). In spite of this upward revision in issue prices, there occurred higher food subsidy burden on the Government. The reason does not lie in changing issue prices but in the level of these prices set. The Central Issue Prices of foodgrains for PDS/RPDS are fixed deliberately much below the economic cost of foodgrains with a view to making foodgrains available to PDS consumers at reasonable prices (Government of India, 1995-96, p. 87). Price setting on foodgrains for distribution through PDS is administered price. While 'the Central Government issues foodgrains to States for PDS at a uniform CIP, the consumer-end retail price fixed by State Governments for the PDS varies considerably between states' (Government of India, 1994-95, p. 80). When the consumer-end PDS prices of foodgrains are lower than CIP, State Governments bear the burden of additional subsidy. 'Depressing administered prices artificially by subsidization from the exchequer only alters the source of price rise; it does not eradicate the possibility of price rise. Subsidies reduce the incentives to producers to compete and reduce costs. In fact, when accompanied by retention pricing, subsidies reward the least efficient producers at the expense of the efficient ones' (Government of India, 1992-93, p. 85).

2.11 Subsidy on Food

Under the system of dual pricing of sugar in operation for some years, the government, at pre-determined prices as levy sugar, acquires 45 per cent of the sugar production. The remaining 55 per cent of the produce are released for sale in the open market. This ratio of levy to free sale sugar has been maintained at 45:55 since 1988-89 (Government of India, 1991-92, Part II, p. 56). The retail issue price of levy sugar distributed through the PDS at Rs. 5.25 per kg. with effect from 1st January, 1989 was raised to Rs. 6.10 per kg. from 24th July, 1991 and further to Rs. 6.90 per kg. from 21st January, 1992 to reduce the burden of subsidy on sugar distribution through the PDS (Government of India, 1991-92, Part II, p. 57). Levy sugar price supplied to PDS consumers had remained unchanged at Rs. 9.05 per kg for three years since February, 1994 in spite of periodic revisions in the statutory minimum price of cane paid to sugarcane growers. Consequently, PDS supply of sugar was heavily subsidized. In order to reduce part of the subsidy the Government raised the issue price of sugar for PDS to Rs. 10.50 per kg. in February 1997. Even then, the PDS retail price was cheaper compared to the market price. The latter ranged between Rs. 15 and Rs. 16.50 per kg (Government of India, 1996-97, p. 77).

Sugar subsidy as a percentage of food subsidy declined during the end of the 1990s. Subsidy on sugar was more than one-tenth of total food subsidy in 1994-95 and declined to 5 per cent in 1997-98 and below it during the following two years of the 1990s (Table 2.18).

Table 2.18: Subsidy on Food and Sugar in India, 1991-2005

(Rs. in Crores)

Year	Food Subsidy*	Food Subsidy as % of GDP	Sugar Subsidy	Sugar Subsidy as % of Food Subsidy	Food Subsidy as % of Central Govt. Expenditure
1991-92	2850		—	—	
1992-93	2800	0.37	—	—	2.27
1993-94	5537	0.64	—	—	3.9
1994-95	5100	0.50	566	11.09	2.8
1995-96	5377	0.45	422	7.84	2.78
1996-97	6066	0.44	900	14.83	2.46
1997-98	7900	0.52	400	5.06	3.23
1998-99	9100	0.52	400	4.39	3.11
1999-2000	9434	0.49	360	3.76	3.03
2000-01	12060	0.58	NA	NC	3.61
2001-02	17499	0.77	NA	NC	4.83
2002-03	24176	0.98	NA	NC	5.17
2003-04 (RE)	25800	0.93	NA	NC	NC
2004-05	17639		NA	NC	NC

Note: * Other than that on Sugar; NA: Not Available; NC: Not Calculated. Sugar Subsidy refers to Sugar year, October- September; —Not Available.

Source: Government of India, 1999-2000, *Economic Survey*, pp. 82, 84.
Government of India, 2000-2001, *Economic Survey*, p. 96.
Government of India, 2001-02, *Economic Survey*, p. 126.
Government of India, 2004-2005, *Economic Survey*, p. 104.
Planning Commission, Government of India, *Tenth Five Year Plan*, 2002-07, Vol. II, p. 368.

Sugar subsidy thus cannot explain the burden on account of subsidy as a whole on food account. Even then questions may come regarding confinement of subsidy to a commodity even when it is not significantly consumed by the income-poor.

In formulating agricultural policy, debates center around short-term welfare gains for the income-poor *via* food subsidies at a public budget cost *vis-à-vis* more public investment. This is primarily because the latter shows the possibilities of higher growth and employment opportunities while the former shows cost or burden on the public exchequer. Also, while providing subsidies, 'eligibility is not determined on the basis of a means test but applies to all households in the neighbourhoods where stores are located; nor is there self-targeting by choice of commodities with high income elasticities for the poor and low to the rich' (Janvry and Subbarao, 1986, p. 78). The need to restrain the burden of subsidy on the central budget calls for a judicious PDS including coverage of items to be distributed, the cross-section of population to be served, and the pricing of the items to be distributed. Regarding selection/exclusion of target groups, a number of measures have been considered. These include exclusion of income tax payers, salaried employees in Government, public and private sector, registered shop-owners, sales tax assessees, telephone owning families, residents of posh housing colonies etc. (Government of India, 1993-94, p. 66). Subsidies arise from the difference between the issue price and the economic cost of FCI. In addition, unwillingness or delay in making necessary correction in the Central Issue Price (CIP) consequent to a rise in the Minimum Support Price (MSP) or procurement price may cause the food subsidy budget to rise significantly. Given the extent of poverty and the necessity of procurement of food stocks for distribution during calamities, withdrawal of food subsidy may be neither desirable nor feasible, at least in the short and medium term. The task then is to impose an upper limit on subsidy.

2.12 Households by Consumption of Cereals Based on NSS Report

Following NSS data (58th Round), average annual per capita consumption of cereals (in real terms) for U.P. stood above national average for both rural and urban regions. Per capita annual consumption of cereals (real) of U.P. stood above both surplus region (Punjab) and deficit region (Kerala). Wheat consumption of U.P. was far ahead of all-India average for both rural and urban regions, while rice consumption was less for each of the regions. Wheat consumption in Punjab was well ahead of U.P. while rice consumption of U.P. was much ahead of that in Punjab. U.P. is also one of the surplus states in wheat production in India. Cereals consumption in Kerala is characterized mainly by rice consumption for both rural and urban regions which on per capita real terms was well ahead of not only all-India average but also ahead of Punjab and U.P. (Table 2.19).

Table 2.19: Average Annual per Capita Consumption of Cereals in Selected States in India (*in kg.*)

States	*Areas*	*Rice*	*Wheat*	*Other/Cereals*	*Total*
Kerala	Rural	104.52	10.56	0.00	115.08
	Urban	87.60	14.16	0.00	101.76
Punjab	Rural	8.88	106.56	1.32	116.64
	Urban	10.08	94.08	0.84	104.88
Uttar Pradesh	Rural	42.84	104.88	2.40	150.24
	Urban	31.80	92.28	0.12	129.84
All India	Rural	78.24	52.08	14.64	144.96
	Urban	56.88	55.08	6.00	117.96

Note : Others include Jowar, Bajra, Maize, Barley, Small Millets and Ragi.

Source : Household Consumer Expenditure & Employment-Unemployment Situation in India, *NSS 58th round report*, 2003.

Following NSS 58th round report (2003) we observe a monotonic increase in per capita consumption of cereals in value terms for rural India when the monthly per capita expenditure (MPCE) brackets are arranged in ascending order. In quantity terms we find a little aberration in higher MPCE brackets where after reaching peak real (quantity per capita) consumption for MPCE bracket (Rs. 5040 to Rs. 5640), consumption started declining a little. In value terms, per capita annual consumption of rice showed monotonic increase with respect to high MPCE brackets, which holds good for wheat also excepting one aberration for MPCE bracket (Rs. 6300 to Rs. 7380). In quantity terms, per capita annual consumption of rice showed monotonically higher figures excepting a little decline for MPCE brackets like Rs. 6300 to Rs. 7380 and Rs. 7380 to Rs. 9300. We find a drastic decline in per capita annual consumption of other items, excluding rice and wheat, in value terms for the top two MPCE brackets, Rs. 9300 to Rs. 11400 and above Rs. 11400. In quantity terms, this decline is not visible. The implication may be that the prices that the higher MPCE brackets pay on other items have got reduced much to lead to reduction in value terms, on the assumption that it is money-based exchange. It is difficult to draw any conclusion from the 'quantity-value' comparisons, i.e., what do the MPCE brackets do when the households decide their consumption-mix. It is, however, clear that higher MPCE brackets spend more on total cereals relative to the lower brackets (Table 2.20).

Table 2.20: Per Capita Annual Consumption of Cereals in Rural India

MPCE (Rs.)	*Quantity (in kg.)*				*Value (in Rs.)*			
	Rice	*Wheat*	*Others*	*Total*	*Rice*	*Wheat*	*Others*	*Total*
0-2700	73.69	26.11	17.69	117.49	539.97	158.23	91.62	789.83
2700-3060	76.49	37.09	17.32	130.91	588.77	228.75	92.84	910.36
3060-3600	77.35	44.29	14.64	136.27	612.81	280.36	81.25	974.41
3600-4080	78.81	46.97	15.74	141.52	662.22	301.83	90.40	1054.45
4080-4560	78.93	51.12	15.25	145.30	669.17	330.62	90.04	1089.83
4560-5040	79.91	51.61	15.25	146.77	697.47	339.28	90.52	1127.28
5040-5640	80.76	52.09	16.23	149.08	719.19	348.43	98.58	1166.20
5640-6300	80.52	58.32	15.25	154.09	747.37	397.84	91.87	1237.08
6300-7380	81.13	56.24	15.98	153.35	777.99	391.62	99.19	1268.80
7380-9300	81.13	57.83	14.40	153.35	803.61	423.22	95.04	1321.87
9300-11400	81.13	62.83	10.86	154.82	836.19	448.96	71.98	1357.13
11400+	77.71	67.59	8.91	154.21	896.70	524.48	58.32	1479.49
All	79.54	52.95	14.88	147.38	727.97	363.19	89.06	1180.23

Note: 'Others' include Jowar, Bajra, Maize, Barley, Small Millets and Ragi.
Source: Household Consumer Expenditure & Employment-Unemployment Situation in India, *NSS 58th round report*, 2003.

Following NSS data (58th round), per capita annual consumption of cereals in urban India in real terms increased monotonically with reference to MPCE (Rs.) brackets in ascending order excepting the bracket Rs. 6000 to Rs. 6900. We do not find any monotonic increase in real consumption (Rs.) of wheat when seen in the context of MPCE brackets in ascending order. For rice consumption in real terms per capita for urban India, the monotonic increase is generally true excepting two MPCE brackets, Rs. 3600 to Rs. 4200 and Rs. 7980 to Rs. 9300. Per capita real consumption of other cereals showed oscillations with reference to MPCE brackets in ascending order, with visible overall decline for high MPCE brackets. What is obvious is that the low MPCE brackets spend more per capita on items like jowar, bajra, maize, ragi etc. relative to the higher MPCE brackets. In quantity terms, per capita annual consumption of cereals in urban India showed variations with respect to MPCE brackets, with visible decline for higher MPCE brackets. The same quantity per capita consumption of all cereals for the lowest MPCE bracket (less than Rs. 3600) and highest (more than Rs. 23100) does not reveal the same consumption mix even within cereals. While the former bracket consumes more of 'more inferior items' like jowar, bajra, maize etc. the latter consumes less of these items, and more of wheat (less inferior items). We do not find any monotonic increase in consumption of rice and wheat with respect to MPCE brackets seen in ascending order (Table 2.21).

Table 2.21: Per Capita Annual Consumption of Cereals in Urban India

MPCE (Rs.)	*Quantity (in kg.)*				*Value (in Rs.)*			
	Rice	*Wheat*	*Others*	*Total*	*Rice*	*Wheat*	*Others*	*Total*
0-3600	53.44	43.68	13.05	110.17	454.94	301.22	82.72	838.87
3600-4200	51.85	66.00	6.71	124.56	439.32	497.64	43.31	980.27
4200-5100	53.68	60.88	9.39	123.95	496.17	451.40	60.02	1007.60
5100-6000	56.97	57.71	8.05	122.73	549.00	442.49	53.92	1045.42
6000-6900	58.56	53.44	9.03	121.02	610.98	429.56	64.78	1105.32
6900-7980	62.22	50.75	7.93	120.90	676.12	419.68	56.36	1152.17
7980-9300	56.36	59.90	5.86	122.12	651.11	508.13	43.68	1202.92
9300-10980	59.54	55.02	6.10	120.66	704.06	489.95	44.53	1238.54
10980-13440	61.73	55.39	4.27	121.39	781.53	502.40	31.11	1315.04
13440-18000	60.76	55.63	3.29	119.68	816.55	535.70	26.96	1379.21
18000-23100	56.97	57.83	3.29	118.10	828.26	581.94	26.11	1436.31
23100 more	51.61	55.27	2.44	109.31	854.73	626.47	22.81	1504.02
All	57.83	56.00	6.10	119.93	689.91	494.59	43.31	1227.81

Note: 'Others' include Jowar, Bajra, Maize, Barley, Small Millets and Ragi.

Source: Household Consumer Expenditure & Employment-Unemployment Situation in India, *NSS 58th round report*, 2003.

2.13 Consumption Mix

As observed by the Planning Commission, dramatic changes in food consumption patterns took place in India in the post-Green Revolution period. Between 1972-73 and 1993-94, the food basket became more diversified, with the share of cereals experiencing a dramatic decline (Planning Commission, 2002-07, Vol. II, p. 365). The increase in percentage share of non-food in India's rural total expenditure during 1973-2000 went parallel to the sharply declining share of agriculture in GDP (Table 2.22).

Generally, rising income is associated with rising expenditure on higher-order (non-food) goods. Thus, the phenomena of reducing income in agriculture and increasing non-food expenditure need cautious explanation, as opposed to the explanation by the Planning Commission that 'this trend towards a more diversified diet is also discernible among the poorest 25 per cent of the population' (Planning Commission, 2002-07, Vol. I, p. 365). The Commission also observed that 'the growth of aggregate demand for cereals in the country can be said to have been kept in check due to two factors—slow down in the pace of population growth and shift in consumer preference towards non-cereals' (Planning Commission, 2002-07, Vol. I, p. 366). What matters really are the income brackets of the population rather than the 'slow down in the pace of population growth' that determines the relative requirement of food and non-food in consumption mix. What is to be examined is the skewness in the distribution of income and productive assets in rural India rather than suggesting at a macro level the preference of the bottommost section of rural population for non-food. Even if there is preference it is yet to get revealed in the market.

Table 2.22: Share of Agriculture and Non-Food in India, 1973-2000

Year	*Share of Agriculture in GDP*	*Share of Non-Food in Rural Expenditure*
1973-74	44.0	25.1
1983	38.7	34.4
1993-94	32.9	36.8
1999-2000	26.9	40.6

Source: Planning Commission, Government of India, *Tenth Five Year Plan*, 2002-07, Vol. I, p. 28.

In the next chapter we will describe the major issues in the Public Distribution System as it functions in Uttar Pradesh, India.

3

Public Distribution System in Uttar Pradesh: Some Issues

In this chapter we will discuss some of the issues related to PDS in U.P. and will also describe the methodology we followed for studying the PDS being practiced in U.P., India. Our aim is to examine the extent to which the PDS succeeded in providing essential commodities to the people living below poverty line (BPL). This includes the non-beneficiary households, i.e., those who have been left out of the system because of being cardless. In our study of U.P. we analysed the working of the delivery mechanism (Centre—State—FCI Godowns—Local FPSs—Target Groups) in this system. The role that the Panchayati Raj Institutions (PRIs) play in ensuring the smooth delivery system and in ensuring food security of the poor was also examined. Finally, we examined if the existing distributive set up was efficient to run the PDS. The reason why we selected U.P. was that it was the second largest state by area with population size ranked first. It is today one of the most underdeveloped states in India that relies more on production of food-grains like wheat and rice. High production has hardly had any impact on eradicating perpetual poverty and hunger of a large section of population in the state. There are, however, intra-state differentials in production and productivity of foodgrains.

In U.P., SC population as percentage of total population (21.1) is ahead of that of India (16.2%) while the ST population in U.P. (as per cent of total) is 0.1, far behind that of all-India (8.1%). Urban population in U.P. (20.8%) is far behind that of all-India (27.8%). Size of households in U.P. (6.5%) is more than that of all-India (5.3%). Sex ratio in U.P. is against women more than it is in case of all-India. Literacy rate in U.P. (56.3%) is behind that of all-India (64.8%). Density of population in U.P. (689) is far more than that of all-India (324). There are district-wise (selected sample) variations in all these variables.

Cultivators as percentage of total workers in U.P. (41.1) are far ahead of that in India (31.6). Agricultural labourers as percentage of total workers in U.P. (24.8) are similar to that in India (26.6). Other workers as percentage of total workers in U.P. (28.5) are much less than that in India (37.6). The rest is covered by workers in household industries. Work participation rate in U.P. (32.5%) is much less than that of all-India (39.3). Main workers as percentage of total workers in U.P. (23.7%) are much less than that of all-India (30.5%). The percentage of non-workers in U.P. (67.5%) is much ahead of that for all-India (60.7%). The rest (main workers and non-workers by percentage subtracted from total workers) is explained by marginal workers. There is a striking similarity in all these rates and percentages when sample (eight districts of U.P.) mean and U.P. as a whole are compared, excepting those for agricultural labour and other workers. There are, however, district-wise variations in all these rates and percentages.

Methodology and Sample

We covered in this study most of the schemes where foodgrains are distributed through TPDS that cover households listed as BPL and APL, and households covered under Antyodaya Yojana and Annapurna Yojana. We covered the eligible non-beneficiaries also who for some reasons remained cardless. There are four regions in U.P. by administrative division, namely, east, west, central and Bundelkhand. We classified all districts based on per capita income above and below the State average income in each region. Four districts have been selected from above the State average and four from below the State average. We selected two districts from each region in which one is developed and the other is underdeveloped.

A composite development index was prepared for each district on the basis of percentage of electrified villages and availability of *pucca* road per lakh population based on equal weightage. If the block was above district index, it was considered developed and if below district index, it was considered underdeveloped. One block from each category had been randomly selected from every selected district. For the urban areas, all the towns were arranged in alphabetical order and one was selected randomly. We selected randomly two villages and two wards from each selected block/town where FPSs existed. We also selected some additional villages/wards to compensate sample loss. We listed the benefited households as we received it from State Supply Department. Similarly we listed the Fair Price Shops (FPSs).

SAMPLE PROCEDURE

Coverage at Different Levels	Sample Size	Methodology
State	Uttar Pradesh	• Purposive Selection, because it is one of the 'BIMARU' States of India and the state produced high quantity of food-grains but existence of hunger is much. • There is no previous state level detailed study on public distribution system and food security.
Districts	8 Districts from all Regions of which 4 Developed and 4 Under-Developed	• Classified all districts based on per capita income above and below the State average income in each (4) regions. • Four districts have been selected from above the State average and four from below the State average. • The two districts from each region in which one is developed and the other is under-developed.
Blocks	16 Blocks from all 8 Selected Districts of which 8 Developed & 8 Under-Developed and two wards from selected (urban) towns	• A composite development index is prepared for each district on the basis of percentage of electrified villages and availability of pucca road per lakh population based on equal weightage. • If the block is above district index, it is considered developed and if below district index, it is considered under-developed. • Both the categories arranged in alphabetical order. • One Block from each category has been randomly selected from every selected district. • For the urban areas, all the towns are arranged in alphabetical order and selected one randomly.
Villages	33 Villages from 16 Selected Blocks and 17 wards from 8 selected Towns	• Listed all villages/wards from each selected block/town where FPSs existed. • Arranged all villages in alphabetical order. • Randomly two villages and two wards have been selected from each selected block / town. • Some additional villages/wards selected to compensate sample loss.
Beneficiaries	960 Beneficiary Households from all selected Villages/Wards	• Taking list of benefited households from State Supply Department or FPS and listed them. • The selection is based on random basis. • Proportionate representation of all beneficiaries under PDS has been covered as per our proposal. • Some additional beneficiary households drawn into the sample to compensate sample loss. In case the target not been covered by the selected villages, some additional villages/wards had been visited.
Non-Beneficiaries	241 Non-Beneficiary eligible Households from all Selected Villages/Wards	• Listed all non-benefited households, who were eligible for any schemes under PDS with the help of FPS, Panchayat, Local people, & self survey and listed them. • 05 non-benefited households have been selected on random basis, and some additional sample taken to compensate sample loss. • If the target had not been covered by the selected villages, additional villages were drawn, Incase it remains not covered, the loss is compensated at district or regional level.
Fair Price Shops	46 FPS dealers from all Selected Villages/wards	The FPS selected, where most of the sampled beneficiaries were availing PDS facilities. In case of Annpurnna Yojana, we covered those FPSs where the beneficiaries had taken their food-grains.

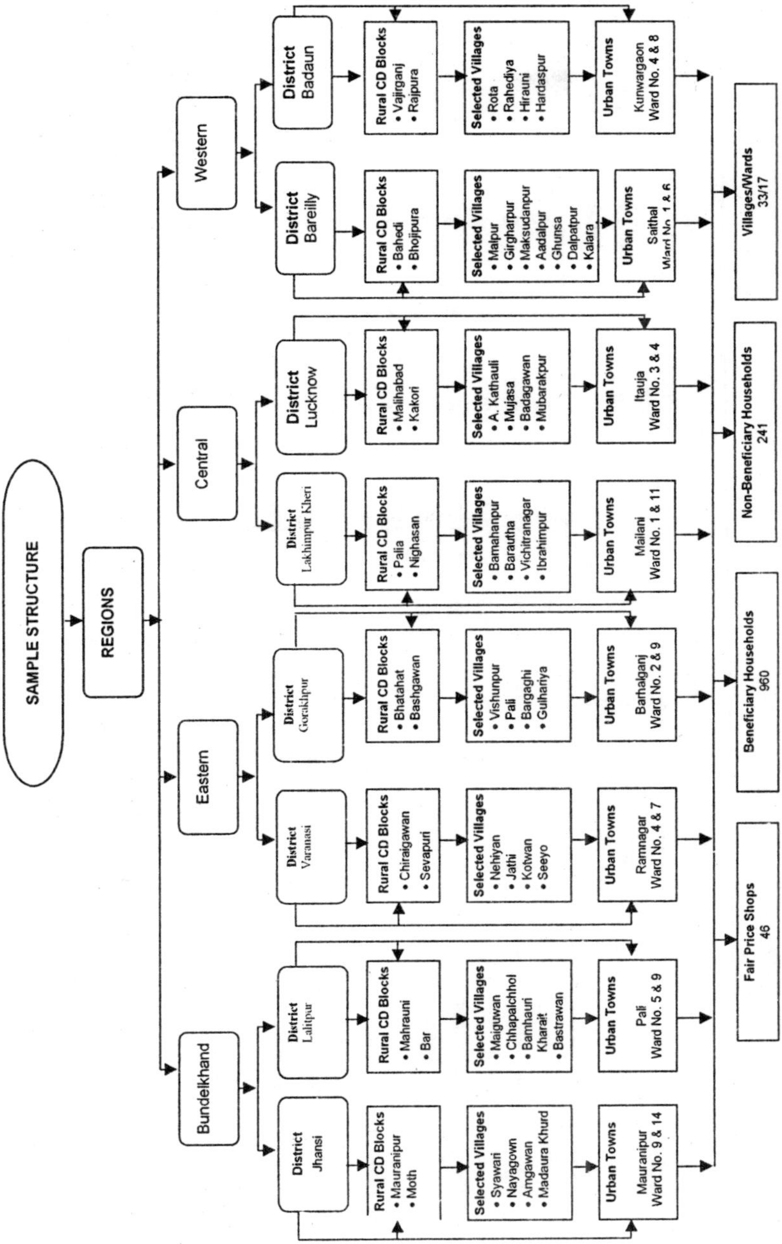

SAMPLE STRUCTURE
REGIONS
Bundelkhand
Eastern
Central
Western
District Jhansi
District Lalitpur
District Varanasi
District Gorakhpur
District Lakhimpur Kheri
District Lucknow
District Bareilly
District Badaun
Rural CD Blocks • Mauranipur • Moth
Rural CD Blocks • Mahrauni • Bar
Rural CD Blocks • Chiraigawan • Sevapuri
Rural CD Blocks • Bhatahat • Bashgawan
Rural CD Blocks • Palia • Nighasan
Rural CD Blocks • Malihabad • Kakori
Rural CD Blocks • Bahedi • Bhojipura
Rural CD Blocks • Vajirganj • Rajpura
Selected Villages • Syawari • Nayagown • Amgawan • Madaura Khurd
Selected Villages • Maiguwan • Chhapalchhol • Bamhauri Kharait • Bastrawan
Selected Villages • Nehiyan • Jathi • Kotwan • Seeyo
Selected Villages • Vishunpur • Pali • Bargaghi • Gulhariya
Selected Villages • Bamahanpur • Barautha • Vichitranagar • Ibrahimpur
Selected Villages • A. Kathauli • Mujasa • Badagawan • Mubarakpur
Selected Villages • Malpur • Girgharpur • Maksudanpur • Aadalpur • Ghunsa • Dalpatpur • Kalara
Selected Villages • Rota • Rahediya • Hirauni • Hardaspur
Urban Towns Mauranipur Ward No. 9 & 14
Urban Towns Pali Ward No. 5 & 9
Urban Towns Ramnagar Ward No. 4 & 7
Urban Towns Barhalganj Ward No. 2 & 9
Urban Towns Mailani Ward No. 1 & 11
Urban Towns Itauja Ward No. 3 & 4
Urban Towns Saithal Ward No. 1 & 6
Urban Towns Kunwargaon Ward No. 4 & 8
Fair Price Shops 46
Beneficiary Households 960
Non-Beneficiary Households 241
Villages/Wards 33/17

Table 3.1: Coverage of the Study

Regions	Districts	Sample Units		Households			Fair Price Shop Dealers	Godowns		Government Functionaries	
		Villages	*Urban Wards*	*Beneficiary Households*	*Non-Beneficiary Households*	*Total*		*Food-grains*	*Kerosene Depots*	*District Level*	*Tehsil Level*
Western	Bariely	6	2	118	18	136	7	3	3	1	3
	Badaun	4	2	120	42	162	5	3	3	1	3
	Total	10	4	238	60	298	12	6	6	2	6
Central	Lakhimpur	4	3	122	30	152	6	3	4	0	2
	Lucknow	3	2	120	31	151	5	3	3	1	3
	Total	7	5	242	61	303	11	6	7	1	5
Bundelkhand	Lalitpur	4	2	120	27	147	6	3	4	1	3
	Jhansi	4	2	120	33	153	6	2	3	1	2
	Total	8	4	240	60	300	12	5	7	2	5
Eastern	Gorakhpur	4	2	120	30	150	6	2	4	0	2
	Varanasi	4	2	120	30	150	5	2	3	1	2
	Total	8	4	240	60	300	11	4	7	1	4
	Grand Total	33	17	960	241	1201	46	21	27	6	20

We listed all eligible non-benefited households with the help of FPS, Panchayat, Local people, and through a pilot survey. If the target had not been covered by the selected villages, additional villages were drawn. In case it remains not covered, the sample loss was compensated at district or regional level.

We covered 960 beneficiary households and 241 non-beneficiary households, 46 FPSs, 33 representatives of Gram Panchayats, 48 foodgrains godowns and 27 kerosene depots, and 26 functionaries from eight selected districts of the state. This is shown in Table 3.1.

In the next chapter we will focus on the observations that unearth PDS-related facts for the districts of UP that we covered.

4

Public Distribution in Uttar Pradesh: Some Facts

In this chapter we will describe the facts that we observed on the Public Distribution System as it has been functioning in U.P. We found regional variations based on selected development indicators in all the eight districts. The density of population is very low in Bundelkhand, and is far behind east, west and central U.P. Urban population is lowest in east U.P., far behind that in west, central and Bundelkhand in that order as percentage of total population. East and west U.P. cover more than three-fourths of total population selected in U.P. Literacy rate in each of the four regions shows similar pattern, between 55.0 and 60.0 per cent. Main workers as percentage of total population is lowest in east U.P. (22.0) and highest in Bundelkhand (27.0). Main workers engaged in agriculture as percentage of total main workers varied between 56.8 per cent for west U.P. and highest for Bundelkhand (74.5). There is tremendous gap regionally in number of employees working in registered factory per lakh population, 64 for Bundelkhand and 413 for west U.P. Per capita net output (in value terms) from commodity production in 1997-98 was highest for west U.P. (Rs. 9,882) and lowest for east U.P. (Rs. 6,269).

4.1 Beneficiary Households

We covered a total of 960 beneficiary households in the sample from eight districts of U.P. more or less equally distributed over all the four regions in the state, namely, east, west, central and Bundelkhand. Each of the selected eight districts had more or less equal number of households in the sample.

Of the total households, 68.4 per cent were rural and 31.6 per cent were urban. Of the rural sample beneficiary households, the minimum was drawn from east U.P. (66.25%) and the maximum from central U.P. (71.1%). For the urban beneficiary households, the minimum percentage was 28.9 drawn from central U.P. and the maximum was 33.7 drawn from east U.P. There was not much district-wise difference by percentages of rural and urban households selected. Table 4.1 shows the sample beneficiary households by blocks, towns and sample units from each of the regions of U.P.

Table 4.1: Sample Beneficiary Households by Blocks, Towns and Sample Units

Region	District	Households Covered						Sample Units			
		Rural		Urban		Total		Blocks	Towns	Villages	Wards
		No.	%	No.	%	No.	%				
Western	Barielly	81	68.6	37	31.4	118	100.0	2	1	5	2
	Badaun	85	70.8	35	29.2	120	100.0	2	1	4	2
	Total	166	69.7	72	30.3	238	100.0	4	2	9	4
Central	Lakhim-pur Kheri	82	67.2	40	32.8	122	100.0	2	1	4	2
	Lucknow	90	75.0	30	25.0	120	100.0	2	1	5	2
	Total	172	71.1	70	28.9	242	100.0	4	2	9	4
Bundel-khand	Lalitpur	80	66.7	40	33.3	120	100.0	2	1	4	2
	Jhansi	80	66.7	40	33.3	120	100.0	2	1	4	2
	Total	160	66.7	80	33.3	240	100.0	4	2	8	4
Eastern	Gorakh-pur	79	65.8	41	34.2	120	100.0	2	1	4	2
	Vāranasi	80	66.7	40	33.3	120	100.0	2	1	4	2
	Total	159	66.25	81	33.75	240	100.0	4	2	8	4
Total Sample		657	68.4	303	31.6	960	100.0	16	8	34	16

Source: Field Survey, 2006.

The total beneficiary households (960) were equally distributed by category of cardholding, namely, BPL, APL, ANP and ANT. The beneficiaries were also equally distributed in all the rural beneficiary households. District-wise each category of households by cardholding was equally distributed into a total of 30, of which 20 were for the rural areas for each district. We covered four categories, thus, adding up to a total of 120 households by cardholding for each district. Thus we followed uniform distribution in selection of beneficiary households by cardholding as shown in Table 4.2.

Table 4.2: Profile of Beneficiary Households by Different Types of Ration Cards

Districts		*BPL*		*APL*		*ANP*		*ANT*		Total	
		Rural	*Total*	*Rural*	*Total*	*Rural*	*Total*	*Rural*	*Total*	*Rural*	*Total*
Barielly	No.	20	30	20	30	21	28	20	30	81	118
	%	24.7	37.0	24.7	37.0	25.9	34.6	24.7	37.0	25.4	100.0
Badaun	No.	20	30	20	30	25	30	20	30	85	120
	%	23.5	35.3	23.5	35.3	29.4	35.3	23.5	35.3	25.0	100.0
Lakhimpur Kheri	No.	20	30	20	30	22	32	20	30	82	122
	%	24.4	36.6	24.4	36.6	26.8	39.0	24.4	36.6	24.6	100.0
Lucknow	No.	20	30	20	30	30	30	20	30	90	120
	%	22.2	33.3	22.2	33.3	33.3	33.3	22.2	33.3	25.0	100.0
Lalitpur	No.	20	30	20	30	20	30	20	30	80	120
	%	25.0	37.5	25.0	37.5	25.0	37.5	25.0	37.5	25.0	100.0
Jhansi	No.	20	30	20	30	20	30	20	30	80	120
	%	25.0	37.5	25.0	37.5	25.0	37.5	25.0	37.5	25.0	100.0
Gorakhpur	No.	20	30	20	30	19	30	20	30	79	120
	%	25.3	38.0	25.3	38.0	24.1	38.0	25.3	38.0	25.0	100.0
Varanasi	No.	20	30	20	30	20	30	20	30	80	120
	%	25.0	37.5	25.0	37.5	25.0	37.5	25.0	37.5	25.0	100.0
Total	No.	160	240	160	240	177	240	160	240	657	960
	%	24.4	36.5	24.4	36.5	26.9	36.5	24.4	36.5	25.0	100.0

Source: Field Survey, 2006.

4.1.1 Demographic Profile of Beneficiary Households

Of all the beneficiary households, 45.2 per cent were in the age bracket 35-60 while 69.0 per cent were in the age bracket 18-60. In rural regions the percentages were 44.6 and 70.3 respectively and in urban region, the respective percentages were 46.5 and 66.0. Of all beneficiary households, the male-female ratio was 59.9:40.1. There were district-wise variations in households by age, gender and rural-urban.

Of the total population in the sample, 53.4 per cent belonged to the age bracket between 15 and 60 years, 23.2 per cent in the age bracket between 7 and 14 years, 14.6 per cent below 6 years and 8.8 per cent above 60 years. For the total population the male-female ratio was 52:48. Of the total population 52.3 per cent was SCs, 27.2 per cent OBCs, 16.9 per cent minority and 2.8 per cent belonged to the general castes.

Sixty-six per cent of the beneficiary households were illiterate, 10.1 per cent had education at the level of high school and above while another 10.1 per cent had attained primary level education.

By poverty indicator, 28.9 per cent were BPL, 26.3 per cent ANT, 16.9 per cent ANP and 27.8 per cent APL.

4.1.2 Occupational Structure of Beneficiary Households

The distribution of main occupations of the beneficiary households show that most of the beneficiaries were engaged as non-agricultural labour (47.3%), followed by cultivation (13.2%), small business (6.0%) and agricultural labour (5.3%). Of all the BPL households, 43.8 per cent were non-agricultural labourers, which included 39.2 per cent from the APL beneficiaries, 42.1 from the ANP and 64.2 from ANT. 25.8 per cent of APL households were cultivators. Joblessness was most for the ANP households (15.4%). The activities of the households by types of cardholding are shown in Table 4.3.

4.1.3 Income Structure of Beneficiary Households

Of all the beneficiary households, 4.0 per cent were 'incomeless', i.e., having no source of income. 66.6 per cent earned income less than Rs. 19,000 per annum, 81.6 per cent below Rs. 25,000 per annum, and 4.1 per cent above Rs. 50,000 per annum. Less than one-fifth of the households earned more than Rs. 25,000 per annum. The annual income of beneficiary households by districts is shown in Table 4.4.

Table 4.3: Main Occupations of Beneficiary Households by Ration Cards

Occupations	*BPL*		*APL*		*ANP*		*ANT*		*Total*	
	No.	*%*	*No.*	*%*	*No.*	*%*	*No.*	*%*	*No.*	*%*
Agriculture	32	13.3	62	25.8	18	7.5	15	6.3	127	13.2
Agricultural labour	18	7.5	8	3.3	8	3.3	17	7.1	51	5.3
Non-Ag Labour	105	43.8	94	39.2	101	42.1	154	64.2	454	47.3
Skilled Labour	21	8.8	4	1.7	7	2.9	10	4.2	42	4.4
Traditional labour	8	3.3	6	2.5	10	4.2	7	2.9	31	3.2
Government service	2	0.8	8	3.3	1	0.4	1	0.4	12	1.3
Private Service	19	7.9	15	6.3	13	5.4	8	3.3	55	5.7
Small Business	2	0.8	2	0.8	0	0.0	3	1.3	7	0.7
Pensioner	0	0.0	6	2.5	15	6.3	2	0.8	23	2.4
Animal husbandry	0	0.0	3	1.3	2	0.8	3	1.3	8	0.8
Small Business	11	4.6	25	10.4	13	5.4	9	3.8	58	6.0
Rickshaw/ Trolley Pulling and Hawking	9	3.8	3	1.3	1	0.4	8	3.3	21	2.2
Bidi Making	0	0.0	0	0.0	2	0.8	1	0.4	3	0.3
No Work	1	0.4	0	0.0	37	15.4	0	0.0	38	4.0
Begging	0	0.0	0	0.0	9	3.8	0	0.0	9	0.9
Weaving	12	5.0	4	1.7	3	1.3	2	0.8	21	2.2
Total	240	100.0	240	100.0	240	100.0	240	100.0	960	100.0

Source: Field Survey, 2006.

For the sample districts considered together the reported average income of the BPL households was more than the reported average income of the APL households. This was explained by the higher percentage of BPL households included in the medium income bracket Rs. 19,000 to Rs. 50,000 per annum relative to that of the APL households. A higher percentage of APL households obviously had been included in the higher income bracket above Rs. 50,000 per annum relative to the inclusion of BPL households. There were variations in the percentages of households by cardholding in different income brackets and hence in estimated average income.

Annual income per beneficiary household on average over all the districts stood at Rs. 18,675, which was a weighted average of the income levels by brackets. The average annual income of the rural households (Rs. 17,918) was less than that of the urban households (Rs. 20,317).

Table 4.4: Annual Income (Rs.) of Beneficiary Households by Districts

District	*Figure in*	*No Income*	*Up to 5000*	*5000-10000*	*10000-19000*	*19000-25000*	*25000-50000*	*50000-1 Lakh*	*>1 Lakh*	*Total*
Barielly	No.	3	10	16	34	23	24	8	0	118
	%	2.5	8.5	13.6	28.8	19.5	20.3	6.8	0.0	100.0
Badaun	No.	7	13	23	42	10	18	5	2	120
	%	5.8	10.8	19.2	35.0	8.3	15.0	4.2	1.7	100.0
Lakhimpur	No.	3	17	24	42	19	14	2	1	122
Kheri	%	2.5	13.9	19.7	34.4	15.6	11.5	1.6	0.8	100.0
Lucknow	No.	3	12	26	46	16	13	3	1	120
	%	2.5	10.0	21.7	38.3	13.3	10.8	2.5	0.8	100.0
Lalitpur	No.	11	8	24	46	17	14	0	0	120
	%	9.2	6.7	20.0	38.3	14.2	11.7	0.0	0.0	100.0
Jhansi	No.	7	2	24	42	21	21	3	0	120
	%	5.8	1.7	20.0	35.0	17.5	17.5	2.5	0.0	100.0
Gorakhpur	No.	1	11	22	37	22	17	6	4	120
	%	0.8	9.2	18.3	30.8	18.3	14.2	5.0	3.3	100.0
Varanasi	No.	3	8	20	53	16	15	4	1	120
	%	`2.5	6.7	16.7	44.2	13.3	12.5	3.3	0.8	100.0
Total	No.	38	81	179	342	144	136	31	9	960
	%	4.0	8.4	18.6	35.6	15.0	14.2	3.2	0.9	100.0

Source: Field Survey, 2006.

The average rural income of the BPL households was reported to be more than that of the APL. The same was reported by the households in urban area by the types of cardholding. The reason was a higher percentage of BPL households in both rural and urban areas included in the income bracket Rs. 19,000 to Rs. 50,000 which was not offset by the higher percentage of households in income bracket above Rs. 50,000 from the APL households. Table 4.5 shows the distribution of beneficiary households by income and region.

66.7 per cent of the beneficiary households had no economic occupations. The productive population was involved in a number of occupations like cultivation (3.8%), labour (19.9%), skilled labour (3.5%), traditional labour (0.9%), animal husbandry (0.4%), service (1.9%), business (2.2%) and pension (0.8%).

54.4 per cent of the population in the sample lived below income per annum per household Rs. 19,000. Another 19.3 per cent earned income per annum between Rs. 19,001 and Rs. 25,000. Thus, 26.3 per cent of the population earned income per annum per household above Rs. 25,000.

Table 4.5: Distribution of Beneficiary Households by Income and Region

Income Category (Rs.)		Rural					Urban				
		BPL	APL	ANP	ANT	Total	BPL	APL	ANP	ANT	Total
No Income	No. of HHs	0	0	27	0	27	1	0	10	0	11
	%	0.0	0.0	15.3	0.0	4.1	1.3	0.0	15.9	0.0	3.6
Up to 5000	Average Income	3600	4200	3235	2600	3259	4800	4800	3189	4800	3470
	No. of HHs	1	5	46	6	58	1	2	19	1	23
	%	0.6	3.1	26.0	3.8	8.8	1.3	2.5	30.2	1.3	7.6
5000-10000	Average Income	7659	8255	7573	8361	8026	7500	8467	7582	7800	7996
	No. of HHs	17	33	37	46	133	2	18	11	15	46
	%	10.6	20.6	20.9	28.8	20.2	2.5	22.5	17.5	18.8	15.2
10000-19000	Average Income	14851	14586	13427	14096	14340	15660	14467	15323	14200	14832
	No. of HHs	65	71	37	69	242	30	18	13	39	100
	%	40.6	44.4	20.9	43.1	36.8	37.5	22.5	20.6	48.8	33.0
19000-25000	Average Income	22119	22560	23220	21700	22226	23012	22484	23500	21818	22630
	No. of HHs	37	20	10	24	91	17	19	6	11	53
	%	23.1	12.5	5.6	15.0	13.9	21.3	23.8	9.5	13.8	17.5
25000-50000	Average Income	33310	33540	32753	31846	33015	34777	34145	30600	31629	33545
	No. of HHs	31	20	17	13	81	26	11	4	14	55
	%	19.4	12.5	9.6	8.1	12.3	32.5	13.8	6.3	17.5	18.2
50000-1 Lakh	Average Income	69400	70114	86800	53400	70800	74800	63240	0	0	65908
	No. of HHs	6	7	3	2	18	3	10			13
	%	3.8	4.4	1.7	1.3	2.7	3.8	12.5	0.0	0.0	4.3
>1 Lakh	Average Income	153600	153300	0	0	153429	0	162000	0	0	162000
	No. of HHs	3	4			7		2			2
	%	1.9	2.5	0.0	0.0	1.1	0.0	2.5	0.0	0.0	0.7
Total	Average Income	23921	22219	11159	15090	17918	25118	27270	9629	16980	20317
	No. of HHs	160	160	177	160	657	80	80	63	80	303
	%	100.0	100.0	100.0	100.0	100.0	100.0	100.0	100.0	100.0	100.0

Source: Field Survey, 2006.

Per capita income per annum for all the beneficiary households was Rs. 3,744. Per capita annual income of each of APL and BPL households was above the grand average at Rs. 3744, while that of each of ANT and ANP was below the grand average. However the reliability of reported income data was doubtful. Table 4.6 shows the per capita annual income of beneficiary households by income brackets.

Table 4.6: Per Capita Annual Income of Beneficiary Households

(By Income Brackets)

Annual Income	*Barielly*	*Badaun*	*Lakhimpur Kheri*	*Lucknow*	*Lalitpur*	*Jhansi*	*Gorakhpur*	*Varanasi*	*Total*
Below Rs. 5000	750	1572	1662	2088	980	686	1600	1680	1385
Rs. 5001-10000	2181	2174	1454	1674	1902	1800	1819	1754	1807
Rs. 10001-19000	2796	2911	3127	2756	2912	3438	2869	2898	2953
Rs. 19001-25000	3916	3725	4008	3860	3121	3919	3246	3378	3627
Rs. 25001-50000	5197	5172	4932	5209	4838	4544	4376	4185	4790
Rs. 50001-1 Lakh	10702	7346	9300	12800	—	6785	6748	11571	8768
Above Rs. 1 Lakh	—	37500	7520	17143	—	—	13969	51000	17556
Total	4249	4096	3465	3501	3012	3684	4120	3722	3744

Source: Field Survey, 2006.

4.1.4 Ownership over Productive Assets of Beneficiary Households

Most of the beneficiary households did not have agricultural productive assets for livelihood support. Only 6.1 per cent had pump sets and 3.5 per cent had ploughs. The ownership over other items like cutting machine, buffalo/bull carts was rare.

Of all the beneficiary households, only 1 per cent had hand-driven carts, 0.8 per cent had tractors, 0.9 per cent had trolley/rickshaw, and 0.7 per cent had sewing machines. Thus the households hardly had ownership over income-generating assets.

As a livelihood support system, the productive animals that the beneficiary households owned included mainly cow, buffalo, goat, ox, horse, hen, and bull.

4.1.5 Living Condition of Beneficiary Households

Only two of the beneficiary households were shelterless and 39.4 per cent of the households had *kuccha* houses. 23.2 per cent had *pucca* houses of which BPL cardholders had 35.4 per cent; APL cardholders had 27.4 per cent, ANP 23.3 per cent, and ANT 13.9 per cent. There were variations in the housing conditions of households by cardholding.

97.8 per cent of the beneficiary households depended on kerosene for light. The rest were dependent on candle. The other methods of illumination like gobar gas, solar light, inverter, and wood were insignificant. The ANT households depended almost wholly on kerosene (99.6%). This was generally true for other types of cardholders also, as is shown in Table 4.7.

Table 4.7: Dependence of Beneficiary Households for Light at Night by Types of Card-Holding

Sources	*BPL*		*APL*		*ANP*		*ANT*		*Total*	
	No.	*%*	*No.*	*%*	*No.*	*%*	*No.*	*%*	*No.*	*%*
Gobar Gas	1	0.4	0	0.0	0	0.0	0	0.0	1	0.1
Solar Light	1	0.4	0	0.0	0	0.0	0	0.0	1	0.1
Battery	0	0.0	1	0.4	1	0.4	3	1.3	5	0.5
Inverter	1	0.4	1	0.4	0	0.0	0	0.0	2	0.2
Kerosene	234	97.5	240	100.0	226	94.2	239	99.6	939	97.8
Candle	35	14.6	24	10.0	13	5.4	22	9.2	94	9.8
Live in Darkness	1	0.4	0	0.0	13	5.4	0	0.0	14	1.5
Wood Burning	1	0.4	0	0.0	0	0.0	0	0.0	1	0.1
Mustard Oil	1	0.4	0	0.0	3	1.3	2	0.8	6	0.6
Total	240	100.0	240	100.0	240	100.0	240	100.0	960	100.0

Source: Field Survey, 2006.

The major fuels that the beneficiary households used for cooking purposes were wood (92.5%) and '*kanda*' (90.8%). Kerosene was not a major fuel for cooking. The use of other types of fuels like coal, electricity, LPG (Gas), leaf etc. for cooking was insignificant by all the households. Table 4.8 shows the fuels used by different types of ration card holders.

4.1.6 Landholding of Beneficiary Households

Of all the beneficiary households, 68.1 per cent were landless. By the types of cardholding, landlessness was reported by 78.8 per cent of all ANP households, 75.4 per cent of all ANT households, 62.1 per cent of the BPL households and 56.3 of the APL households. The average landholding (ownership) for those who owned land was 1.5 acre, which varied by cardholding. Table 4.9 shows the beneficiary households by landholding by types of ration cards.

Table 4.8: Fuels Used by Different Types of Ration Card Holders

	BPL		*APL*		*ANP*		*ANT*		*Total*	
	No.	*%*	*No.*	*%*	*No.*	*%*	*No.*	*%*	*No.*	*%*
Wood	226	94.2	211	87.9	223	92.9	228	95.0	888	92.5
Kanda*	213	88.8	204	85.0	222	92.5	233	97.1	872	90.8
Kerosene	5	2.1	6	2.5	2	0.8	3	1.3	16	1.7
Stone Coal	9	3.8	3	1.3	5	2.1	2	0.8	19	2.0
Wood Coal	1	0.4	3	1.3	4	1.7	3	1.3	11	1.1
LPG	16	6.7	34	14.2	8	3.3	3	1.3	61	6.4
Electricity	3	1.3	0	0.0	0	0.0	0	0.0	3	0.3
Gobar Gas	0	0.0	2	0.8	0	0.0	2	0.8	4	0.4
Leaf etc.	1	0.4	0	0.0	1	0.4	2	0.8	4	0.4
Total	240	100.0	240	100.0	240	100.0	240	100.0	960	100.0

* Cow dung cake

Source : Field Survey, 2006.

Table 4.9: Beneficiary Households by Landholding by Types of Ration Cards

(*Land in Acre*)

Sample		*Total Land holding*		*Landless Households*	*Total Households*
		HHs	*Total Land*		
BPL	No.	91	112.6	149	240
	%	37.9	100.0	62.1	100.0
APL	No.	105	220.2	135	240
	%	43.8	100.0	56.3	100.0
ANP	No.	51	53.8	189	240
	%	21.3	100.0	78.8	100.0
ANT	No.	59	66.0	181	240
	%	24.6	100.0	75.4	100.0
Total	No.	306	452.5	654	960
	%	31.9	100.0	68.1	100.0

Source : Field Survey, 2006.

4.1.7 Availability of Basic Amenities in Selected Villages

As reported by the Panchayat representatives, 78.8 per cent of the selected villages had link roads, 6.1 per cent were connected with main road, and 3.0 per cent had only *kuccha* roads. On average, electricity per day was available in the sample villages for 6.67 hours that varied across districts. Electricity was available within 1 km in all the sample villages, public telephone was available within 1 km in 31 of the total (33) villages, FPS was available for 30 villages within 1 km, 66.6 per cent of the foodgrain godowns were located beyond 10 km from the selected villages; 93.9 per cent of the foodgrain godowns were located beyond 5 km, 54.5 per cent of the oil depots were located beyond 10 km; 93.9 per cent of the oil depots were located beyond 5 km, 51.5 per cent of the mandi samity/purchase centres were located beyond 10 km; 78.8 per cent of the mandi samity/purchase centers were located beyond 5 km 54.5 per cent of the weekly markets are located within 3 km, 45.4 per cent of the permanent markets were available within 3 km.

In all the villages, primary schools are located within a distance of 1 km and 90.9 per cent of the villages have Anganwadi/Balwadi within 1 km. No PHC is available within 1 km. Unregistered medical practitioners ('*Jhola Chhap*' doctors) are available within 1 km. distance in 72.7 per cent of the selected villages. 63.6 per cent of the PHCs are available beyond 5 km and 39.3 per cent of the registered doctors/clinics are available beyond 5 km from the selected villages.

4.2 Households as Borrowers by Types of Ration Cards

Of all the beneficiary households, 21.1 per cent had outstanding loans. 33.8 per cent of the BPL households were borrowers followed by 20.4 per cent ANT type households, 17.5 per cent of APL and 12.9 per cent of ANP households. A district-wise beneficiary household as borrowers by types of ration cards is shown in Table 4.10.

Table 4.10: Beneficiary Households as Borrowers by Types of Ration Cards

District	*BPL*		*APL*		*ANP*		*ANT*		*Total*	
	No.	*%*	*No.*	*%*	*No.*	*%*	*No.*	*%*	*No.*	*%*
Barielly	8	9.9	7	16.7	4	12.9	13	26.5	32	15.8
Badaun	11	13.6	13	31.0	6	19.4	10	20.4	40	19.7
Lakhimpur Kheri	5	6.2	6	14.3	5	16.1	6	12.2	22	10.8
Lucknow	7	8.6	2	4.8	0	0.0	2	4.1	11	5.4
Lalitpur	14	17.3	6	14.3	1	3.2	10	20.4	31	15.3
Jhansi	12	14.8	4	9.5	2	6.5	5	10.2	23	11.3
Gorakhpur	16	19.8	1	2.4	2	6.5	1	2.0	20	9.9
Varanasi	8	9.9	3	7.1	11	35.5	2	4.1	24	11.8
Loanee*	81	33.8	42	17.5	31	12.9	49	20.4	203	21.1
Not Taken Loan*	159	66.3	198	82.5	209	87.1	191	79.6	757	78.9
Total HHs	240	100.0	240	100.0	240	100.0	240	100.0	960	100.0

*Percentage calculated on total sample.

Source: Field Survey, 2006.

4.2.1 PDS at the Level of Beneficiary Households

94.5 per cent of the rural and 95.0 per cent of the urban beneficiary households reported that 'eligibility' as a criterion was followed while issuing different types of ration cards. The other factors why and how the households received different types of ration cards were connections, pressure, paying bribe, personal relations and working as vote bank.

In the process of helping to prepare/access ration cards distributed across households by cardholding, the major support came from family members, Gram Pradhan, Panchayat Secretary, and village development officer. The others who helped were friends and neighbours, members of Nagar Panchayat, staff of Supply Department, advocate etc. Across cardholding, there were differences in the percentages of beneficiary households reporting help in the process of getting cards.

Ignorance was the major response of most of the households when asked if they had knowledge about being listed in BPL. Ignorance about being listed in BPL was similar in each of urban and rural regions for households over cardholding.

4.2.2 Households who had More Than a Single-type Ration Card

17.2 per cent of the households had more than a single-type ration card, of which 70.3 per cent were in the rural region and 29.7 per cent in the urban region. Of the total rural beneficiary households, 17.6 per cent had more than one type of ration card. Of the total urban beneficiary households, 16.2 per cent had more than one type of ration card. Of the rural households having ration cards of more than one type, the maximum was for ANP (66.4%) and the minimum was for APL (10.34%). Of the urban households having ration cards more than one type, the maximum was for ANP (73.5%) and the minimum was for ANT (4.1%). The number of households having more than one ration card by region is shown in Table 4.11.

4.2.3 Households which had Fake Ration Cards

Of all the beneficiary households, 19.7 per cent had fake cards, which was 19.8 per cent in rural and 19.5 per cent in urban region. Of all the BPL households, fake cardholding covered 9.2 per cent, which was 9.2 for APL, 52.9 for the ANP and 7.5 for the ANT. There were variations in fake cardholding by region by cardholding.

Table 4.11: Number of Households having More than One Ration Card by Region

Households	*Urban*		*Rural*		*Total*	
	No.	*%*	*No.*	*%*	*No.*	*%*
BPL	4	8.16	13	11.21	17	10.30
APL	7	14.29	12	10.34	19	11.52
ANP	36	73.47	77	66.38	113	68.48
ANT	2	4.08	14	12.07	16	9.70
Total*	49	16.17	116	17.66	165	17.19
Total HHs	303	100.00	657	100.00	960	100.00

Note: * % based on total Households and others are Households having more than one Ration Card.

Source: Field Survey, 2006.

9.9 per cent of all beneficiary households paid bribe for receiving ration cards, which was 8.9 per cent for rural and 12.0 per cent for urban region. This percentage varied across households by cardholding. Over -all, for APL the coverage of households paying bribe was least relative to the households of other categories by cardholding.

More than 60.0 per cent of the beneficiary households reported to have paid bribe to agencies/persons to get their ration cards issued. Of the receivers of bribe paid, the central person was the Panchayat Secretary, followed by NP, Gram Pradhan, teacher, and Supply Department. It seemed as if all the catalysts helping the eligible beneficiaries were involved in sharing bribe.

4.3 Routes of Fulfilment of Essential Commodities

Excepting kerosene, the fulfilment of requirement of all the other essential items like rice, wheat and sugar were mostly met from the market. For wheat, the market satisfied 67.8 per cent of the total requirement, which was 55.6 per cent in case of rice and 78.8 per cent in case of sugar. 82.6 per cent of requirement of kerosene was met by the FPSs and only 12.4 per cent were met by the market. Self-production was a major factor for both rice and wheat in meeting the requirement. For wheat it was 18.3 per cent while for rice it was 11.4 per cent. FPSs met only 11.5 per cent of requirement of wheat, which was 33.2 per cent in case of rice. FPSs met 18.6 per cent of requirement of sugar.

There were variations in requirements of essential commodities met by alternative routes like market, FPSs and self-production by categories of cardholding. There was no self-production of kerosene and generally market response to supply of kerosene was rare in rural areas, so that the role of FPSs was most prominent in case of kerosene.

As percentage of fulfilment of average annual requirement of wheat, the percentage of self-production was highest in case of APL (33.1%) followed by that by BPL (17.6%). The same pattern was true for rice. Self-production of sugar was nil for APL and ANP and negligible for BPL and ANT type households. Self-production thus determined to some extent the fulfilment of total consumption requirement in case of rice and wheat more in the case of APL, as shown in Table 4.12.

In the rural region 22.7 per cent of the requirement for wheat was met from self-production which was 7.8 per cent in the urban region. The respective percentages were 13.5 and 7.7 for rice, 0.9 and 0 for sugar. Since there was no self-production of kerosene the requirement of kerosene had to be met either by the market or by FPSs or remain unfulfilled. FPSs fulfilled 11.0 per cent of requirement of wheat in rural region, which was 33.4 per cent for rice, 19.2 for sugar and 80.5 for kerosene. The respective percentages of fulfilling wheat requirement met by FPSs for urban region were 12.2, 32.7, 17.5 and 86.7 for the four regions. Most of the requirements of commodities excepting kerosene were met from the market in each of the rural and urban regions. Table 4.13 shows the routes of fulfilment of average annual requirement of commodities in the rural and urban regions of the sample population.

Fulfilment of per capita requirement of essential commodities by different routes by cardholding in quantity (kg./lt.) terms shows the following:

For all the households by cardholding, requirement satisfied by the market remained the dominant route for all types of cardholders for each of rice, wheat and sugar. As usual, the market was insignificant in satisfying kerosene requirement over households by cardholding. This is shown in Table 4.14.

For each district, market satisfied most of the requirements excepting kerosene. Self-production, though positive, was not at all a significant factor in explaining fulfilment of consumption requirements excepting to some extent rice.

The supply points covered self-production, market supply (including wage labour and kind payment) and supply from FPSs.

Table 4.12: Average Annual Requirement of Commodities: Routes of Fulfilment (By Card Holding)

(Quantity in kg.)

	Routes	BPL		APL		ANP		ANT		Total	
		Qty.	%	Qty.	%	Qty.	%	Qty.	%	Qty.	%
Wheat	Self-Production	114.9	17.6	231.3	33.1	41.5	9.3	69.2	9.9	114.2	18.3
	Purchase from Market	472.8	72.5	451.0	64.5	287.2	64.3	481.5	68.9	423.1	67.8
	Fulfilment from Wages	12.4	1.9	17.9	2.6	6.8	1.5	20.0	2.9	14.3	2.3
	FPS	90.0	13.8	1.8	0.3	66.1	14.8	129.4	18.5	71.8	11.5
	Requirement	652.3	100.0	699.0	100.0	446.8	100.0	699.3	100.0	624.3	100.0
Rice	Self-Production	34.7	11.6	79.4	21.6	9.5	4.8	15.3	4.3	34.7	11.4
	Purchase from Market	140.3	47.0	284.8	77.5	136.2	69.5	113.4	32.3	168.7	55.6
	Fulfilment from Wages	3.5	1.2	5.6	1.5	3.5	1.8	9.1	2.6	5.5	1.8
	FPS	132.1	44.3	3.9	1.1	47.1	24.0	215.5	61.3	100.6	33.2
	Requirement	298.3	100.0	367.6	100.0	196.1	100.0	351.4	100.0	303.3	100.0
Sugar	Self-Production	0.3	0.6	0.0	0.0	0.0	0.0	0.6	1.5	0.2	0.6
	Purchase from Market	27.1	68.9	54.5	96.9	16.6	80.7	25.8	62.6	31.3	78.8
	Fulfilment from Wages	0.0	0.0	0.0	0.0	0.1	0.4	0.1	0.3	0.0	0.1
	FPS	10.5	26.8	1.2	2.1	3.8	18.5	13.6	33.1	7.4	18.6
	Requirements	39.3	100.0	56.3	100.0	20.6	100.0	41.2	100.0	39.7	100.0
Kerosene Oil	Purchase from Market	4.9	11.0	5.8	12.0	4.0	12.7	6.2	14.0	5.2	12.4
	Fulfilment from Wages	0.1	0.2	0.0	0.0	0.1	0.2	0.0	0.0	0.0	0.1
	FPS	37.7	84.8	38.2	80.0	26.0	82.8	36.9	83.2	34.8	82.6
	Requirement	44.4	100.0	47.8	100.0	31.4	100.0	44.4	100.0	42.2	100.0

Source: Field Survey, 2006.

Table 4.13: Average Annual Requirement of Commodities: Routes of Fulfilment (By Region)

Com-modities	Routes	Rural		Urban		Total	
		Quantity	%	Quantity	%	Quantity	%
Wheat	Self-Production	145.8	22.7	45.7	7.8	114.2	18.3
	Purchase from Market	401.6	62.7	469.6	79.8	423.1	67.8
	Fulfilment from Wages	18.9	2.9	4.3	0.7	14.3	2.3
	FPS	70.8	11.0	74.0	12.6	71.8	11.5
	Annual Requirement	640.9	100.0	588.3	100.0	624.3	100.0
Rice	Self-Production	38.8	13.5	25.7	7.7	34.7	11.4
	Purchase from Market	149.4	51.9	210.3	62.5	168.7	55.6
	Fulfilment from Wages	7.5	2.6	1.0	0.3	5.5	1.8
	FPS	96.3	33.4	110.1	32.7	100.6	33.2
	Annual Requirement	288.1	100.0	336.4	100.0	303.3	100.0
Sugar	Self-Production	0.3	0.9	0.0	0.0	0.2	0.6
	Purchase from Market	28.7	77.9	36.9	80.4	31.3	78.8
	Fulfilment from Wages	0.0	0.1	0.1	0.2	0.0	0.1
	FPS	7.1	19.2	8.0	17.5	7.4	18.6
	Annual Requirement	36.8	100.0	45.9	100.0	39.7	100.0
Kerosene Oil	Purchase from Market	5.6	14.0	4.3	9.3	5.2	12.4
	Fulfilment from Wages	0.0	0.0	0.1	0.2	0.0	0.1
	FPS	32.4	80.5	40.3	86.7	34.8	82.6
	Annual Requirement	40.2	100.0	46.5	100.0	42.2	100.0

Source: Field Survey, 2006.

Table 4.14: Per Capita Average Annual Requirement of Commodities: Routes of Fulfilment

(In kg./lt)

Commodities	Routes	BPL	APL	ANP	ANT	Total
Wheat	Self-Production	20.0	41.8	12.3	13.3	23.0
	Purchase from Market	82.2	81.6	85.3	92.3	85.2
	Fulfilment from Wages	2.2	3.2	2.0	3.8	2.9
	FPS	15.7	0.3	19.6	24.8	14.5
	Requirement	113.4	126.4	132.7	134.1	125.7
Rice	Self-Production	6.0	14.4	2.8	2.9	7.0
	Purchase from Market	24.4	51.5	40.5	21.7	34.0
	Fulfilment from Wages	0.6	1.0	1.1	1.7	1.1
	FPS	23.0	0.7	14.0	41.3	20.3
	Requirement	51.9	66.5	58.2	67.4	61.1
Sugar	Self-Production	0.0	0.0	0.0	0.1	0.0
	Purchase from Market	4.7	9.9	4.9	4.9	6.3
	Fulfilment from Wages	0.0	0.0	0.0	0.0	0.0
	FPS	1.8	0.2	1.1	2.6	1.5
	Requirement	6.8	10.2	6.1	7.9	8.0
Kerosene	Purchase from Market	0.8	1.0	1.2	1.2	1.1
	Fulfilment from Wages	0.0	0.0	0.0	0.0	0.0
	FPS	6.6	6.9	7.7	7.1	7.0
	Requirement	7.7	8.6	9.3	8.5	8.5

Source: Field Survey, 2006.

Thus, our balance equation is:

Supply ≥ Demand (Requirement),

where Supply = Self-production + Market Supply + FPSs Supply.

In self-production, rice and wheat were important items, which was zero for kerosene. Thus, 'FPSs supplied' kerosene determined total consumption of the same when the market response to requirement of kerosene at the lowest end of consumption was either non-existent or negligible. Only rice and wheat were distributed for fulfilling consumption requirements from wages in kind (Table 4.15).

There was general deficit (requirement > supply) for kerosene, but the fact remained that across income brackets requirement of kerosene was met mostly by FPSs. As considered in an ascending order, we found increasing requirement of kerosene per annum for higher income brackets and increasing quantity met by FPSs.

We found generally lower percentage of wheat requirement met by FPSs at the highest income brackets (above Rs. 50,000 per annum) and very low percentage at the level of incomeless households. For the households in the income bracket between Rs. 50,000 and Rs. One Lakh, the percentage requirement fulfilled by the FPSs was 4.9 for wheat, 11.8 for rice, 7.8 for sugar, and 86.5 for kerosene. It was surprising how the incomeless households managed to get priced items from the FPSs. As opposed to this, for the households in the lower income bracket between Rs. 10,000 and Rs. 19,000, the FPSs supplied fulfilment of requirement for wheat was 12.5, for rice 40.0, for sugar 19.4 and for kerosene 84.3.

The contribution (supply) of FPSs in fulfilment of consumption requirements of essential commodities was more in lower income brackets relative to what it was in higher income brackets (Table 4.16).

4.4 Target of Ration Cards for Distribution and Year-wise Variations

Target of the ration cards for distribution set for each district and overall declined for BPL type. For ANP type cards, the target set for distribution declined overall. For ANT type cards for distribution, the target set increased overall. There are district-wise variations in the targets set for cards by types for distribution.

Table 4.15: Per Capita Average Annual Requirement and Their Fulfilment from Different Sources

(In kg./lt. District-wise)

	Routes	*Barielly*	*Badaun*	*Lakhimpur Kheri*	*Lucknow*	*Lalitpur*	*Jhansi*	*Gorakh pur*	*Varanasi*	*Total*
Wheat	Self-Production	39.3	36.2	16.0	9.1	39.1	34.4	11.4	2.0	23.0
	Purchase from Market	53.4	100.7	91.7	88.7	114.4	110.3	67.5	62.7	85.2
	Fulfilment from Wages	1.4	1.9	7.0	0.0	0.5	3.6	4.6	3.6	2.9
	FPS	15.7	17.0	11.2	14.5	16.8	17.1	10.5	13.7	14.5
	Requirement	117.5	144.6	126.4	114.6	171.1	166.0	94.1	82.7	125.7
Rice	Self-Production	26.3	3.8	10.4	6.5	0.5	0.0	6.5	1.2	7.0
	Purchase from Market	34.0	45.0	35.1	31.1	38.7	18.3	43.9	25.0	34.0
	Fulfilment from Wages	1.8	0.0	3.0	0.0	0.1	0.0	2.0	1.5	1.1
	FPS	15.1	17.5	23.3	22.7	22.7	17.7	16.0	27.3	20.3
	Requirement	73.2	66.5	69.6	59.5	60.3	35.0	68.2	55.1	61.1
Sugar	Self-Production	0.3	0.0	0.0	0.0	0.0	0.0	0.0	0.0	0.0
	Purchase from Market	8.7	10.3	6.9	5.6	5.5	4.7	4.6	4.2	6.3
	Fulfilment from Wages	0.0	0.0	0.0	0.0	0.0	0.0	0.0	0.0	0.0
	FPS	1.9	0.7	2.2	1.1	1.0	2.1	0.9	2.1	1.5
	Requirement	11.4	11.1	9.1	6.8	6.5	6.7	5.6	6.7	8.0
Kerosene Oil	Purchase from Market	1.4	1.2	2.2	1.2	1.3	0.6	0.2	0.3	1.1
	Fulfilment from Wages	0.0	0.0	0.0	0.0	0.0	0.0	0.0	0.0	0.0
	FPS	5.9	6.4	7.1	8.0	7.9	9.0	6.1	6.1	7.0
	Requirement	7.4	8.5	9.5	9.4	9.3	10.0	7.2	7.2	8.5

Source: Field Survey, 2006.

Table 4.16: Average Annual Requirement of Commodities: Fulfilment from Different Routes (By Income Brackets, in Rs.)

	Routes	No Income	Up to 5000	5000-10000	10000-19000	19000-25000	25000-50000	50000-1 Lakh	>1 Lakh	Total
/heat	Self-Production	0.0	5.7	23.0	129.0	199.5	150.0	191.0	655.6	114.2
	Purchase from Market	60.3	162.0	409.7	412.1	519.9	566.1	668.7	435.6	423.1
	Fulfilment from Wages	5.8	11.9	11.9	12.3	10.8	30.4	9.7	22.2	14.3
	FPS	25.5	54.8	76.7	79.3	69.2	79.5	44.5	55.6	71.8
	Requirement	139.2	260.1	524.2	631.9	781.3	827.9	913.9	1068.9	624.3
₹ice	Self-Production	0.0	0.0	6.2	33.2	58.3	41.0	93.5	444.4	34.7
	Purchase from Market	20.4	70.2	164.5	145.5	214.4	223.5	402.4	277.8	168.7
	Fulfilment from Wages	2.6	10.3	7.6	2.9	4.9	5.5	12.9	11.1	5.5
	FPS	20.0	25.4	110.4	118.5	97.5	113.2	68.4	72.2	100.6
	Requirement	46.3	108.9	288.4	296.2	356.3	381.7	577.3	733.3	303.3
ugar	Self-Production	0.0	0.0	0.0	0.4	0.4	0.0	0.0	0.0	0.2
	Purchase from Market	3.5	9.8	29.1	29.4	35.9	36.4	64.1	143.6	31.3
	Fulfilment from Wages	0.0	0.2	0.0	0.1	0.0	0.0	0.0	0.0	0.0
	FPS	1.5	1.9	6.9	7.5	8.1	10.3	5.4	24.2	7.4
	Requirement	5.5	11.5	36.6	38.7	44.1	48.1	69.2	174.4	39.7
'osene	Purchase from Market	1.3	0.9	4.4	5.1	6.5	8.2	3.6	14.4	5.2
	Fulfilment from Wages	1.0	0.2	0.0	0.0	0.0	0.0	0.0	0.0	0.0
	FPS	11.9	20.6	34.4	36.1	38.0	39.6	42.5	35.1	34.8
	Requirement	18.1	22.9	39.8	42.8	46.8	50.9	49.1	72.7	42.2

Source: Field Survey, 2006.

4.4.1 Ration Cards by Types

As reported by the Government functionaries at the district level, for 2005-06, 76.7 per cent of all cards were APL type, from the rest BPL covered 15.6 per cent, ANP 0.9 per cent and ANT 6.8 per cent. For 2006-07, 76.9 per cent of all cards were APL, the rest under BPL (13.7%), ANP (0.8%) and ANT (8.5%). The last three types may be considered under 'poor' category. There are district wise variations in the types of cards distributed.

For 2005-06 the percentage deviation in the number of ration cards distributed from the number of households as per census 2001 was 47.9, that is, cards less from the census households for all the selected districts covered. For 2006-07, the percentage was 48.4. The district-wise deviation was always positive for each district (Table 4.17):

Table 4.17: Deviation in Number of Ration Cards from the Number of Households as per Census 2001

Districts	*2005-06*			*2006-07*			*HHs as per Census 2001*
	Total No. of Ration Cards	*Deviation from Census 2001*		*Total No. of Ration Cards*	*Deviation from Census 2001*		
		No.	*%*		*No.*	*%*	
Bareilly	858813	304052	54.8	859101	304340	54.9	554761
Badaun	735746	264590	56.2	735757	264601	56.2	471156
Lucknow	859706	215437	33.4	861791	217522	33.8	644269
Lalitpur	217001	50989	30.7	215757	49745	30.0	166012
Jhansi	397068	107205	37.0	415232	125369	43.3	289863
Varanasi	712012	281361	65.3	705780	275129	63.9	430651
Total	3780346	1223634	47.9	3793418	1236706	48.4	2556712

Source: Field Survey, 2006.

4.4.2 Distance of FPSs from Residences of Households: Their Frequency of visiting FPSs

For 84.0 of the beneficiary households in rural areas, the distance of the FPSs from the residence of the households was within 1 km. For the urban areas, for 84.5 per cent of the households, the FPS was within 1 km from the residence.

Most of the households reported need-based visit of FPSs and visit based on cash income earned. The reasons cited by the households for not visiting the FPSs on a regular basis have been mentioned in Box 4.1.

Box 4.1: Reasons for Households not going to FPSs on a Regular Basis

Reasons
Items do not come every month
FPSs do not distribute items
FPS had been closed
ANP had been closed
No requirement of foodgrains
Prices are increased by FPS Dealer
No provision on APL Ration Card
Non-availability of Money

Source: Field Survey, 2006.

It is difficult to draw any conclusion if the price board was visible in the FPSs as one-half of the beneficiary households reported visibility and the other half reported invisibility. The cardholders revealed confusion by reporting both visibility and invisibility of the same price board on the unique location/FPS wall. The illiteracy and hence reported irrelevance of price chart for them made situations worse.

4.5 Allocation, Lifting and Distribution of Commodities

For kerosene it was cent per cent distribution as percentage of lifting and cent per cent as percentage of allotment. Generally, what was lifted was distributed as reported by the functionaries. This was reported in cases of BPL rice, BPL wheat, ANT rice, ANT wheat, ANP wheat, and sugar. In case of sugar in districts Badaun, Jhansi and Varanasi, lifting remained much less than allotment. However, in these districts cent per cent of sugar allotted was distributed. Generally there were no district-wise variations in the lifting and distribution data of the items under different types of cardholding (Table 4.18).

4.6 Demand, Availability and Supply of Foodgrains and Kerosene

As reported by the Godown-in-charge for 2005-06, the stock/availability on average was higher than estimated demand for each of rice, wheat and sugar. Supply of these items was marginally less than demand in cases of wheat and sugar. For rice, supply equalled estimated demand.

Supply of each item was less than stock for each of the items, implying addition to stock for release for the next year. There are district-wise differences in each of demand, stock and supply for each of these items. There was no general dearth of stock/availability relative to demand and what was to be supplied (Table 4.19).

Table 4.18: Commodities Allotted, Lifted and Distributed for the Districts in 2005-06

(*Figure in %*)

Items	*Status*	*Bareilly*	*Badaun*	*Lucknow*	*Lalitpur*	*Jhansi*	*Varanasi*	*Total*
BPL Rice	Distributed	100.0	98.7	100.0	100.0	99.9	95.2	93.8
	Lifted	100.0	98.7	100.0	100.0	99.9	95.2	93.8
	Allotment	100.0	100.0	100.0	100.0	100.0	100.0	100.0
BPL Wheat	Distributed	100.0	97.9	100.0	100.0	98.4	89.8	99.2
	Lifted	100.0	97.9	100.0	100.0	99.0	89.8	99.3
	Allotment	100.0	100.0	100.0	100.0	100.0	100.0	100.0
ANT Rice	Distributed	100.0	100.0	100.0	100.0	99.9	99.9	94.3
	Lifted	100.0	100.0	100.0	100.0	99.9	99.9	94.3
	Allotment	100.0	100.0	100.0	100.0	100.0	100.0	100.0
ANT Wheat	Distributed	100.0	100.0	100.0	100.0	99.1	99.9	99.9
	Lifted	100.0	100.0	100.0	100.0	99.7	99.9	100.0
	Allotment	100.0	100.0	100.0	100.0	100.0	100.0	100.0
ANP Wheat	Distributed	100.0	100.0	100.0	100.0	100.0	100.0	100.0
	Lifted	100.0	100.0	100.0	100.0	100.0	100.0	100.0
	Allotment	100.0	100.0	100.0	100.0	100.0	100.0	100.0
Sugar	Distributed	100.0	89.7	100.0	100.0	93.6	90.8	98.3
	Lifted	100.0	89.7	100.0	100.0	93.8	90.8	98.3
	Allotment	100.0	100.0	100.0	100.0	100.0	100.0	100.0
Kerosene	Distributed	100.0	100.0	100.0	100.0	100.0	100.0	100.0
	Lifted	100.0	100.0	100.0	100.0	100.0	100.0	100.0
	Allotment	100.0	100.0	100.0	100.0	100.0	100.0	100.0

Note: Data reported by functionaries of concerned districts.

Source: Field Survey, 2006.

Stock of kerosene on average in oil depot in 2005-06 was higher than demand, overall and for each district. For five districts out of the selected eight, supply by depot equalled demand from FPSs. For the remaining three districts, supply was a little less than demand (Table 4.20).

Table 4.19: Demand, Stock and Supply of Foodgrains in Godowns (2005-06) (As Reported by Foodgrains Godown-in-charge)

(*Quantity in quintall*)

Districts	*Figure in*	*Wheat*			*Rice*			*Sugar*		
		Supply	*Stock*	*Demand*	*Supply*	*Stock*	*Demand*	*Supply*	*Stock*	*Demand*
Bareilly	Quantity	553.0	562.2	555.3	615.3	628.0	616.0	52.6	52.6	53.1
	%	99.6	101.2	100.0	99.9	101.9	100.0	99.1	99.1	100.0
Badaun	Quantity	2135.9	2135.9	2135.9	2122.8	2122.8	2122.8	849.9	849.9	849.9
	%	100.0	100.0	100.0	100.0	100.0	100.0	100.0	100.0	100.0
Lakhimpur Kheri	Quantity	311.5	383.6	311.5	514.4	594.5	514.4	67.9	72.7	67.9
	%	100.0	123.1	100.0	100.0	115.6	100.0	100.0	107.0	100.0
Lucknow	Quantity	160.1	163.7	160.1	244.7	276.2	244.7	44.4	47.1	44.4
	%	100.0	102.3	100.0	100.0	112.8	100.0	100.0	106.1	100.0
Lalitpur	Quantity	244.8	254.0	244.4	248.3	261.4	249.7	38.1	38.5	38.2
	%	100.2	103.9	100.0	99.5	104.7	100.0	99.9	101.0	100.0
Jhansi	Quantity	327.0	399.9	342.3	316.2	349.2	332.7	56.4	60.5	58.4
	%	95.5	116.8	100.0	95.0	104.9	100.0	96.6	103.7	100.0
Gorakhpur	Quantity	202.6	237.9	202.6	405.1	453.2	405.1	76.2	78.2	76.2
	%	100.0	117.4	100.0	100.0	111.9	100.0	100.0	102.7	100.0
Varanasi	Quantity	220.9	220.9	262.2	448.3	476.5	448.3	64.1	64.1	75.6
	%	84.2	84.2	100.0	100.0	106.3	100.0	84.8	84.8	100.0
Total	Quantity	612.5	636.0	616.8	689.4	714.4	689.3	104.7	106.5	105.8
	%	99.3	103.1	100.0	100.0	103.6	100.0	99.0	100.7	100.0

Source: Field Survey, 2006.

Table 4.20: Demand, Stock and Supply of Kerosene Oil by Oil Depots (2005-06) (As Reported by Kerosene Depot-in-Charge)

(Quantity in kl)

District	*Supply*		*Stock/Availability*		*Demand*	
	Quantity	*%*	*Quantity*	*%*	*Quantity*	*%*
Bareilly	2159.7	100.0	2215.8	102.6	2159.7	100.0
Badaun	2656.0	100.0	2666.9	100.4	2656.0	100.0
Lakhimpur Kheri	759.0	100.0	846.7	111.6	759.0	100.0
Lucknow	1826.1	100.0	2005.9	109.8	1826.1	100.0
Lalitpur	1861.6	99.8	1938.2	103.9	1866.2	100.0
Jhansi	1750.5	98.7	1898.6	107.0	1774.0	100.0
Gorakhpur	2141.3	99.6	2191.4	101.9	2150.1	100.0
Varanasi	2113.7	100.0	2281.8	108.0	2113.7	100.0
Total	1863.5	99.7	1955.0	104.6	1868.3	100.0

Source: Field Survey, 2006.

4.6.1 Supply of Foodgrains under Different Schemes

Based on data on average supply of foodgrains to TPDS and welfare schemes for 2005-06, we offer the following observations:

- Only one-tenth of the supply of foodgrains (rice and wheat) was distributed under the welfare schemes. 90.5 per cent of these items were supplied under TPDS.
- Of the supply for TPDS, the ratio for wheat and rice was 48:52. Of the supply for welfare schemes, the ratio was 40:60. We find district-wise variations in the ratios in which wheat and rice are supplied under TPDS and welfare schemes.
- For each of Lakhimpur Kheri and Gorakhpur, the supply of foodgrains for TPDS was more than 95.0 per cent (Table 4.21).

4.7 Existence of Households under BPL and APL Category

As estimated by Gram Panchayats, of total households in the selected villages, 29.4 per cent are from SCs, which is 71.2 per cent from BPL and 28.8 per cent from APL. The selected SC households as percentage of total households vary over districts.

In the rural region, FPSs fulfilled 11.1 per cent of the requirement of wheat which was 33.4 per cent for rice, 18.8 per cent for sugar and 80.3 per cent for kerosene. In the urban region, FPSs fulfilled 12.6 per cent

Table 4.21: Average Supply of Foodgrains under Different Schemes (2005-06) (As Reported by Godown-in-Charge and Depot-in-Charge)

(Quantity in Quintal)

Districts	*Figure in*	*TPDS*			*Welfare Schemes*			*Total*
		Wheat	*Rice*	*Total*	*Wheat*	*Rice*	*Total*	
Bareilly	Quantity	53216.6	58475.4	111691.9	3167.2	5002.6	8169.8	119861.7
	%	44.4	48.8	93.2	2.6	4.2	6.8	100.0
Badaun	Quantity	214489.6	210501.7	424991.3	19461.4	35670.0	55131.4	480122.7
	%	44.7	43.8	88.5	4.1	7.4	11.5	100.0
Lakhimpur Kheri	Quantity	30151.7	49995.1	80146.8	998.5	2890.0	3888.4	84035.3
	%	35.9	59.5	95.4	1.2	3.4	4.6	100.0
Lalitpur	Quantity	22533.1	22214.5	44747.5	1930.7	2975.1	4905.8	49653.3
	%	45.4	44.7	90.1	3.9	6.0	9.9	100.0
Jhansi	Quantity	36512.7	35792.9	72305.6	1773.4	2437.9	4211.3	76516.9
	%	47.7	46.8	94.5	2.3	3.2	5.5	100.0
Gorakhpur	Quantity	20313.5	39163.8	59477.3	1013.6	2058.3	3071.9	62549.3
	%	32.5	62.6	95.1	1.6	3.3	4.9	100.0
Total	Quantity	68270.1	74120.0	142390.1	5869.9	9065.0	14934.8	157324.9
	%	43.4	47.1	90.5	3.7	5.8	9.5	100.0

Source: Field Survey, 2006.

of the requirement of wheat which was 32.6 per cent for rice, 17.7 per cent for sugar and 86.6 per cent for kerosene. While the contribution of FPSs in fulfilment of requirement of all the essential items excepting kerosene was very low, its support role was significant (Table 4.22).

Table 4.22: Per Capita Average Annual Requirement of Commodities: Fulfilment from Different Routes

(By Region, in kg)

Commodities	*Routes*	*Rural*	*Urban*	*Total*
Wheat	Self-Production	27.5	9.5	18.5
	Purchase from Market	75.8	97.8	86.8
	Fulfilment from Wages	3.6	0.9	2.2
	FPS	13.4	15.4	14.4
	Annual Requirement	120.9	122.6	121.8
Rice	Self-Production	7.3	5.4	6.3
	Purchase from Market	28.2	43.8	36.0
	Fulfilment from Wages	1.4	0.2	0.8
	FPS	18.2	22.9	20.6
	Annual Requirement	54.4	70.1	62.2
Sugar	Self-Production	0.1	0.0	0.0
	Purchase from Market	5.4	7.7	6.6
	Fulfilment from Wages	0.0	0.0	0.0
	FPS	1.3	1.7	1.5
	Annual Requirement	6.9	9.6	8.3
Kerosene Oil	Purchase from Market	1.1	0.9	1.0
	Fulfilment from Wages	0.0	0.0	0.0
	FPS	6.1	8.4	7.3
	Annual Requirement	7.6	9.7	8.6

Source: Field Survey, 2006.

4.8 Households' Propensity to Purchase Foodgrains from Market

Households decided to buy essential commodities mainly based on purchasing power at a particular point of time. The other determinants included seasonal need and survival. Availability of cash income based propensity to purchase from the market explained the major role of the market-led fulfilment of requirements across households by card holdings. Actually it is a combination of need and purchasing power that mostly explains the propensity of the households by cardholding to buy from the market.

4.8.1 Foodgrains Purchased by Households from Open Market (on Credit Basis)

58.2 per cent of the beneficiary households purchased foodgrains from the open market on credit basis, which was 67.5 for BPL, 65.4 for ANT, 58.3 for the ANP and 41.7 for the APL. Of all the households reporting credit-based purchase of foodgrains from alternative sources, 97.5 per cent depended on local shopkeeper, 25.9 per cent on community and 4.5 per cent on FPS dealers. Thus, the households reported multiple sources of dependence for credit-based purchase of foodgrains from open market.

4.9 Benefits Derived through PDS

The best performance of PDS by coverage of BPL households was revealed in case of kerosene where on average each household received 3.2 lt per month at the price per lt Rs. 11.20. The frequency of visit to FPSs for kerosene by BPL households was five that was more or less uniform over districts. There was not much difference between rural and urban regions so far as availability of kerosene was concerned from FPSs by quantity, price and frequency of visit to FPSs. The performance of PDS in case of distribution of wheat for BPL households revealed average quantity drawn at 10.4 kg at a price per kg Rs. 5.45 with a frequency of visit of households three (number of times the households visit the FPSs). The performance of PDS in case of distribution of rice for BPL households revealed average quantity drawn at 17.3 kg at a price per kg Rs. 6.66 with a frequency of visit of households three. The frequency varied over districts from lowest at two to highest at six. For sugar for BPL households the average quantity drawn was 1.4 kg at a price per kg Rs. 14.65 with a frequency of two.

The best performance of PDS by coverage of ANT households was revealed in case of kerosene where on average each household received 3.1 lt. per month at price per unit Rs. 11.05. There was not much difference between rural and urban regions so far as availability of kerosene was concerned from FPSs by quantity, price and frequency of visit to FPSs. The performance of PDS in case of distribution of wheat for ANT households revealed average quantity drawn at 12.3 kg at a price per kg Rs. 2.32. The performance of PDS in case of distribution of rice for ANT households revealed average quantity drawn at 22.3 kg at a price per kg Rs. 3.30. For sugar for ANT households the average quantity drawn is 1.4 kg at a price per kg Rs. 14.65.

The ANP households got wheat and kerosene, the former on average 6.8 kg per month and the latter 0.6 lt. at an average price of Rs. 11.30. The rural average quantity of wheat drawn by ANP households was 7.1 kg while the urban average quantity was 5.9 kg. The respective percentages for kerosene were 11.40 lt. and 10.75 lt There were district wise minor variations in the reported quantity of wheat and kerosene drawn by ANP households over districts and regions by rural and urban within each district.

The performance of PDS by coverage of APL households in case of kerosene showed on average each household receiving 3.0 lt per month at price per unit Rs. 11.0. There was not much difference between rural and urban regions so far as availability of kerosene was concerned from FPSs by quantity, price and frequency of visits of FPSs by the households.

Based on actual quantity available during the second half of 2006 to the beneficiary households under BPL and ANT schemes, we derived the gap between actual available quantity of foodgrains and provision. Under BPL the gap was 57.5 per cent, which is 53.2 per cent for the urban and 60.1 per cent for the rural region so far as provision and actual availability of foodgrains over last six months (end 2006) was concerned. Under Antyodaya the gap was 18.2 per cent, which was 9.6 per cent for the urban and 22.4 per cent for the rural region so far as provision and actual availability of foodgrains over the reference period was concerned. There were district-wise variations in the percentages in the gap between provision and availability calculated over this period. There were rural-urban variations in the gap between provision and availability.

4.10 Reasons for Households being Deprived of Essential Commodities

15.0 per cent of all the BPL households did not receive wheat, 14.2 per cent did not receive rice, 23.8 per cent did not receive sugar and 0.4 per cent did not receive kerosene during a reference period of second half of 2006. Of all the ANT households, 1.7 per cent did not receive wheat, 0.8 per cent did not receive rice, 34.2 per cent did not receive sugar, and 0.4 per cent did not receive kerosene. Of all the ANP households, 32.5 per cent did not receive wheat and 73.3 per cent did not receive kerosene. 9.6 per cent of APL households did not receive kerosene. Some of the same households were deprived of a number of items.

82.6 per cent of the beneficiary households reported no problems in purchase of items from the FPSs. Most of those who reported problems cited non-availability of money (purchasing power) as the major reason. The other reasons cited by the households included long distance of the FPS from the residence, non-information about distribution, absence of the households' members, bad quality of items and non-requirement. There were variations in the reported reasons for non-purchase by cardholding.

The reasons cited by the households for non-purchase of items from the FPSs during the last six months of 2006 included mainly non-distribution of items. The other reasons included non-arrival of items for distribution, non-distribution of rice and wheat, distance of the FPSs, short period of distribution, non-preparation (non-availability) of ration cards, absence of the household in the village while items were distributed/card were issued, post-distribution non-availability etc.

The reasons for not purchasing sugar from FPSs have been mentioned in Box 4.2.

Box 4.2: Reasons for not Purchasing Sugar from FPSs

Reasons
Item never comes
Non-distribution every month
Never distributed in any month
Not received due to non-availability of Money
Distributed during only festivals
Dealer opines ineligibility of item-seekers
Not needed

Source: Field Survey, 2006.

4.11 Adequacy of Quantity of Kerosene Oil Distributed

Around 70.0 per cent of the beneficiary households reported adequacy of quantity of kerosene oil that they received from FPSs for household consumption. For BPL households, 75.8 per cent reported adequacy which was 72.5 for ANP households, 69.2 per cent for ANT households and 62.1 per cent for APL households. 77.6 per cent of the rural and 66.4 per cent of the urban households reported adequacy of kerosene oil so far as requirement was concerned.

The average price of kerosene oil per lt purchased from the open market was reported to be Rs. 25.57. For households by cardholding, BPL reported to pay Rs. 25.27 per lt and APL Rs. 26.06. The ANP households paid Rs. 26.54 and ANT Rs. 24.74. Thus, the reported price per unit for kerosene per lt from the open market did not vary much, the range of variation being Rs. 1.80 per lt. There were little district-wise variations in the reported price per lt of kerosene oil purchased from the open market.

The gap between open market price and FPS supplied price of kerosene was reported to be Rs. 9.47 per lt that showed a percentage price gap of 58.82 between open market and FPS. In this case, the absolute price gap was Rs. 3.40. There was not much difference in the price paid by households across cardholding so far as purchase from open market was concerned. In case when the cardholders went to other dealers they are not attached to, they had to pay higher varying prices.

4.12 Effect of Withdrawal of Sugar and Kerosene from PDS

In case sugar and kerosene were withdrawn from the PDS, most of the households reported that they would be adversely affected. This percentage was 92.8 for kerosene and 26.3 for sugar. The necessity of kerosene, thus, was felt much more by the households. In the rural region 92.4 per cent and in the urban region 93.7 per cent would be adversely affected if kerosene were withdrawn from the PDS. Considered over both rural and urban regions combined, this percentage for BPL was 97.5, for APL 93.8, for ANP 81.7 and for ANT 98.3. Separately for each of rural and urban regions these percentages showed the same pattern. In the rural region 26.3 per cent and in the urban region 26.1 per cent would be adversely affected if sugar were withdrawn from the PDS. Considered over both rural and urban regions combined, this percentage for BPL was 30.4, for APL 5.8, for ANP 22.1 and for ANT 46.7. For rural APL, withdrawal of sugar did not have much adverse effect which was true for urban APL where only 2.5 per cent reported to be adversely affected if sugar were withdrawn.

In case PDS was restricted to only distributing rice and wheat, 86.1 per cent would remain unsatisfied, which would be 87.1 per cent in urban and 85.7 per cent in rural region. Of those who still would remain satisfied, the maximum percentage was reported from rural ANP (29.4%), followed by urban ANP (20.6%) and urban APL (20.0%). There were variations in the reported extent of satisfaction by cardholding in case the items other than rice and wheat were withdrawn.

The reasons for non-satisfaction of households for providing only food-grains through PDS have been mentioned in Box 4.3.

Box 4.3: Reasons for Non-satisfaction of Households for Providing Only Foodgrains as per Household Requirement

Reasons
Price of kerosene is very high in open market
Kerosene is not available at other places
Kerosene is inescapable for family
Compulsion to use Diesel for light at night, if kerosene would be withdrawn
Living in darkness if kerosene would be withdrawn
Increased family expenses if kerosene will be withdrawn
Foodgrains self-produced

Source: Field Survey, 2006.

4.13 Annapurna Yojana

69.2 per cent of the beneficiary households under Annapurna Yojana were female. The most prominent catalyst for selection of households as beneficiaries under Annapurna Yojana was the Panchayat. In the urban region, the most prominent catalyst was the Supply Department. The other catalysts were Lekhpal and FPS dealer. Of all the Annapurna beneficiary households, 54.2 per cent attained age above 65 years, which was 52.5 per cent in rural and 58.7 per cent in urban region.

Eligibility was the most important factor in determining the inclusion under Annapurna Yojana, as opined by 73.8 per cent of the households, followed by support of Panchayats. The other factors, though negligible, included approach, local pressure, bribing, and vote bank in Panchayat elections.

Most of the beneficiary households denied that the eligible households were not getting benefits or that the non-eligible households were deriving benefits under Annapurna Yojana. However, some beneficiary households reported that some of the eligible households remained excluded from the net of Annapurna. Most of the beneficiary households reported that they would be facing problems in survival in case Annapurna Yojana was stopped.

4.14 Antyodaya Yojana

91.3 per cent of the households reported that they would be adversely affected in terms of livelihood if not covered by Antyodaya Yojana. The types of adverse effect on livelihood for each of rural and urban region in case Antyodaya Yojana is closed included increased hunger, increased poverty, debt and poor economic condition (Box 4.4).

Box 4.4: Types of Adverse Effect of Non-Availability of Antyodaya Yojana on Livelihood

Area	*Types of Adverse Effect*
Rural and Urban	Under Debt Poor Economic Condition Purchase at High Market Price Increased Poverty Increased Hunger

Source: Field Survey, 2006.

The most prominent catalyst for selection of households as beneficiaries under Antyodaya Yojana was the Panchayat. In the urban region, the most prominent catalyst was the supply department followed by Lekhpal and FPS dealer. The reasons behind the eligible households not getting the benefits of Antyodaya cards have been mentioned in Box 4.5.

Box 4.5: Perception about Eligible Beneficiary not Getting Benefits of Antyodaya Yojana

Area	*Perception*
Rural	Poverty Low Allotment of Cards Physically Absent during issuing Cards Lack of Approach Do not give Bribe Ignorance
Urban	Poverty Personal Relation Low Allotment of Cards Physically Absent during issuing Cards Lack of Approach Do not give Bribe Groupism Ignorance

Source: Field Survey, 2006.

87.9 per cent of the beneficiary households denied inclusion of non-eligible households in the net of Antyodaya. The reasons why and how non-eligible households got selected in the Antyodaya Yojana included personal connections, local pressure, bribe, and pressure from officials.

4.15 Perception of Beneficiary Households Regarding Performance of PDS

We got varying responses from the beneficiary households on the indicators that we considered for performance of PDS in U.P. These indicators included manipulation in measurement of items during delivery, providing benefits to close persons, FPS dealers keeping government officials in their favour, distributable items lifted but not brought to villages where the FPS is located, FPS dealers involved in black marketing, changing the quality of items, dealers involved in corruption with the help of Panchayat.

One-third of the beneficiary households rejected the idea of involvement of dealers in corruption in alliance with Panchayat. Half of the households reported involvement of the dealers in such corruption regularly and occasionally. One-sixth of the households reported ignorance. Ignorance was a major factor in cases of dealers keeping government officials in favour and involvement in black marketing. From the viewpoint of the beneficiaries, the factors that were reported most were manipulation in measurement (Table 4.23).

4.15.1 Satisfaction Level of Beneficiary Households

Most of the households reported satisfaction regarding distribution of items through FPSs under PDS. In case of distribution of kerosene the extent of satisfaction was most for all the categories, BPL, APL and ANT. Generally, the BPL households were less satisfied with the distribution of items relative to that by ANT. Excepting kerosene, the extent of satisfaction of the beneficiary households so far as quantity of items distributed by the FPSs was very low across households by cardholding.

The reasons for households not satisfied with quantity of items distributed have been mentioned in the Box 4.6.

4.15.2 Weaknesses and Strength of PDS Perceived by Beneficiary Households

The weaknesses in PDS perceived by the beneficiary households centered on the FPS dealer, followed by high level Government officials and Gram Pradhan. The weaknesses were also inherent in the role of Panchayat Secretary, MLA, DM, Lekhpal and Supply Department. There were variations in the percentages of households by cardholding that revealed opinion on the weaknesses in PDS.

Table 4.23: Performance of Public Distribution System Based on Some Selected Indicators (Based on Perception of Beneficiary Households)

Indicators		*Regu-larly*	*Occas-ionally*	*Never*	*Ignor-ance*	*NR*	*Total*
Short measurement during delivery	No.	380	304	248	27	1	960
	%	39.6	31.7	25.8	2.8	0.1	100.0
Pretended for delivery	No.	253	339	342	25	1	960
	%	26.4	35.3	35.6	2.6	0.1	100.0
Give more benefits to close persons	No.	401	251	223	84	1	960
	%	41.8	26.1	23.2	8.8	0.1	100.0
Dealers keep officials in their favour	No.	383	196	161	219	1	960
	%	39.9	20.4	16.8	22.8	0.1	100.0
Lift items without bringing in village	No.	66	210	447	236	1	960
	%	6.9	21.9	46.6	24.6	0.1	100.0
Involved in black marketing	No.	225	234	293	207	1	960
	%	23.4	24.4	30.5	21.6	0.1	100.0
Change the quality of items	No.	21	159	640	139	1	960
	%	2.2	16.6	66.7	14.5	0.1	100.0
Mixed other thing in foodgrains	No.	21	132	672	134	1	960
	%	2.2	13.8	70.0	14.0	0.1	100.0
Involved in corruption with the help of Panchayat	No.	260	213	324	162	1	960
	%	27.1	22.2	33.8	16.9	0.1	100.0

Source: Field Survey, 2006.

Box 4.6: Reasons for Households Not Satisfied with Quantity of Items Distributed

Reasons
Quantity distributed less than requirement
High prices
Less quantity given by FPS Dealer
Nothing is received for a long time (many months)
Items not received regularly
Not lifted due to lack of money
Only one item (Rice or Wheat) distributed by the Dealer
Having ANP or APL Card

Source: Field Survey, 2006.

Of those who perceived weaknesses in PDS, the most important reason cited was corruption. If we consider sharing benefits in bribe and corruption in issuing ration cards, then effective extent of corruption would be much higher. The other reasons cited by the households included non-distributing items through FPSs, marketing in the open/black (market), fault/cheating in weight while distributing items, non-checking, poor quality, higher price than what was fixed, availability less than requirement, and irregular distribution (Box 4.7).

Box 4.7: Reasons for Perceived Weaknesses in PDS

Reasons
Corruption in issuing Ration Cards
Black marketing with the help of officials
Food-grains not distributed every month
Manipulation in measurement by FPS dealers
No FPS in the village due to non-initiative of GP
Actual checking not done
Discrimination among poor households
Non-poor households grab foodgrains
High price of commodities
Quality of foodgrains poor

Source: Field Survey, 2006.

4.15.3 Consumer Rights, Awareness and Complaints

Ignorance of the beneficiary households was the most important factor when the question centered on the rights of them as consumers to check the records of FPS dealers. So far as checking stock register was concerned, 87.3 per cent were ignorant about any such rights, which were for 87.2 per cent of the households when it was checking sale register, 87.4 per cent when it was checking ration card or shop register and 87.5 per cent when it was checking allotment and actual distribution.

Less than one per cent in case of each revealed that they knew the rights-based access to commodities under PDS. More than 10.0 per cent in case of each type of register and distribution did not know the rights-based approach. There were variations in these percentages for households over cardholding reporting on the question, with somewhat more consciousness in case of APL households though at a very low level.

Of all the beneficiary households, 85.4 per cent reported that no local vigilance committee had been formed in the memorable past, the percentage being 87.1 for the urban households and 84.6 per cent for the rural households.

96.4 per cent of the complaints against the FPS dealers remained non-registered, which was 96.7 per cent in rural and 95.7 per cent in urban areas. These percentages did not vary much over households by the types of cardholding. After complaints made against FPS dealers Officials visited and left with no action like recording complaints, Supply Inspectors came for inspection and it ended there.

4.16 Non-Beneficiary Households: Sample Profile

Of all the non-beneficiary households, 79.2 per cent were from the rural region and the rest urban. Of these households, 56.4 per cent were SCs, 20.7 per cent OBCs, 15.4 per cent minority and 7.5 per cent general castes (Table 4.24).

4.16.1 Coverage of Population

Of total population in the sample households, 52.4 per cent were male and the rest female. Of total population from the sample households, 55.6 per cent were SCs, 19.4 per cent OBCs, 17.2 per cent minorities and the rest 7.8 per cent from general castes. The household size was five for all the districts taken together and for each of rural and urban regions, for all the caste categories excepting the OBCs. A little more than half of the total population from the sample constituted the productive age group.

4.16.2 Educational Level of Non-Beneficiary Households

38.7 per cent of the population from the sample were illiterate, 22.4 per cent were in the age bracket below 6 years. Only 9.0 per cent of the population had education at the level of high school certificate and above. Only 0.1 per cent of the population had technical education. Of all the literate population from the sample, male female ratio was 60:40. For each of the caste categories, male literacy was higher than female literacy.

4.16.3 Occupational Structure of Non-Beneficiary Households

Of all the urban non-beneficiary households, 54.0 per cent constituted non-agricultural labourers, which was 69.6 per cent for the rural region. Cultivation covered 7.9 per cent of the rural households which was 4.0 per cent for the urban households. Agricultural labour covered 4.7 per cent of rural households which was 4.0 per cent for urban households. There was not much difference in the types of occupations for non-beneficiary households in rural and urban areas (Table 4.25).

Table 4.24: Non-Beneficiary Households by Caste and Region

Caste	Region		Barielly	Badaun	Lakhim-pur Kheri	Lucknow	Lalitpur	Jhansi	Gorakh-pur	Varanasi	Total
SC	Urban	No.	—	5	9	3	4	—	—	—	21
		%	—	33.3	30.0	30.0	66.7	—	—	—	42.0
	Rural	No.	8	15	7	11	14	24	25	11	115
		%	53.3	55.6	35.0	52.4	66.7	88.9	83.3	36.7	60.2
	Total	No.	8	20	16	14	18	24	25	11	136
		%	44.4	47.6	53.3	45.2	66.7	72.7	83.3	36.7	56.4
OBC	Urban	No.	—	2	1	2	1	4	—	—	10
		%	—	13.3	10.0	20.0	16.7	66.7	—	—	20.0
	Rural	No.	2	8	5	4	7	2	5	7	40
		%	13.3	29.6	25.0	19.0	33.3	7.4	16.7	23.3	20.9
	Total	No.	2	10	6	6	8	6	5	7	50
		%	11.1	23.8	20.0	19.4	29.6	18.2	16.7	23.3	20.7
Minority	Urban	No.	3	5	0	0	1	2	—	—	11
		%	100.0	33.3	0.0	0.0	16.7	33.3	—	—	22.0
	Rural	No.	5	4	7	6	—	—	—	4	26
		%	33.3	14.8	35.0	28.6	—	—	—	13.3	13.6
	Total	No.	8	9	7	6	1	2	—	4	37
		%	44.4	21.4	23.3	19.4	3.7	6.1	—	13.3	15.4
General	Urban	No.	0	3	0	5	—	—	—	—	8
		%	0.0	20.0	0.0	50.0	—	—	—	—	16.0
	Rural	No.	0	0	1	0	—	1	0	8	10
		%	0.0	0.0	5.0	0.0	—	3.7	0.0	26.7	5.2
	Total	No.	0	3	1	5	—	1	0	8	18
		%	0.0	7.1	3.3	16.1	—	3.0	0.0	26.7	7.5
Total	Urban	No.	3	15	10	10	6	6	0	0	50
		%	100.0	100.0	100.0	100.0	100.0	100.0	100.0	100.0	100.0
	Rural	No.	15	27	20	21	21	27	30	30	191
		%	100.0	100.0	100.0	100.0	100.0	100.0	100.0	100.0	100.0
	Total	No.	18	42	30	31	27	33	30	30	241
		%	100.0	100.0	100.0	100.0	100.0	100.0	100.0	100.0	100.0

Source: Field Survey, 2006

Table 4.25: Main Occupations of Non-Beneficiary Households by Region

Area	*Occupations*	*Barielly*	*Badaun*	*Lakhim-pur Kheri*	*Lucknow*	*Lalitpur*	*Jhansi*	*Gorakh-pur*	*Varanasi*	*Total*
Urban	Agriculture	33.3	6.7	—	—	—	—	—	—	4.0
	Agri. Labour	—	6.7	—	10.0	—	—	—	—	4.0
	Non-Agri. Labour	66.7	40.0	90.0	10.0	66.7	83.3	—	—	54.0
	Traditional Labour	—	20.0	—	—	—	—	—	—	6.0
	Service	—	6.7	10.0	20.0	—	16.7	—	—	10.0
	Animal Husbandry	—	—	—	10.0	16.7	—	—	—	4.0
	Small Business	—	20.0	—	50.0	16.7	—	—	—	18.0
	Total No.	3	15	10	10	6	6	—	—	50
	Total %	100.0	100.0	100.0	100.0	100.0	100.0	—	—	100.0
Rural	Agriculture	13.3	25.9	10.0	—	4.8	7.4	3.3	—	7.9
	Agri. Labour	13.3	11.1	5.0	14.3	—	—	—	—	4.7
	Non-Agri. Labour	60.0	48.1	65.0	76.2	90.5	85.2	76.7	56.7	69.6
	Traditional Labour	—	—	—	4.8	4.8	—	—	—	1.0
	Service	—	3.7	—	—	—	—	16.7	26.7	7.3
	Pensioner	—	3.7	—	—	—	—	—	3.3	1.0
	Animal Husbandry	—	—	—	—	—	3.7	3.3	0.0	1.0
	Small Business	6.7	7.4	20.0	—	—	—	—	3.3	4.2
	Weaving/Sewing	—	—	—	—	—	—	—	6.7	1.0
	Begging	6.7	—	—	4.8	0.0	3.7	—	3.3	2.1
	Total No.	15	27	20	21	21	27	30	30	191
	Total %	100.0	100.0	100.0	100.0	100.0	100.0	100.0	100.0	100.0
Total	Agriculture	16.7	19.0	6.7	—	3.7	6.1	3.3	—	7.1
	Agri. Labour	11.1	9.5	3.3	12.9	—	—	—	—	4.6
	Non-Agri. Labour	61.1	45.2	73.3	54.8	85.2	84.8	76.7	56.7	66.4
	Traditional Labour	—	7.1	0.0	3.2	3.7	—	—	—	2.1
	Service	—	4.8	3.3	6.5	—	3.0	16.7	26.7	7.9
	Pensioner	—	2.4	—	—	—	—	—	3.3	0.8
	Animal Husbandry	—	—	—	3.2	3.7	3.0	3.3	0.0	1.7
	Small Business	5.6	11.9	13.3	16.1	3.7	—	—	3.3	7.1
	Weaving/Sewing	—	—	—	—	—	—	—	6.7	0.8
	Begging	5.6	—	—	3.2	—	3.0	—	3.3	1.7
	Total No.	18	42	30	31	27	33	30	30	241
	Total %	100.0	100.0	100.0	100.0	100.0	100.0	100.0	100.0	100.0

Source: Field Survey, 2006.

Of all the non-beneficiary households, 66.4 per cent were engaged as non-agricultural labourer, while only 4.6 per cent as agricultural labourer, and 7.1 per cent as cultivator. The other occupations like traditional labour, animal husbandry, weaving/sewing, and small business encompassed very small percentage of total households. For most of the non-beneficiary households, supplementary occupations covered activities like animal husbandry, weaving/sewing, small business, agricultural and non-agricultural labour.

31.7 per cent of total non-beneficiary population constituted working population engaged mainly as non-agricultural labour. The other occupations included traditional labour, agricultural labour, cultivation, animal husbandry, small business, rickshaw/trolley pulling, and working as hawkers.

4.16.4 Income Structure of Non-Beneficiary Households

Of all the non-beneficiary households, 0.8 per cent was incomeless. In the urban region 66.0 per cent of the non-beneficiary households earned income below Rs. 19,000 per annum, that was 78.5 per cent in the rural region. Half of all the households earned income per annum between Rs. 10,001 and Rs. 19,000. More than three-fourths of the households earned income per annum below Rs. 19,000. In the lowest income brackets the percentage of households was higher in rural region while in the higher income brackets the percentage was higher in urban region (Table 4.26).

Of all the earning population from the sample, earning male population constituted 25.6 per cent and earning female population constituted 7.8 per cent. Of all the earning population from the sample, earning male population constituted 25.6 per cent and earning female population constituted 7.8 per cent.

4.16.5 Living Condition of Non-Beneficiary Households

There was no 'incomelessness' among non-beneficiary households in urban region as opposed to its presence in rural region. The percentage of non-beneficiary households earning less than Rs. 19,000 was 71.3. Of all non-beneficiary households, 79.7 per cent were landless. Excepting very few, none of the non-beneficiary households had income-generating productive assets. Kerosene as a means of fuel for cooking purposes was generally absent in both rural and urban regions. Most of the households in both the regions used multiple fuels like wood and '*kanda*' (cow dung cake) for cooking. Most of the non-beneficiary households had no ration cards for a period between two and ten years. They needed cards because of income poverty, and landlessness in rural region. Necessity of kerosene oil was a major factor for need of ration cards for both the urban and rural regions.

Table 4.26: Annual Income of Non-Beneficiary Households by Region

Area	Annual Income		Barielly	Badaun	Lakhimpur Kheri	Lucknow	Lalitpur	Jhansi	Gorakhpur	Varanasi	Total
Urban	Upto Rs. 5000		—	—	10.0	—	—	—	—	—	2.0
	Rs. 5001-10000		—	13.3	10.0	—	83.3	16.7	—	—	18.0
	Rs. 10001-19000		33.3	53.3	70.0	50.0	16.7	16.7	—	—	46.0
	Rs. 19001-25000		33.3	20.0	10.0	30.0	—	50.0	—	—	22.0
	Rs. 25001-50000		33.3	6.7	—	—	—	16.7	—	—	6.0
	Rs. 50001-1 Lac		—	6.7	—	10.0	—	—	—	—	4.0
	Above Rs. 1 Lac		—	—	—	10.0	—	—	—	—	2.0
	Total	No.	3	15	10	10	6	6	—	—	50
		%	100.0	100.0	100.0	100.0	100.0	100.0	—	—	100.0
Rural	Incomeless		6.7	—	—	—	—	3.7	—	—	1.0
	Upto Rs. 5000		6.7	7.4	5.0	4.8	9.5	—	—	6.7	4.7
	Rs. 5001-10000		26.7	29.6	30.0	42.9	33.3	29.6	6.7	0.0	23.0
	Rs. 10001-19000		53.3	37.0	30.0	38.1	47.6	51.9	80.0	56.7	50.8
	Rs. 19001-25000		—	14.8	5.0	9.5	4.8	7.4	—	6.7	6.3
	Rs. 25001-50000		—	11.1	25.0	—	4.8	7.4	6.7	26.7	11.0
	Rs. 50001-1 Lac		6.7	—	—	—	—	—	6.7	—	1.6
	Above Rs. 1 Lac		—	—	5.0	4.8	—	—	—	3.3	1.6
	Total	No.	15	27	20	21	21	27	30	30	191
		%	100.0	100.0	100.0	100.0	100.0	100.0	100.0	100.0	100.0
Total	Incomeless		5.6	—	—	—	—	3.0	—	—	0.8
	Upto Rs. 5000		5.6	4.8	6.7	3.2	7.4	—	—	6.7	4.1
	Rs. 5001-10000		22.2	23.8	23.3	29.0	44.4	27.3	6.7	—	22.0
	Rs. 10001-19000		50.0	42.9	43.3	41.9	40.7	45.5	80.0	56.7	49.8
	Rs. 19001-25000		5.6	16.7	6.7	16.1	3.7	15.2	—	6.7	9.5
	Rs. 25001-50000		5.6	9.5	16.7	—	3.7	9.1	6.7	26.7	10.0
	Rs. 50001-1 Lac		5.6	2.4	—	3.2	—	—	6.7	—	2.1
	Above Rs. 1 Lac		—	—	3.3	6.5	—	—	—	3.3	1.7
	Total	No.	18	42	30	31	27	33	30	30	241
		%	100.0	100.0	100.0	100.0	100.0	100.0	100.0	100.0	100.0

Source: Field Survey, 2006.

In the urban region, 42.0 per cent of the households lived in *kuccha* houses, which was 47.6 per cent in rural region. 6.0 per cent of the households in urban region lived in 'huts' which was for 13.1 per cent households in rural region (Table 4.27).

Table 4.27: Housing Condition of Non-Beneficiary Households by Region

Region	Status	Barielly	Badaun	Lakhim-pur Kheri	Lucknow	Lalitpur	Jhansi	Gorakh-pur	Varanasi	Total
Urban	*Pucca*	100.0	20.0	—	70.0	16.7	50.0	—	—	34.0
	Semi-*Pucca*	—	20.0	—	10.0	50.0	33.3	—	—	18.0
	Kuccha	—	60.0	70.0	20.0	33.3	16.7	—	—	42.0
	Hut	—	—	30.0	—	—	—	—	—	6.0
	Total No.	3	15	10	10	6	6	—	—	50
	Total %	100.0	100.0	100.0	100.0	100.0	100.0	—	—	100.0
Rural	*Pucca*	20.0	22.2	15.0	9.5	9.5	11.1	46.7	23.3	20.9
	Semi-*Pucca*	40.0	29.6	5.0	4.8	19.0	18.5	10.0	23.3	18.3
	Kuccha	33.3	33.3	40.0	52.4	61.9	66.7	36.7	53.3	47.6
	Hut	6.7	14.8	40.0	33.3	9.5	3.7	6.7	—	13.1
	Total No.	15	27	20	21	21	27	30	30	191
	Total %	100.0	100.0	100.0	100.0	100.0	100.0	100.0	100.0	100.0
Total	*Pucca*	33.3	21.4	10.0	29.0	11.1	18.2	46.7	23.3	23.7
	Semi-*Pucca*	33.3	26.2	3.3	6.5	25.9	21.2	10.0	23.3	18.3
	Kuccha	27.8	42.9	50.0	41.9	55.6	57.6	36.7	53.3	46.5
	Hut	5.6	9.5	36.7	22.6	7.4	3.0	6.7	—	11.6
	Total No.	18	42	30	31	27	33	30	30	241
	Total %	100.0	100.0	100.0	100.0	100.0	100.0	100.0	100.0	100.0

Source: Field Survey, 2006.

Of all the non-beneficiary households, 46.5 per cent had kuccha houses 11.6 per cent of all the non-beneficiary households had 'hut' (cottage).

Of all the non-beneficiary households, 98.8 per cent used kerosene for lighting at home that was similar for both rural and urban houehholds. The other sources of lighting at home were candle, battery and mustard oil. Living in darkness existed in rural region that was absent in urban region.

Kerosene as a means of fuel for cooking purposes was generally absent in both rural and urban regions. Most of the households in both the regions used multiple sources like wood and '*kanda*' (cow dung cake) for cooking.

4.16.7 Productive and Non-Productive Assets Owned by Non-Beneficiary Households

Excepting very few households, none of the non-beneficiary households had income-generating productive assets like tractor, '*atta chakki*', pump set, thresher, and trolley. The only asset that the non-beneficiary households had in the urban region was rickshaw. Overall, the non-beneficiary households were assetless that could have offered scope for income.

The non-beneficiary households owned some productive animals like cow, ox, calf, buffalo, hen, and goat. Of all these households, 79.7 per cent were landless. Of the remaining households having land, most were in possession of land less than one acre per household, the percentage for SCs being 8.1, for OBCs 16.0, for minority 5.4 and for general castes 16.7. Excepting one household in district Bareilly, nobody was reported to have land more than 5.0 acres (Table 4.28).

Table 4.28: Land Ownership of Non-Beneficiary Households by Castes

Caste	*Land Ownership in Acre*	*Barielly*	*Badaun*	*Lakhim-pur Kheri*	*Lucknow*	*Lalitpur*	*Jhansi*	*Gorakh-pur*	*Varanasi*	*Total*
SC	Landless	100.0	65.0	87.5	100.0	77.8	70.8	80.0	100.0	81.6
	Below 1 Acre	—	25.0	—	—	5.6	4.2	16.0	—	8.1
	1-2.5 Acre	—	5.0	12.5	—	16.7	16.7	4.0	—	8.1
	2.5-5.0 Acre	—	5.0	—	—	—	8.3	—	—	2.2
	Total No.	8	20	16	14	18	24	25	11	136
	Total %	100.0	100.0	100.0	100.0	100.0	100.0	100.0	100.0	100.0
OBC	Landless	—	40.0	100.0	100.0	75.0	100.0	40.0	85.7	72.0
	Below 1 Acre	—	40.0	—	—	—	—	60.0	14.3	16.0
	1-2.5 Acre	50.0	20.0	—	—	25.0	—	—	—	10.0
	Above 5.0 Acre	50.0	—	—	—	—	—	—	—	2.0
	Total No.	2	10	6	6	8	6	5	7	50
	Total %	100.0	100.0	100.0	100.0	100.0	100.0	100.0	100.0	100.0
Minority	Landless	62.5	88.9	85.7	100.0	100.0	100.0	—	100.0	86.5
	Below 1 Acre	12.5	11.1	—	—	—	—	—	—	5.4
	1-2.5 Acre	25.0	—	—	—	—	—	—	—	5.4
	2.5-5.0 Acre	—	—	14.3	—	—	—	—	—	2.7
	Total No.	8	9	7	6	1	2	—	4	37
	Total %	100.0	100.0	100.0	100.0	100.0	100.0	—	100.0	100.0
General	Landless	—	100.0	100.0	100.0	—	—	—	50.0	72.2
	Below 1 Acre	—	—	—	—	—	—	—	37.5	16.7
	1-2.5 Acre	—	—	—	—	—	100.0	—	12.5	11.1
	Total No.	—	3	1	5	—	1	—	8	18
	Total %	—	100.0	100.0	100.0	—	100.0	—	100.0	100.0
Total	Landless	72.2	66.7	90.0	100.0	77.8	75.8	73.3	83.3	79.7
	Below 1 Acre	5.6	23.8	—	—	3.7	3.0	23.3	13.3	10.0
	1-2.5 Acre	16.7	7.1	6.7	—	18.5	15.2	3.3	3.3	8.3
	2.5-5.0 Acre	—	2.4	3.3	—	—	6.1	—	—	1.7
	Above 5.0 Acre	5.6	—	—	—	—	—	—	—	0.4
	Total No.	18	42	30	31	27	33	30	30	241
	Total %	100.0	100.0	100.0	100.0	100.0	100.0	100.0	100.0	100.0

Source : Field Survey, 2006.

In the urban region, 92.0 per cent of the non-beneficiary households were landless, which was 76.4 per cent in the rural region. The ownership over land in urban region did not cross 2.5 acres, whereas in the rural region the range of land ownership was from landlessness to more than 5.0 acres.

Of all these households, 16.6 per cent had outstanding loans, which was 8.0 per cent in urban region and 18.8 per cent in the rural region. The average (per household) outstanding loan over all the non-beneficiary households as borrowers at the end of 2006 stood at Rs. 14,838, which was Rs. 15,014 for rural region and Rs. 13,250 for urban region (Table 4.29).

Table 4.29: Average Outstanding Loan of Non-Beneficiary Households by Caste and Region

Caste	*Barielly*	*Badaun*	*Lakhim-pur Kheri*	*Lucknow*	*Lalitpur*	*Jhansi*	*Gorakh-pur*	*Varanasi*	*Total (Rs.)*
SC	5000	15429	15000	—	12250	13667	15000	14250	13913
OBC	15000	8000	—	—	7500	—	3000	10000	8688
Minority	20000	30600	—	—	—	—	—	5000	25429
General	—	—	6000	—	—	—	—	20000	13000
Urban	—	16000	5000	—	—	—	—	—	13250
Rural	13333	19750	15500	—	11300	13667	11000	12750	15014
Total (Rs.)	13333	19000	12000	—	11300	13667	11000	12750	14838

Source: Field Survey, 2006.

4.16.8 Migration of Households

Of all the non-beneficiary households, 12.0 per cent reported migration, which was 14.1 per cent from the rural region and 4.0 per cent from the urban region. Non-availability of work in the locality was the major cause. This was the push factor. The pull factors for migration from rural region included wage work in brick field, service, searching for enhanced income, accompanying contractor (for paid work elsewhere) and business. For urban region, there was no reported push factor. Migration was dominantly a rural phenomenon and that too because of deruralization (push factors).

4.16.9 Reasons for Cardlessness

More than one-tenth of these households did not have cards for more than ten years, the percentage of such households being 11.5 in rural region and 12.0 in urban region. 79.2 per cent of the households did not have ration cards for a period between two and ten years. This was for 79.0 per cent of the households in rural and 80.0 per cent of the households in urban region. 42.9 per cent of the households in rural region had no ration cards for a period 6 to 10 years, which was true for 16.0 per cent of the households in urban region (Table 4.30).

Table 4.30: Households having No-Ration Card by Region

Region	Year	Barielly	Badaun	Lakhim-pur Kheri	Lucknow	Lalitpur	Jhansi	Gorakh-pur	Varanasi	Total
Urban	Up to 1 year	—	20.0	10.0	—	—	—	—	—	8.0
	2 To 5 years	100.0	40.0	60.0	70.0	100.0	66.7	—	—	64.0
	6 To 10 years	—	20.0	20.0	20.0	—	16.7	—	—	16.0
	Above 10 years	—	20.0	10.0	10.0	—	16.7	—	—	12.0
	Total No.	3	15	10	10	6	6	—	—	50
	Total %	100.0	100.0	100.0	100.0	100.0	100.0	—	—	100.0
Rural	Up to 1 year	13.3	3.7	5.0	9.5	—	3.7	6.7	30.0	9.4
	2 To 5 years	40.0	33.3	65.0	14.3	33.3	55.6	26.7	26.7	36.1
	6 To 10 years	40.0	51.9	25.0	71.4	42.9	29.6	50.0	33.3	42.9
	Above 10 years	6.7	11.1	5.0	4.8	23.8	11.1	16.7	10.0	11.5
	Total No.	15	27	20	21	21	27	30	30	191
	Total %	100.0	100.0	100.0	100.0	100.0	100.0	100.0	100.0	100.0
Total	Up to 1 year	11.1	9.5	6.7	6.5	—	3.0	6.7	30.0	9.1
	2 To 5 years	50.0	35.7	63.3	32.3	48.1	57.6	26.7	26.7	41.9
	6 To 10 years	33.3	40.5	23.3	54.8	33.3	27.3	50.0	33.3	37.3
	Above 10 years	5.6	14.3	6.7	6.5	18.5	12.1	16.7	10.0	11.6
	Total No.	18	42	30	31	27	33	30	30	241
	Total %	100.0	100.0	100.0	100.0	100.0	100.0	100.0	100.0	100.0

Source: Field Survey, 2006.

As reported by the Panchayat/Supply Department, the reasons for non-issuing ration cards for the households included absence of the representative of the household while the process of card-making was on, name not included in BPL list, no new introduction of cards, and voting factor. New card not being issued explained a high percentage of exclusion of households in both rural and urban regions. Voting as an explanatory factor was insignificant in both the rural and urban regions.

Most of the non-beneficiary households needed ration cards because of poverty. The major factor that explained the need of ration cards in rural region was landlessness. Necessity of kerosene oil was a major factor for need of ration cards in urban region.

The catalysts responsible for non-making of ration cards have been mentioned in Box 4.8.

Box 4.8: Catalysts Responsible for Non-making of Ration Cards (Perception of the Households)

Area	*Catalysts*
Urban	Elected Panchayat Member Secretary/Lekhpal FPS Dealer Supply Department
Rural	Elected Panchayat Member Secretary/Lekhpal Self FPS Dealer Supply Department

Source: Field Survey 2006.

The reasons for non-issuing ration cards have been mentioned in Box 4.9.

Box 4.9: Reasons for Non-making of Ration Cards (Perception of the Households)

Area	*Reasons*
Urban	Lack of Approach The voice of poor not heard Low allotment of Cards Don't give Bribe No Permanent house in Village Voting system
Rural	Non-initiative of Pradhan Lack of Approach The voice of poor not heard Process is going on Low allotment of Card Don't give Bribe No Permanent house in Village Groupism Absent during Card making Period Only One Card Issue in a Family Voting system

Source: Field Survey, 2006.

4.16.10 Requirement of Essential Commodities

The average consumption requirement of wheat per month per non-beneficiary household was reported to be 47 kg. This was 48 kg for rural region and 43 for urban region. The average consumption requirement of rice per month was reported to be 21 kg which was the same for rural and urban regions. The average requirement of kerosene per month per household was 3 lt which was 3 lt for rural region and 4 lt for urban region.

The market price of wheat per kg was Rs. 8.7 for rural region and Rs. 8.8 for the urban region. The market price of rice per kg was Rs. 9.4 for rural region and Rs. 10.5 for the urban region. The market price per kg of rice and wheat varied over regions, rural and urban, and over districts, though the reported price gap was not significant.

In this chapter we studied the Public Distribution System in U.P. as observed through our study of eight selected districts of the state, from the point of view of the people at whom the system is targeted. In the next chapter we will discuss the role of the local bodies and public institutions which are responsible for ensuring the availability and accessibility of essential commodities to the target recipients of the welfare measure of the government, based on our observations of the PDS functioning in the selected districts of U.P.

5

Role of Local Bodies and Public Institutions in PDS

In this chapter we will discuss the functioning of local bodies and public institutions like the Fair Price Shop dealers, the Gram Panchayats, the Godown Owners and the Government Officials-in-charge of PDS in the eight selected districts of the state and also the relationships between these bodies for ensuring the smooth and proper functioning of the Public Distribution System.

5.1 Fair Price Shops

The Fair Price Shops which distribute the essential commodities to the beneficiaries of PDS are at the centre of the functioning of the public distribution system. In the study we covered 46 FPSs for assessing their functions, role and responsibility, and the problems they face.

The FPSs were equally distributed across all the districts covered. 64.3 per cent of the selected FPS dealers belonged to SCs and backward castes, and 13.0 per cent belonged to the minority category. All the sample FPS dealers were literate. Most of the FPS dealers were aged below 60 and more than two-thirds were between 35 and 60 years. Of the FPS dealers in the age bracket 35-60, more than one-third had been running the shops for a period between 10 and 15 years. More than one-fourth of the FPS dealers were in the age bracket 21-35, half of whom had been running the shops between one and five years. One-sixth of all FPS dealers had more than 20 years experience.

5.1.1 Problems of FPS Dealers in Getting Dealership

The problems cited by the FPS dealers in getting dealership focused mainly on political support and connections, necessary payment of bribe to the Supply Department for preparation of documents/File and payment of bribe to other officials. The FPS dealers had to frequently visit Government officials at different levels to get their work done.

5.1.2 Average Number of Households Attached with FPS

We considered three years, i.e., 2004 to 2006, for examining the number and types of cards served by the FPS dealers. On average one FPS dealer served a total of 741 cards. We found monotonic increase in the average number of ration cards served by an FPS dealer with the exception of BPL. There were intra-district variations in average number of cards by types and in the average number of each type of cards served (Table 5.1).

Table 5.1: Average Number of Ration Cards Served per FPS

Time Point/ Year	*Category of Ration Cards*	*Bareilly*	*Badaun*	*Lakhimpur Kheri*	*Lucknow*	*Lalitpur*	*Jhansi*	*Gorakhpur*	*Varanasi*	*Total*
Apr-2004	BPL	160	138	92	207	157	261	226	88	171
	APL	382	501	498	528	235	353	287	598	412
	ANP	10	12	12	15	15	11	22	34	16
	ANT	33	40	68	47	43	65	82	39	51
	Total	586	690	670	797	451	690	618	758	651
Apr-2005	BPL	143	118	251	272	147	179	200	152	183
	APL	362	516	680	668	221	291	290	788	471
	ANP	10	12	14	15	14	24	23	32	18
	ANT	37	60	134	133	58	72	105	72	84
	Total	552	705	1080	1089	440	566	618	1045	755
Apr-2006	BPL	296	0	211	252	136	157	180	139	182
	APL	525	0	680	702	193	410	281	788	508
	ANP	0	0	15	14	15	11	28	29	21
	ANT	20	0	133	154	70	107	113	85	107
	Total	841	0	1039	1122	413	685	602	1042	818
Average on Total	BPL	199	85	185	244	147	199	202	126	179
	APL	423	339	619	633	216	351	286	725	464
	ANP	7	8	14	15	14	15	24	32	18
	ANT	30	33	112	112	57	81	100	66	81
	Total	660	465	929	1003	435	647	613	948	741

Source: Field Survey, 2006.

5.1.3 Requirement, Availability and Distribution of Commodities as Reported by FPS Dealers

5.1.3.1 Rice and Wheat for BPL Households

Based on the report by the FPS dealers on requirement, availability and distribution of rice and wheat under BPL, 99.5 per cent of requirement of rice was available in 2004-05, which was 98.9 in 2005-06. 98.9 per cent of requirement of wheat was available in 2004-05, which was cent per cent in 2005-06. Requirement of rice in 2005-06 was nearly double of that in 2004-05; requirement of wheat in 2005-06 was 12.1 per cent more than what it was in 2004-05. Distribution of rice as a percentage of availability in 2004-05 was 99.5 over all the districts which was 96.5 per cent in 2005-06 (Table 5.2).

5.1.3.2 Rice and Wheat under Antyodaya Yojana

Based on the report by FPS dealers, availability as a percentage of requirement under Antyodaya Yojana was cent per cent for rice in 2004-05 and 99.3 per cent in 2005-06. The corresponding percentages for wheat were 98.8 and 98.9. Requirement of rice under Antyodaya in 2005-06 was 2.5 times what it was in 2004-05, while of wheat it was nearly double.

5.1.3.3 Wheat under Annapurna Yojana

Based on the information provided by the FPS dealers, 92.6 per cent of requirement of wheat in 2004-05 under Annapurna Yojana was made available of which 99.4 per cent had been distributed. The corresponding figures for 2005-06 were 92.8 and 99.9 per cent.

5.1.3.4 Distribution of Sugar

In 2004-05, considered over all the selected districts, 98.2 per cent of sugar required had been available. Of the available sugar, 99.5 per cent had been distributed.

5.1.3.5 Distribution of Kerosene

For 2004-05, considered over all the selected districts, 78.3 per cent required was available, of which 99.6 per cent had been distributed. For 2005-06, 81.6 per cent of requirement had been available with the dealers, of which 99.7 per cent had been distributed.

Table 5.2: Requirement, Availability and Distribution of Rice and Wheat per FPS Dealer under BPL

(*Quantity in kg.*)

Districts	Figure in	Year 2004-05						Year 2005-06					
		Rice			Wheat			Rice			Wheat		
		Distributed	Available	Required	Distributed	Available	Required	Distributed	Available	Required	Distributed	Available	Required
Bareilly	No.	11158	18159	18987	17493	26733	27691	18887	29789	30727	35176	35788	35788
	%	58.8	95.6	100.0	63.2	96.5	100.0	61.5	96.9	100.0	98.3	100.0	100.0
Badaun	No.	19816	19816	19816	25750	25750	25750	23294	23294	23294	38708	38708	38708
	%	100.0	100.0	100.0	100.0	100.0	100.0	100.0	100.0	100.0	100.0	100.0	100.0
Lakhimpur	No.	NA	NA	NA	37562	37562	39410	54790	54790	57250	NA	NA	NA
Kheri	%	NA	NA	NA	95.3	95.3	100.0	95.7	95.7	100.0	NA	NA	NA
Lucknow	No.	35209	35209	35209	48567	48567	48567	63441	63441	63441	74179	74179	74179
	%	100.0	100.0	100.0	100.0	100.0	100.0	100.0	100.0	100.0	100.0	100.0	100.0
Lalitpur	No.	23523	23523	23523	29784	29784	29784	28946	28946	28946	40473	40473	40473
	%	100.0	100.0	100.0	100.0	100.0	100.0	100.0	100.0	100.0	100.0	100.0	100.0
Jhansi	No.	24187	24214	24214	36633	36631	36631	34314	34325	34325	51417	51417	51417
	%	99.9	100.0	100.0	100.0	100.0	100.0	100.0	100.0	100.0	100.0	100.0	100.0
Gorakhpur	No.	24753	24753	24753	24239	24306	24306	43444	43490	43490	29328	29328	29328
	%	100.0	100.0	100.0	99.7	100.0	100.0	99.9	100.0	100.0	100.0	100.0	100.0
Varanasi	No.	16790	16790	16790	22020	22020	22020	40020	40020	40020	15045	15045	15045
	%	100.0	100.0	100.0	100.0	100.0	100.0	100.0	100.0	100.0	100.0	100.0	100.0
Total	No.	19437	20308	20411	27504	31419	31770	38392	39762	40187	35553	35630	35630
	%	95.2	99.5	100.0	86.6	98.9	100.0	95.5	98.9	100.0	99.8	100.0	100.0

Note: Availability and Distribution each is calculated as per cent of Requirement. NA = Not Available.

Source: Field Survey, 2006.

5.1.3.6 Lifting of Items from Godown

Two-thirds of the total FPS dealers reported to have received items for distribution from the concerned Godown. The reasons for non-receipt of items regularly (every month) by the FPS dealers are mentioned in Box 5.1.

Box 5.1: Non-Lifting of Items Every Month (Reasons Reported by FPS Dealers)

Reasons
Stock finished at concerned Godown
Depot/Food Godown often closed
Godown in-charge often threatened to cancel the licence
Kerosene oil not given by Depot one month per year
Visited the Godown/Depot frequently for lifting of allotment
Sugar not received during last two years

Source: Field Survey, 2006.

There were district-wise and item-wise variations in the delay (number of days spent between money deposited and items received by the FPS dealers).

5.1.4 Actual Sale Price of Commodities Distributed to Households by Cardholding and Costs Involved

Rice under BPL and Antayodaya Yojana

Actual sale price charged by the FPS dealer is the purchase price that the consumers pay. This price is the sum of purchase price from the Godown plus costs on logistics plus compensating the quantity lost (price surrendered) at the Godown (because of a number of reasons).

- *For BPL rice per unit (kg.)*: Actual Sale Price (Rs. 6.62) = Purchase Price from Godown (Rs. 6.09) + Cost on Logistics (Rs. 0.41) + Cost compensated for Quantity loss at Godown (Rs. 0.11).
- *For ANT rice per unit (kg.)*: Actual Sale Price (Rs. 3.41) = Purchase Price from Godown (Rs. 2.94) + Cost on Logistics (Rs. 0.41) + Cost compensated for Quantity loss at Godown (Rs. 0.05).

The reported purchase price for each of BPL and ANT rice was fixed and lifted at the fixed rate across all the selected districts.

Cost on logistics includes items like loading/unloading, transportation, weighing and other expenses like paying bribe. The Godown level deduction in quantity means the FPS dealer had to pay a portion to some of the officials/operators for smooth lifting of items (Table 5.3).

Table 5.3: Actual Sale Price of Rice under BPL and Antyodaya Yojana

(On per kg. item in Rs.)

Districts	*Purchase Price from Godown*		*Expenditure on Logistics*				*Items Lost at Godown (Quantity and Cost)*			*Actual Sale Price*	
	ANT Rice	*BPL Rice*	*Loading/ Unloading*	*Trans-portation*	*Weighing*	*Other expenses*	*Quantity*	*ANT Cost*	*BPL Cost*	*ANT Rice*	*BPL Rice*
Bareilly	2.94	6.09	0.03	0.16	0.08	0.40	0.03	0.08	0.16	3.69	6.92
Badaun	2.94	6.09	0.05	0.10	0.01	0.00	0.02	0.06	0.12	3.16	6.37
Lakhimp Kheri	2.94	6.09	0.03	0.14	0.02	0.10	0.02	0.05	0.10	3.28	6.48
Lucknow	2.94	6.09	0.06	0.12	0.00	0.23	0.04	0.11	0.22	3.45	6.72
Lalitpur	2.94	6.09	0.05	0.16	0.01	0.43	0.01	0.03	0.06	3.61	6.79
Jhansi	2.94	6.09	0.03	0.10	0.00	0.04	0.01	0.03	0.07	3.15	6.34
Gorakhpur	2.94	6.09	0.05	0.10	0.03	0.15	0.02	0.06	0.12	3.32	6.54
Varanasi	2.94	6.09	0.05	0.15	0.00	0.05	0.01	0.02	0.04	3.21	6.38
Total	2.94	6.09	0.04	0.13	0.04	0.20	0.02	0.05	0.11	3.41	6.62

Source: Field Survey, 2006.

Wheat under BPL and Antayodaya Yojana

- *For BPL wheat per unit (kg.)*: Actual Sale Price (Rs. 5.07) = Purchase Price from Godown (Rs. 4.59) + Cost on Logistics (Rs. 0.39) + Cost compensated for Quantity loss at Godown (Rs. 0.09).
- *For ANT wheat per unit (kg.)*: Actual Sale Price (Rs. 2.37) = Purchase Price from Godown (Rs. 1.94) + Cost on Logistics (Rs. 0.39) + Cost compensated for Quantity loss at Godown (Rs. 0.04).

The reported purchase price for each of BPL and ANT wheat was fixed and lifted at the fixed rate across all the selected districts. The reported (actual) sale price of wheat for each of BPL and ANT varies across districts (Table 5.4).

Table 5.4: Actual Sale Price of Wheat under BPL and Antyodaya Yojana

(*per kg. in Rs.*)

Districts	Purchase Price from Godown		Expenditure on Logistics				Items Lost at Godown (Quantity and Cost)			Actual Sale Price	
	ANT Wheat	BPL Wheat	Loading/ Unloading	Trans-portation	Weighing	Other expenses	Quantity	ANT Cost	BPL Cost	ANT Wheat	BPL Wheat
Bareilly	1.94	4.59	0.03	0.16	0.03	0.40	0.03	0.05	0.12	2.61	5.33
Badaun	1.94	4.59	0.05	0.10	0.01	0.00	0.02	0.04	0.09	2.14	4.84
Lakhimpucr Kheri	1.94	4.59	0.03	0.14	0.02	0.10	0.02	0.03	0.07	2.26	4.95
Lucknow	1.94	4.59	0.06	0.12	0.00	0.23	0.04	0.07	0.17	2.42	5.17
Lalitpur	1.94	4.59	0.05	0.16	0.01	0.43	0.02	0.03	0.07	2.61	5.30
Jhansi	1.94	4.59	0.03	0.10	0.00	0.04	0.02	0.03	0.07	2.14	4.83
Gorakhpur	1.94	4.59	0.05	0.10	0.03	0.15	0.02	0.04	0.10	2.31	5.01
Varanasi	1.94	4.59	0.05	0.15	0.00	0.05	0.00	0.00	0.01	2.19	4.85
Total	1.94	4.59	0.04	0.13	0.02	0.20	0.02	0.04	0.09	2.37	5.07

Source: Field Survey, 2006.

Sale Price of Sugar

- *For Sugar per unit (kg.)*: Actual Sale Price (Rs. 14.07) = Purchase Price from Godown (Rs. 13.44) + Cost on Logistics (Rs. 0.3) + Cost compensated for Quantity loss at Godown (Rs. 0.2).

The reported purchase price of sugar was fixed and lifted at the fixed rate across all the selected districts. The reported (actual) sale price of sugar varied over districts. The cost on logistics as well as cost on items lost varied over districts (Table 5.5).

Sale Price of Kerosene

- *For Kerosene per unit (lt)*: Actual Sale Price (Rs. 10.56) = Purchase Price from Depot (Rs. 9.82) + Cost on Logistics (Rs. 0.7) + Cost compensated for Quantity loss at Depot (Rs. 0.0).

The reported purchase price at the Depot level of Kerosene varied over districts. The reported (actual) sale price of Kerosene also varied over districts. There was no reported quantity lost at the Depot level. There was, however, loss on account of logistics overall and across districts (Table 5.6).

Table 5.5: Actual Sale Price of Sugar

(On per kg. item in Rs.)

Districts	Purchase Price from Godown	Expenditure on Logistics				Items Lost at Godown (Quantity and Cost)		Actual Sale Price
		Loading/ Unloading	Trans-portation	Weighing	Other expenses	Quantity	Cost	
Bareilly	13.44	0.0	0.2	0.0	0.2	0.02	0.3	14.18
Badaun	13.44	0.1	0.1	0.0	0.0	0.02	0.3	13.87
Lakhimpur Kheri	13.44	0.0	0.1	0.0	0.1	0.00	0.0	13.77
Lucknow	13.44	0.1	0.1	0.0	0.2	0.04	0.5	14.40
Lalitpur	13.44	0.1	0.2	0.0	0.4	0.01	0.2	14.26
Jhansi	13.44	0.0	0.1	0.0	0.0	0.00	0.0	13.66
Gorakhpur	13.44	0.0	0.1	0.0	0.3	0.03	0.4	14.29
Varanasi	13.44	0.1	0.2	0.0	0.1	0.00	0.0	13.72
Total	13.44	0.0	0.1	0.0	0.2	0.02	0.2	14.07

Source: Field Survey, 2006.

Table 5.6: Actual Sale Price of Kerosene

(Per Litre in Rs.)

Districts	Purchase Price from Deport	Expenditure on Logistics				Deducted Quantity at Depot		Actual Sale Price
		Loading/ Unloading	Trans-portation	Weighting	Other expenses	Quantity	Value	
Bareilly	9.81	0.1	0.6	0.0	0.0	0.00	0.00	10.59
Badaun	9.75	0.1	0.9	0.1	0.0	0.00	0.00	10.82
Lakhimpur Kheri	9.85	0.1	0.4	0.0	0.0	0.00	0.00	10.32
Lucknow	9.78	0.1	0.4	0.0	0.0	0.00	0.00	10.31
Lalitpur	9.78	0.1	0.7	0.0	0.0	0.00	0.00	10.55
Jhansi	9.85	0.1	0.3	0.0	0.0	0.00	0.00	10.21
Gorakhpur	9.80	0.1	0.5	0.0	0.0	0.00	0.00	10.41
Varanasi	9.90	0.1	0.6	0.0	0.0	0.00	0.00	10.58
Total	9.82	0.1	0.5	0.1	0.0	0.00	0.00	10.56

Source: Field Survey, 2006.

5.1.5 Price Hike by FPS Dealers Because of Enhanced Cost in Logistics

The FPS dealers reported that they felt compelled to fix sale price more than the price fixed by the Government in the PDS because of the costs that they incur on loading/unloading, and transportation. 78.3 per cent of the FPS dealers reported sale by price hike because of additional cost on logistics.

5.1.6 Sale Price of Commodities Reported by FPS Dealers

The actual sale price charged by the FPS dealers on all the items distributed for the BPL and ANT cardholders exceeded the Government announced price per unit of the items, as reported by the dealers (Table 5.7).

Table 5.7: Price Gap in Commodities

Items	*BPL*		*ANT*	
	Govt. Price (Rs.)	*Actual Sale Price (Average)*	*Govt. Price (Rs.)*	*Actual Sale Price (Average)*
Rice	6.15	6.37	3.00	3.03
Wheat	4.65	4.97	2.00	2.15
Sugar	13.50	13.85	13.50	13.82
Kerosene	10.00	10.62	10.00	10.61

Source: Field Survey, 2006.

5.1.7 Utilization of Post-Distribution Balance Items

For 84.8 per cent of the FPS dealers, the stock (post-availability) was released (stock exhausted with no balance) in case of kerosene. For sugar, it was 71.7 per cent, wheat 58.7 per cent and rice 39.1 per cent. FPS, thus, functioned well for kerosene, and extremely poorly for rice. FPS dealers reportedly distributed balance rice among poor households. The report of sale in the open (black) market was least in case of kerosene and highest in case of rice. In case of kerosene, there was no carry forward for the next month, which happened in case of other items.

5.1.8 Quality of Commodities Reported by FPS Dealers

89.1 per cent of the dealers reported quality 'good' for kerosene, which was reported by 69.6 per cent for wheat, 58.7 per cent for sugar and 37.0 per cent for rice. 'Bad' quality in foodgrains meant 'broken', 'dirty', and 'soiled'.

5.1.9 Working Period of FPSs per Month

Two-thirds of the FPS dealers reported opening of FPS just on arrival of items; one-fourth of the dealers reported to open the shop every day; one-sixth of the dealers reported to open the shop on arrival of customers.

The role of Regional Food Controller in checking FPSs was almost absent. Similarly, the role of Administrative Officer, ADO, Lekhpal was negligible as vigilance catalyst over FPS. Officials of Supply Department did not pay much attention towards the necessity of vigilance over FPS.

5.1.10 Relationship of FPS Dealers with Consumers and Supply Department

Most of the FPS dealers were satisfied with the consumers of all types. The reasons for non-satisfaction of the FPS dealers regarding different types of consumers are cited in Box 5.2.

Box 5.2: Reasons for Non-satisfaction of FPS Dealers with the Consumers

Reasons
Abuse the dealers Consumers do not come timely for lifting the items Demand more quantity of all items Do not believe that ANP Yojana has been closed

Source: Field Survey, 2006.

More than four-fifths of FPS dealers were completely satisfied with the Supply Department. The reason for 'partial' satisfaction of the FPS dealers with the Supply Department was that the Department had to be paid bribe money for each work done every month.

5.1.11 Role of Panchayats as Viewed by FPS Dealers

Panchayat is the major controller of PDS. The control exercised by the Panchayats in regulating PDS is shown in Box 5.3.

In the urban areas, the FPS dealers reported local administration grabbing individual benefits which was reported less in rural areas. 40.0 per cent of the urban FPS dealers reported inactive local administration, whereas in rural areas Panchayats were reportedly very active.

The reasons why most of the FPS dealers considered Panchayat-controlled PDS 'bad' are cited in Box 5.4.

Box 5.3: Control over the PDS by the Panchayats by Activities (Opinion of FPS Dealers)

Opinion
Verify the stock each month
Pressurize to give more kerosene oil to their closer people
Monitor the distribution system
Grab 20 kg sugar for each PRIs member
Grab individual benefits in cash or kind
Impose unnecessary pressure on the dealer
Cooperate at the time of distribution of items
Control the demand of dominant people

Source: Field Survey, 2006.

Box 5.4: Panchayat-Controlled PDS Considered 'Bad' (Reasons Reported by FPS Dealers)

Reasons
Take individual benefit in cash or kind
Create interruption in distribution of items
Impose unnecessary pressures
Take money for verification
Issue token for getting items to own people
Create Factions in village
Threaten to cancel the dealership

Source: Field Survey, 2006.

The reasons why the FPS dealers considered Panchayat-controlled PDS 'good' are cited in Box 5.5.

Box 5.5: Panchayat-Controlled PDS Considered Good (Reasons Reported by FPS Dealers)

Reasons
Individual security
Understanding local people
Cooperating in distribution of items
Defending from Punishment by government officials
Controlling dominant people/ criminals

Source: Field Survey, 2006.

5.1.11 Problems Reported and Suggestions Offered by FPS Dealers

Paying Bribe to Supply Department

58.7 per cent of the FPS dealers reportedly did not pay bribe (money) to the officials of Supply Department to continue dealership in future. Of those who paid, the average money paid was Rs. 1422, which had to be paid every month. The person who received the bribe money was the Supply Inspector (Table 5.8).

Table 5.8: Bribe Paid per FPS Dealer, Duration and the Receivers (Report by FPS Dealers)

Districts	*Average Amount Paid**	*Duration of Payment*		*Amount Given to Whom*	
		Every Month	*NR*	*Supply Inspector*	*NR*
Bareilly	860	1	0	1	0
Badaun	700	1	0	1	0
Lakhimpur Kheri	800	3	0	3	0
Lucknow	3950	4	0	4	0
Lalitpur	1500	1	0	1	0
Jhansi	533	3	0	3	0
Gorakhpur	500	2	0	2	0
Varanasi	500	1	1	1	1
Total	1422	16	1	16	1

* It depends on allotment of commodities to FPS dealer.

Source: Field Survey, 2006.

5.1.11.1 Problems Faced in Running Dealership

The major difficulties faced by the FPS dealers in running the shop included the incompatibility between high demand and low allotment, illegal demand of political party leaders, low commission, and cardless customers' pressure. One-tenth of the dealers reported 'loot' by officials in the name of vigilance (Box 5.6).

5.1.11.2. Complaints Reported Regarding Foodgrains Godown and Kerosene Depot

71.7 per cent of the FPS dealers did not complain against foodgrains godown and kerosene depot. The major complains by the dealers included manipulated measurement of items by quantity delivered by the Godown and Depot, and commission paid by the dealers on the items lifted (Box 5.7).

Box 5.6: Difficulties Faced by the FPS Dealers in Running FPS (Reported by FPS Dealers)

Problems
Low commission High cost for lifting and carrying of items Illegal demand from political (ruling) leaders Inner-fighting during the distribution of Items Given bribe in cash and kind to local Panchayat members and officials Officials robbed in the name of checking Problems in distribution due to high demand and low allotment No incentive on MDM and Annapurna items Card-less (non-beneficiary) pressurized to take items

Source: Field Survey, 2006.

Box 5.7: Complaints Reported by FPS Dealers during the Lifting of Commodities from Foodgrain Godown/ Kerosene Depot

Complaints
Take commission on each unit of items False measurement of items by quantity/weight Kerosene not distributed throughout the year Foodgrain of poor quality delivered FPS dealer has to pay Rs. 30 per quintal of BPL rice and wheat for transportation Cost

Source: Field Survey, 2006.

5.1.12 Suggestions of FPS Dealers

The major measures suggested by the FPS dealers for implementation by the Government included raising the rate of commission, ensuring commission on Mid-day Meal, ensuring allotment based on consumers' demand, enhanced allotment of Kerosene oil, covering transportation cost of the dealer, stopping bribes paid to the officials, adding new items to be distributed along with the existing ones through the FPS (Box 5.8).

Box 5.8: Suggestions of FPS Dealers for Implementation

Suggestions
Rate of commission for FPS dealer should be increased
Provision for monthly honorarium for FPS dealer should be made
Allotment of kerosene oil should be increased
Transportation cost of the dealer should be compensated
Commission on MDM should be fixed
Special fund to FPS dealer should be provided by Government
Bribe must be stopped at each level
Distribution of additional items should be entrusted with the FPS shop
Provision should be developed for home delivery of PDS commodities
Allotment must be based on consumers' demand
Political interference should be stopped
Ration cards should be issued to all households
Cut allotted foodgrains and kerosene from godown/depot must be stopped
Proper quality and measurement should be ensured at each level
Checking/verification should not be biased

Source: Field Survey, 2006.

5.2 Gram Panchayat

65.0 per cent of the rural beneficiary households opined that the Gram/ Nagar Panchayats did not take any initiatives for the improvement of the PDS, the percentage being 73.3 for the urban households. While 25.4 per cent of the households in rural region reported positive initiatives by Panchayats, 11.6 per cent households in urban region reported the same.

21.0 per cent of the beneficiary households reported contributions of Gram Panchayats in terms of issuing ration cards, checking FPSs every month, helping the consumers at the time of distribution, and informing the households about arrival of items (Box 5.9).

67.6 per cent of the beneficiary households reported ignorance as the reason why the Gram Panchayats did not initiate any efforts for betterment of PDS. Of those reporting, the focus was on FPS dealers' involvement in corruption with the help of Gram Pradhan or Gram Panchayat, Panchayats having no problems from the FPSs, and Panchayats taking bribe from the FPS dealer every month. Thus, the major reasons centred on the nexus between the FPS dealer and the Panchayat (Gram Pradhan). The other reasons included local power structure, and use of the poor people as vote bank (Box 5.10).

Box 5.9: Contributions of Gram Panchayats in PDS as Reported by Beneficiary Households

Contributions
Issued the Ration Cards
Opened the FPS within village
Checked FPS every month
Informed the beneficiary about arrival of items
Inspected the arrival of items at FPS
FPS Dealership was allotted through a committee
Help the consumers during distribution

Source: Field Survey, 2006.

Box 5.10: Reasons why the Gram Panchayats do not Initiate any Efforts for Betterment of PDS

- Do not live in village
- FPS dealer involved in corruption with the help of Gram Pradhan or Gram Panchayat
- All are engaged in leadership
- Only interest in the Vote Bank
- In case the GP performs right duty, extra income of GP is stopped
- Panchayats have no problems with FPS
- Distribution is good
- Panchayats have no time to do public work
- Panchayats take bribe each month
- Discarded by Gram Pradhan because of not casting vote in his favour
- Ignorance
- Panchayats give more benefits to their own persons

Source: Field Survey, 2006.

5.2.1 Role of Gram Panchayats

The role of Gram Panchayats in PDS as perceived by households in the eight selected districts is mentioned in Box 5.11.

The policy of the Government of India aims at strengthening local governance through the Panchayats to solve the problems at the grassroots level with the participation of local people. So far as the PDS is concerned, the Government of India has empowered the Panchayats for formation of vigilance committee at local level, appointment of FPS dealer, selection of beneficiary households, and verification of distribution of items among others.

Box 5.11: Role/Tasks of Panchayats in PDS (Perception of the Households)

Region	Role/Tasks
Urban	Card Making
Rural	Card Making Distribute Oil Watching Distribution Cooperate in Distribution Circulate Information of Distribution Ensure Distribution of Items for Cardless Persons

Source: Field Survey 2006.

In order to examine this, we interviewed 33 members from Panchayats in selected 33 villages in U.P. of which 36.4 per cent were Pradhans, 27.3 per cent were 'Pradhanpatis', and the rest were members of Panchayats and others. 'Others' meant members of BDC and ex-Pradhan. Excepting one there was no illiteracy among the representatives of Panchayats.

The Gram Panchayats selected the households for distribution of BPL cards based on poverty, landlessness and *kaccha* house. The Gram Panchayats selected the households as beneficiaries of Antyodaya Yojana based on landlessness, single member family, and poorest of the poor. The Gram Panchayats selected the households as beneficiaries under Annapurna Yojana based on helplessness, aged above 65 years and incomelessness.

The officials of Revenue Department (Lekhpal) were mainly engaged in verification of eligibility of beneficiaries, followed by Block officials and Supply Inspectors.

The major reasons for cardlessness of eligible households were reported to be absence of the potential beneficiary while card-making was on, low target for the village, name not found in BPL list, division of family, and discriminatory role of Panchayats.

45.0 per cent of all the representatives from Panchayats acknowledged existence of people who suffered from day-to-day hunger. The reasons for persistence of poverty in the selected villages during the 2001-06 have been mentioned in Box 5.12.

The major reasons cited by Panchayat representatives for persistence of problems in PDS were 'low allotment of items', 'low allotment of ration cards', 'corruption among government officials', 'non-receipt of full quota by FPS dealer', 'black marketing of items', and 'FPS remaining closed most of the days'.

Box 5.12: Persistence of Poverty in Village, 2001-06 (Opinion of Gram Panchayats)

- Division of Family/Property
- Low income/rising prices
- Big size of family/increased population
- Low awareness
- Illiteracy
- Wrong implementation of schemes
- Low productivity of land
- High dependence on wage labour

Source: Field Survey, 2006.

5.3 Kerosene Depots and Foodgrains Godowns

We covered 27 kerosene oil depots and 21 foodgrains godowns covering all the selected districts.

- In case of oil depots we got responses from a number of categories of respondents like partners in business, proprietorship, and manager/accountant.
- In case of foodgrain godowns we got responses from a number of categories of respondents like Godown-in-charge, senior marketing inspector and supply inspector.

About Depot-in-Charge

- More than one-third had work/job experience for a period more than 12 years at a stretch.
- A little less than one-fifth had experience of less than one year.
- Most of the depot-in-charge in the sample had job experience of more than three years.

About Godown-in-Charge

- No Godown-in-charge had job experience of more than three years.
- The differences in job experience between the two categories were natural because while the oil depot-in-charge was privately managed, the Godown-in-charge was managed by Government personnel subject to transfer by location.

5.3.1 Storage Capacity of Foodgrains Godowns and Kerosene Depots

One-third of the Foodgrain Godowns had storage capacity between 23 and 50 Mt, while another one-third had capacity between 50 and 80 Mt. 95.5 per cent of the Foodgrain Godowns had storage capacity below 120 Mt. (Table 5.9).

Table 5.9: Storage Capacity of Regional Foodgrain Godown (As Reported by Godown-in-charge and Depot-in-charge)

Storage (Capacity in MT)	*Figure in*	*Bareilly*	*Badaun*	*Lakhimpur Kheri*	*Lucknow*	*Lalitpur*	*Jhansi*	*Gorakhpur*	*Varanasi*	*Total*
23-50	No.	0	2	0	2	3	0	0	0	7
	%	0.0	66.7	0.0	66.7	100.0	0.0	0.0	0.0	33.3
50-80	No.	1	0	1	1	0	0	2	2	7
	%	33.3	0.0	33.3	33.3	0.0	0.0	100.0	100.0	33.3
80-120	No.	1	1	2	0	0	1	0	0	5
	%	33.3	33.3	66.7	0.0	0.0	50.0	0.0	0.0	23.8
>120	No.	1	0	0	0	0	1	0	0	2
	%	33.3	0.0	0.0	0.0	0.0	50.0	0.0	0.0	9.5
Total	No.	3	3	3	3	3	2	2	2	21
	%	100.0	100.0	100.0	100.0	100.0	100.0	100.0	100.0	100.0

Source: Field Survey, 2006.

As reported by the depot-in-charge, half of the depots had storage capacity per depot between 15 and 20 k. lt. (Table 5.10).

5.3.2 Sources of the Regional Godowns and Depots to Lift Items

The kerosene oil depots in the sample lifted oil from IOC (66.7%), BPCL (25.9%) and HPCL (7.4%). There were no multiple sources for the Depots. The foodgrain Godowns lifted items mainly from FCI (66.7%), RFC (57.1%), PCF (47.6%) and SFC (4.8%). There were multiple sources for lifting items. In total, for godowns, 52.4 per cent was lifted from SWC (state pool) and 28.6 from CWC (central pool).

5.3.3 FPS Dealers Attached with Foodgrains Godowns and Kerosene Depots

On average one depot served 109 FPSs. Generally the depot owners/ managers perceived that the number of FPSs that each was allotted to serve was normal. On average one foodgrain Godown served 95 FPSs (Table 5.11).

Table 5.10: Storage Capacity of Kerosene Oil Depots (As Reported by Depot-in-charge)

Storage Capacity (in k. lit.)	*Figure in*	*Bareilly*	*Badaun*	*Lakhim-pur Kheri*	*Lucknow*	*Lalitpur*	*Jhansi*	*Gorakh-pur*	*Varanasi*	*Total*
15-20	No.	1	0	1	0	3	3	3	2	13
	%	33.3	—	25.0	—	75.0	100.0	75.0	66.7	48.1
20-30	No.	0	0	1	1	1	0	1	0	4
	%	—	—	25.0	33.3	25.0	—	25.0	—	14.8
30-40	No.	0	0	1	0	0	0	0	1	2
	%	—	—	25.0	—	—	—	—	33.3	7.4
40-50	No.	1	1	1	1	0	0	0	0	4
	%	33.	33.3	25.0	33.3	—	—	—	—	14.8
>50	No.	1	2	0	1	0	0	0	0	4
	%	33.3	66.7	—	33.3	—	—	—	—	14.8
Total	No.	3	3	4	3	4	3	4	3	27
	%	100.0	100.0	100.0	100.0	100.0	100.0	100.0	100.0	100.0

Source : Field Survey, 2006.

Table 5.11: Average Number of FPSs Attached to Godowns and Depots (Perception of Godown-in-charge and Depot-in-charge regarding the Number of FPSs Attached)

(*Figure in Numbers*)

Districts	*Kerosene*					*Foodgrains*				
	Average No. of FPSs Attached per Depot	*More*	*Less*	*Normal*	*Total*	*Average No. FPSs Attached per Godown*	*More*	*Less*	*Normal*	*Total*
Bareilly	112	0	1	2	3	153	0	0	3	3
Badaun	163	0	0	3	3	110	0	0	3	3
Lakhimpur Kheri	25	0	0	4	4	71	0	1	2	3
Lucknow	76	0	1	2	3	77	0	0	3	3
Lalitpur	119	1	0	3	4	64	0	0	3	3
Jhansi	62	0	0	3	3	88	1	0	1	2
Gorakhpur	139	0	1	3	4	80	0	0	2	2
Varanasi	133	1	0	2	3	105	0	0	2	2
Total	109	2	3	22	27	95	1	1	19	21

Source: Field Survey, 2006.

The foodgrain Godown and the oil depot were authorized to supply items to blocks, tehsils and directly to FPSs.

5.3.4 Management of Stock in Godowns and Depots after Distribution

For 44.4 per cent of the depots, no balance remained post-distribution. For 42.9 per cent of the Godowns, no balance remained post-distribution (Table 5.12).

Table 5.12: Utilization/Management of the Stock Post-Distribution of Items to FPS Dealers (As Reported by Godown-in-charge and Depot-in-Charge)

Type of Items	*Utilization/Management*	*Total (All Districts)*
Kerosene	Remain balance in stock and initiate sale on order	25.9
	Remain in balance	11.1
	Ignorance	18.5
	No Balance against allotment	44.4
	Total	100.0
Food Grains	Remain balance in stock and initiate sale on order	33.3
	Adjusted in next month	14.3
	Ignorance	9.5
	No Balance against allotment	42.9
	Total	100.0

Source: Field Survey, 2006.

5.3.5 Corrective Measures if the FPS Dealers not Satisfied with Quality of Items

In case the FPS dealers were not satisfied with the quality of items to be lifted by them, the responsibility of the Godown-in-charge was either to change the item or to convince them about the quality. Two-thirds of the Godown-in-charge opined that the distributable items were not poor and 28.6 per cent reported that they changed the items if available.

5.3.6 Loss of Foodgrains and Kerosene due to Management Inadequacy

While most of the Godown-in-charges reported loss of foodgrains due to inadequate management facility, half of the kerosene oil depot owners/managers reported loss in kerosene for the same cause (Table 5.13).

Table 5.13: Loss of Foodgrains and Kerosene per Year due to Management Inadequacy (As Reported by Godown-in-charge and Depot-in-charge)

(Figure in %)

Districts	*Depot-in-charge*			*Godown-in-charge*		
	Loss	*No Loss*	*Total*	*Loss*	*No Loss*	*Total*
Bareilly	66.7	33.3	100.0	0.0	100.0	100.0
Badaun	33.3	66.7	100.0	0.0	100.0	100.0
Lakhimpur Kheri	25.0	75.0	100.0	0.0	100.0	100.0
Lucknow	100.0	0.0	100.0	0.0	100.0	100.0
Lalitpur	50.0	50.0	100.0	33.3	66.7	100.0
Jhansi	0.0	100.0	100.0	0.0	100.0	100.0
Gorakhpur	50.0	50.0	100.0	0.0	100.0	100.0
Varanasi	66.7	33.3	100.0	0.0	100.0	100.0
Total	48.1	51.9	100.0	4.8	95.2	100.0

Source: Field Survey, 2006.

Of the depot owners/managers who reported loss in kerosene, the major reason cited was the variation in temperature between the time of filling (in the company) and the delivery at depot in addition to the leakage problem at filling point during delivery. Regarding the loss in items, the Godown-in-charge cited reasons like inadequate capacity of the Godown and location of the Godown at different places (Table 5.14).

Table 5.14: Reasons for Loss of Foodgrains and Kerosene (As Reported by Godown-in-charge and Depot-in-charge)

Reasons	*Kerosene Depot*		*Foodgrain Godown*	
	No.	*%*	*No.*	*%*
Temperature variation between the time of Filling (company) and delivery (depot)	9	69.2	0	0.0
Leakage problem at filling point during delivery	3	23.1	0	0.0
Density variation between company and depot	1	7.7	0	0.0
Inadequate capacity of Godown	0	0.0	1	100.0
Godown situated at different places	0	0.0	1	100.0
NR	2	15.4	0	0.0
Total	13	100.0	1	100.0

NR: Non-Response.

Source: Field Survey, 2006.

As reported by the representatives of oil depot and Godown-in-charge, none of the regional manager, accountant-in-charge/district-in-charge, district supply officer, and regional food controller ever inspected the kerosene oil depot. All the identified catalysts assigned to inspect the Godowns inspected, with the highest inspection reported in case of the SDM.

5.3.7 Coordination among Supply Department, FPS Dealers, Oil Depots and Godown-in-Charge

Three-fourths of the depot representatives opined that the coordination among the Supply Department, FPS dealers and Depot-in-charge was good, while the rest argued for the necessity for improvement. Four-fifths of the Godown representatives opined that the coordination among the Supply Department, FPS dealers and Godown-in-charge was good, while the rest argued for the necessity for improvement.

5.3.8 Problems and Suggestions of Food-grain Godowns and Kerosene Depots-in-Charge

The major problems reported in case of depots included pressures and responsibilities imposed by government functionaries, higher officials in the government suspecting the depots staff, short duration fixed for distribution of oil, high price gap between kerosene oil and diesel leading to black marketing of kerosene. The major problems reported by the Godowns included government officials suspecting the Godowns staff, and inadequate capacity of Godown.

The major suggestions offered by the Depot-in-charge for improvement of the system pointed at the role of the higher level officials who were expected to be sensitive. The other suggestions included decision on fixing a date for FPS dealers to lift oil, controlling those FPS dealers who used to derive illegal benefits, reducing Government control over the FPS dealers.

The major suggestions for improvement offered by the Godown-in-charge included controlling the FPS dealers who used to derive illegal benefits, in addition to enhanced delivery limit and prompt transportation services (Table 5.15).

The major suggestion provided by the Depot-in-charge for improvement of distribution of kerosene oil under PDS centered on enhanced incentives to the FPS dealers, fixing quota for the wholesale dealer, provision of distribution of LPG along with kerosene from the depot, increased incentives of the depot owners, and establishing depot at block level.

Table 5.15: Suggestions by Godown-in-charge and Depot-in-charge for Improvement

Suggestions	*Kerosene*		*Foodgrains*	
	No.	*%*	*No.*	*%*
Lifting date for FPS dealer should be decided	2	28.6	1	25.0
Higher level officer must understand problems of staff	5	71.4	0	0.0
Needed clear communication among all functionaries	1	14.3	1	25.0
Needed reduced government formality for execution by FPS dealers	1	14.3	0	0.0
Increased delivery limit of foodgrains/ Prompt transportation services	0	0.0	1	25.0
Controlling those FPS dealers who take illegal benefits	2	28.6	2	50.0
Distributing items through creation of government depot		0.0	1	25.0
Total	7	100.0	4	100.0

Source : Field Survey, 2006.

The major suggestions provided by the Godown-in-charge for improvement of distribution of kerosene oil under PDS centred on enhanced incentives to the FPS dealers, increased incentives of the Godown staff, establishing Godown at block level, ensuring supply of foodgrains within the district, improving the transportation services and controlling the contractors involved in carrying the items (Table 5.16).

5.4 Government Functionaries

We collected information on PDS from 26 functionaries of which 20 were supply inspectors and 6 were district supply officers (DSOs). Most of these officials opined that the name of the FPS dealer should be proposed by Gram Sabha, followed by the criterion of education and minimum saving in bank, no criminal allegation, must complete 21 years, having an FPS in a rural area with a population minimum 4000, and that FPS should be set up in a location and dealer appointed following Government Order.

Table 5.16: Suggestions for Improvement of PDS (As Reported by Godown-in-charge and Depot-in-charge)

Suggestions	Kerosene		Foodgrains	
	No.	%	No.	%
Increase the incentives of FPS Dealers	2	28.6	2	33.3
Provision should be made for distribution of LPG along with kerosene Oil to depot owners	1	14.3	0	0.0
Allotment/quota should be fully fixed for wholesale dealer	2	28.6	0	0.0
Provision should be made for home delivery of items to FPS dealers	1	14.3	0	0.0
Increase the incentives of oil depot owner	1	14.3	1	16.7
Kerosene should be distributed only to BPL households	1	14.3	0	0.0
Establish depot/Godown at block level	1	14.3	1	16.7
Increase the allotment of items	1	14.3	0	0.0
Supply of foodgrains and kerosene should be within the district	0	0.0	2	33.3
Issue the BPL & ANT Ration Cards to actual beneficiaries	0	0.0	1	16.7
Improve the transportation services and control the contractors involved in carrying the commodities	0	0.0	1	16.7
Total Respondents given suggestions	7	25.9	6	28.6
Respondents with no suggestions	20	74.1	15	71.4
Total Sample	27	100.0	21	100.0

Note: The suggestions calculated on total Respondents given suggestions and other percentage calculated on total sample.

Source: Field Survey, 2006.

Of 26 functionaries, 21 did not suggest amendments in selection of norms for FPS dealer. This may imply that the prevailing norms were all right. This may also imply inertia in suggesting amendments. The suggested amendments included withdrawing the prevailing rights of the PRIs regarding FPS dealers, making minimum qualification for the dealer high school standard and above, and making reservation policy easier.

The major norm prevailing for issuing BPL cards to the households revolved around household income that had to be below Rs. 19,884 per annum in rural and Rs. 25,564 per annum in urban region. The other norms included issuing BPL cards to households who were in unorganized/informal sector.

On the eligibility criteria under Antyodaya Yojana, most of the officials opined in favour of landlessness, no pucca house and no income-generating assets. Some opined in favour of fixing the criteria based on households headed by widow, no permanent occupation or no income support. A few others opined in favour of households who received no pension and no loan from formal sector.

On the eligibility criteria under Annapurna Yojana, most of the officials opined in favour of persons who attained 65 years. Some opined in favour of persons who did not get any pension. Most of the functionaries opined in favour of those who had no income support and who were helpless.

5.4.1 Monitoring Methods Adopted for Betterment of PDS

The methods adopted by the Government functionaries included different levels of control that covered consumers, FPS dealers, regional offices and regional Godown/Depot. Most of the functionaries reported that they follow three-tier monitoring system at all the levels mentioned. It was also reported that the SDM, BDOs and tehsildar used to regularly monitor at all the levels under their respective jurisdictions. Excepting at the level of the consumers, it was reported that the supply inspectors, ARO, DSO etc. used to perform physical verification of items (Table 5.17).

5.4.2 Problems of Government Functionaries

The problems faced by the Government functionaries in conducting necessary duties, as reported by them, are mentioned in Box 5.13.

Box 5.13: Problems Faced by the Officials in Conducting Duties (As reported by the Functionaries)

Problems
It was difficult to do duty due to political interference Shortage of staff in the supply department Staff demoralized due to non-promotion in the department Subordinates dominate over the higher level officials of the department No active support from other departments Insecurity and deprivation from service benefits

Source: Field Survey, 2006.

Table 5.17: Monitoring Methods Adopted for Betterment of PDS (As Reported by the Functionaries)

Methods	*Consumers*		*FPS Dealers*		*Regional Offices*		*Regional Godown/Depot*	
	No.	*%*	*No.*	*%*	*No.*	*%*	*No.*	*%*
Distribution system verified by asking consumers about it	10	38.5	2	7.7	0	0.0	1	3.8
Followed the government order strictly	0	0.0	2	7.7	1	3.8	3	11.5
Physical verification by Supply Inspector, Lekhpal, ARO, DSO etc.	0	0.0	1	3.8	4	15.4	1	3.8
Follow three-tier checking and monitoring system	14	53.8	19	73.1	17	65.4	20	76.9
Verified by the SDM, BDOs, Tehsildar, etc.	3	11.5	3	11.5	4	15.4	4	15.4
Monitoring through vigilance committee	2	7.7	2	7.7	2	7.7	1	3.8
Steps taken regarding complaint against FPS Dealer through FIR, Cancellation, Suspension of Shop etc.	0	0.0	3	11.5	0	0.0	0	0.0
No Response	1	3.8	0	0.0	0	0.0	0	0.0
Total	26	100.0	26	100.0	26	100.0	26	100.0

Source: Field Survey, 2006.

5.4.3 Suggestions of Government Functionaries for Better Functioning of PDS

Most of these suggestions by Government functionaries focused on increased allotment and hence fulfilling the requirements of the consumers, increasing the target of ANT and BPL ration cards for each district, increased quantity of wheat to be distributed at the level of consumers, creation of awareness among consumers based on 'rights', increased allotment of kerosene for distribution (Box 5.14).

Box 5.14: Suggestions to Improve PDS by Provision of Items (Suggestions of Functionaries)

Suggestions
Increase the allotment and fulfilled the requirement of consumers Increase the quantity of wheat at household level Increase the allotment of kerosene for the district Increase the quantity of sugar at household level Create awareness among consumers regarding their rights

Source: Field Survey, 2006.

Suggestions for improvement of PDS as perceived by the functionaries have been cited in Box 5.15.

Box 5.15: Suggestions for Improvement of PDS by Administration

Suggestions
Entrust all the responsibility with a single department Ensure Allotment based on local needs Increase the incentive of FPS dealers Withdraw the ANT scheme and launch single BPL Ration Card to all poor households Stop the unnecessary interference of Gram Pradhans and Politicians Provide transportation facility and field allowance for FPS dealers Give the honorarium to FPS dealers

Source: Field Survey, 2006?

The following chart shows the administrative structure of the supply department in U.P.

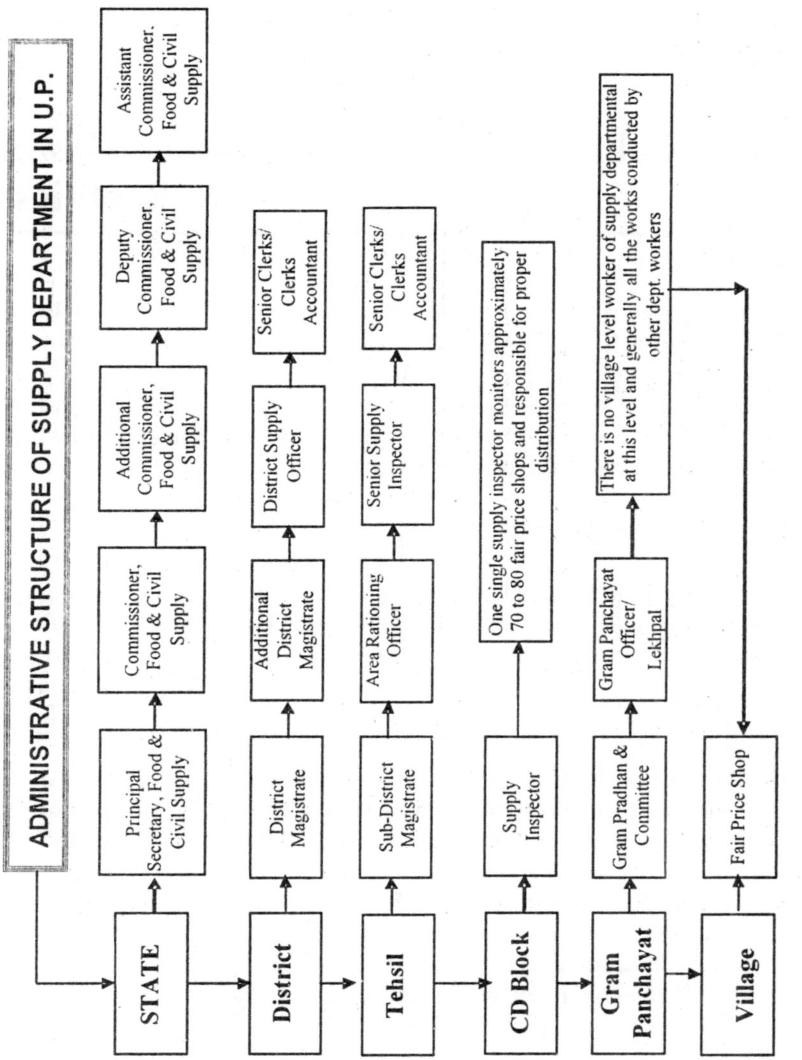
ADMINISTRATIVE STRUCTURE OF SUPPLY DEPARTMENT IN U.P.
STATE
Principal Secretary, Food & Civil Supply
Commissioner, Food & Civil Supply
Additional Commissioner, Food & Civil Supply
Deputy Commissioner, Food & Civil Supply
Assistant Commissioner. Food & Civil Supply
District
District Magistrate
Additional District Magistrate
District Supply Officer
Senior Clerks/ Clerks Accountant
Tehsil
Sub-District Magistrate
Area Rationing Officer
Senior Supply Inspector
Senior Clerks/ Clerks Accountant
CD Block
Supply Inspector
One single supply inspector monitors approximately 70 to 80 fair price shops and responsible for proper distribution
Gram Panchayat
Gram Pradhan & Committee
Gram Panchayat Officer/ Lekhpal
There is no village level worker of supply departmental at this level and generally all the works conducted by other dept. workers
Village
Fair Price Shop

6

Public Distribution in Uttar Pradesh: Micro Realities

In this chapter we offere our observations on the public distribution system at the district level based on interviews with beneficiary and non-beneficiary households, representatives of Gram Panchayats, Fair Price Shop dealers, government functionaries, foodgrains Godown-in-charge and kerosene Depot-in-charge. This qualitative data aims at throwing light on the micro realities of the PDS in U.P.

6.1 District: Bareili

In the Bareili district we observed no standard criteria for categorizing families living Above Poverty Line (APL) or Below Poverty Line (BPL). The Village Development Department had decided that families whose income was less than Rs. 11,500 per annum would be identified as BPL. The state Supply Department however did not consider families with income per annum between Rs. 9,001 and Rs. 11,500 as BPL.

In none of the villages did the Gram Panchayat have a final list of BPL families based on some definite criteria. The tentative lists that were found with some Gram Panchayats had the following shortcomings:

- The number of BPL families was found to change often, the reason being that the Pradhan kept adding people of his own choice to the list.
- The economic/family register of the BPL families was never found to be updated.
- In some villages many lists of BPL families were found.
- In some villages instead of a complete description of all the family members, only the name of the head of the family and the number of members in his family was mentioned in the list.

In all the selected villages the number of ration cards of various types mentioned in the records was much more than the actual number of people having ration cards. The Lekhpal/Patwari of the Revenue Department responsible for issuing ration cards took bribes between Rs. 100 and Rs. 500 per card and issued ration cards without judging the economic condition of the households. These ration cards were not mentioned in the records of the FPS dealers, Supply Department or the Gram Panchayat. The pressure of the powerful people and of the elected representatives of the village or the Lekhpal/Patwari also compelled them to issue these cards.

It was observed that in the selected villages the items were distributed only during a period of one to seven days per month. Later on the items were sold by the FPS dealers in the open market at market prices. The villagers were not given prior information regarding the arrival of essential commodities and the period till when they would be supplied. Either they themselves went to the shop to find out when the supplies would be coming or they got the information when they saw neighbours drawing their quota.

The supply of provisions for such a short duration arbitrarily decided by the FPS dealers deprived many poor people from having access to the facilities of the PDS because of the work pressure that prevented them from taking leave, illness in the family, or non-availability of cash to buy the commodities.

We found a high discrepancy between the actual stock and the amount mentioned in the stock register of the Fair Price Shops. The educational level of most of the FPS dealers was very low, which prevented them from maintaining correct accounts. Most FPS dealers did not have adequate space in their shops to store the allotted kerosene oil and the food grains. The image of the FPS dealers among the local community was found to be dubious. The long-duration dealership by years of many FPS dealers led to their monopolistic behaviour.

In most villages the Panchayats were not playing proper role in facilitating the PDS.

- No vigilance committee had been constituted by the Gram Panchayats in any village to ensure proper functioning of the PDS.
- BPL and ANT cards were being issued arbitrarily in the villages with the connivance of the Panchayats.
- The power to verify the distribution of commodities by the FPS dealers every month and to cancel the ration shops under special

circumstances empowered the Panchayats to extract money or favour from the FPS dealers and giving false verification certificates. The Pradhans also got between Rs. 2,000 and Rs. 4,000 from the FPS dealers newly selected by them.

- The Pradhans had very little knowledge about the welfare schemes or policies of the government that were in practice. Neither were they aware of the functions and duties of the Panchayats.

In urban areas the entire responsibility of the PDS, from issuing ration cards to ensuring proper distribution of the commodities, lay with the Supply Department. However, in practice the Supply Department passed on its responsibilities to the FPS dealers and did not bother to check whether the FPS dealers were performing their duties properly or not. Often the card holders did not receive any information regarding the arrival of the commodities. This obstructed them from drawing their entitlements, facilitating the FPS dealers to supply some of the commodities to his close people and siphon off the rest.

Case Study

Name : Jashoda Devi
Age : 80 years
Caste : Kashyap (BC)
Development Block: Bhojipura
Village: Dalpatpur

Jashoda Devi's son works as a Chowkidar earning Rs. 1,500 per month. There are seven members in the family. Jashoda devi's family has an Annapurna card and one Antyodaya card. The Annapurna card is issued in Jashoda devi's name and she has been using the card since the last four years. In addition, she has been getting an old age pension of Rs. 1,800 per year since 1992. The family also owns 0.70 acres of land which has been leased out for seven years at Rs. 10,000. According the policy of the government, a person can get the benefit of only one scheme—either the old age pension scheme or the Annapurna scheme. But the family's close relationship with the Pradhan, who belongs to the same caste, enabled Jashoda Devi to get both the benefits. It is interesting that there has been no verification of any of the two schemes in the last so many years.

In the villages Malahpur, Girdharpur, Makmudpur and Adalpur in the Baheri Tehsil, none of the BPL card holders had received wheat, rice or sugar for a long period. The FPS dealers reported that the henchmen of the local MLA took away all the commodities meant for the BPL card holders. The FPS dealers were asked to fill up the register with false entries to camouflage that the commodities had been distributed illegally. They also gave each FPS dealer Rs. 50 per quintal to keep quiet. According to the FPS dealers, the top officials of the district and the Supply Department were aware of this. The departments of the PDS and the MPs and MLAs considered the distributable commodities to be their own resources and manipulated with the supplies and allotment, which prevented the Supply Department from taking independent decisions. Thus we found 'political rigging' in the domain of PDS in the district.

The Godown-in-charge of the Bareilly Sadar district alleged that the men of the local MP and MLA visited the Godown occasionally and pressurized him to give them Rs. one lakh and above. He then compensated the money by selling the foodgrains meant for the cardholders in the open market.

The BPL card holders questioned why the government should discriminate in the pricing of the same commodities when both types of card holders, BPL and ANT, were equally poor. The FPS dealers reported that this difference often led the BPL card holders to insist that they were charged at the same rate as the ANT card holders.

The Supply Department had not been given complete freedom by the administration to perform its duties like issuing cards, identifying BPL families, verification of commodities and amount distributed and so on. This resulted in inconsistencies at the village level.

In the absence of magisterial power, the district Supply Officer had to remain dependent on the District Magistrate or the Tehsildars for action if he came across any incident of irregularity. In such an event he had to forward it to the administrative officers for necessary action. Often political pressure or bribery at the administrative level helped the culprits to get away.

The administration had fixed the target number of BPL and ANT families while raising the income level below which families should be considered BPL or Antyodaya. This brought many more families under the net of BPL card holders but led to a divergence between the number of BPL families and the number of cards that had to be issued.

The Supply Department did not have a master list of BPL families per village, which made it difficult to judge the accuracy of ration cards.

The state gave a target of BPL, ANT and ANP cards to each district, which was proportionately distributed among the villages in the districts. Many regions which did not have eligible families were also allotted these cards while the regions which had more BPL households did not get the requisite number. The grassroots implementing bodies also did not like to surrender the cards allotted in their villages.

Most of the FPS dealers could not provide an accurate estimate of their income per month. Each FPS dealer was regularly allotted the exact quantity of commodities that he was supposed to distribute, except for kerosene oil. This implied that there was no irregularity in the supply of essential commodities from the side of the administration. The problem started after allotment when the FPS dealers, in spite of political pressure on them, diverted the supplies to the open market. Thus there was adequate supply of commodities in the open market but at prices much higher than that fixed by the government. The poor economic condition of the people however prevented them from having access to these commodities. Many of these families were found to buy the essential commodities on credit from the grocer, borrow money at high rates from money lenders to sustain their families, or mortgage themselves to the big farmers by working for long hours at low wage rates till their loans were repaid.

6.2 District: Badaun

An alternative system parallel to the PDS for collecting the allotted quota of essential commodities and distribution of this quota by the FPS dealer was found to be in operation in the selected Tehsil and development block of this district. The MPs, MLAs, Block Pramukhs and the leaders of various political parties were involved in the running of this parallel system. The aim of this group was to extort money at each stage of the distribution of kerosene oil and foodgrains in order to strengthen their own people financially. The members of this group were so powerful that no officer could protest against their activities. The main reasons were the feelings of social insecurity and the fear of transfer.

The supply of kerosene oil and foodgrains was quite regular at the district and regional level depots and godowns. The chain from the godowns to the FPS dealers and ultimately to the consumers, however, was filled with corruption and irregularities in which a large number of people including government officials, political leaders and Gram Pradhans were deeply involved. We observed no vigilance committees and no consumer committees at any level of the distribution system like district level, village level, and hamlet level to make it work efficiently. In the selected villages we found most of the FPSs being run either by the local power elite or by those having connections with remote power elite. The FPS dealers were on good terms with the Pradhans who was supposed to verify regularly that the distribution was being done correctly. This system facilitated their misconduct in distribution. The poor, illiterate and 'right-unconscious' card holders remained victims because of the FPS dealers and the village Pradhans.

The FPS dealer in the town Kuargaon who took care of the shop known as Badaun Kendriya Upbhokta Sahakari Bhandar Ltd., reported that the elected members of the Nagar Panchayat used to send 'small chits of paper' through their 'special' people directing the shopkeeper to give them extra quantities of food grains and kerosene oil. The shopkeeper felt compelled to comply with their wishes out of fear.

In Ward No. 8 of town Kuargaon most of the ANT card holders were never allotted sugar and the BPL card holders were never allotted sugar and wheat. Apart from kerosene oil, they were given only 15 kg of rice at Rs. 6.50 per kg.

In the Rahedia village in Wazirganj development block, the Fair Price Shop was located in a 10′ × 10′ tin shed. The FPS dealer had an allotment of 93 quintals foodgrains and 5,000 litres kerosene. It was difficult to manage the stock in such a tiny space. The FPS dealer 'managed' it by paying Rs. 500 to Rs. 1,000 as bribe every month when the Lekhpal and Kanungo visited the shop for checking. The powerful people of the village used to take away around 20 litres of kerosene 'free' every month, thus depriving eligible card holders from getting their entitlement.

In some of the villages like Rota and Rahedia in the district, the FPS dealer had taken away the ration cards of almost all the people through the Pradhan many years ago, ostensibly for renewal. He used to give whatever he liked to the people as and when he felt like.

The Supply Department had shifted the card holders of the whole village to the Fair Price Shop in the adjoining village apparently because the number of consumers was too large for the shop in that village. But the main reason was that the FPS dealer of that village was not a part of the village Pradhan's coterie. Due to this the Pradhan was not getting any share of the profits earned by the FPS dealer. The Pradhan thus manufactured the opinion of a few card holders to complain against the FPS dealer to the Supply Department which led to the cancellation of his licence. The FPS dealer of the shop to which the card holders were now attached was closely associated with the

Pradhan. The Pradhan was thus assured of a regular share of the surplus. The FPS dealer provided no information to the card holders regarding the arrival of commodities in his shop. The cardholders were used to finding the shop closed or that the commodities were not available. They gradually gave up hope of getting the commodities at prices lower than market pries and had stopped going to the FPS.

In the rural areas the majority of the card holders got their cards issued with the help of the village Pradhan. He charged each of them Rs. 100 to Rs. 200 per card but after the cards were ready the Pradhan handed them over to the influential people of the village rather than to those for whom they were meant. While the people belonging to the Pradhan's group were issued ANT cards, the others were issued APL or BPL cards. In the selected villages it was observed that all new Gram Pradhans changed the existing ration cards by categories according to his own wishes. The desire that motivated him was to provide maximum benefits to his 'close' people. If the FPS dealer happened to belong to the new Pradhan's group his shop was allowed to run, but if he did not support the new Pradhan, circumstances were created to get his license cancelled.

In the villages Hiraini and Hardaspur, both located in the Rajpuri development block in the Gugar Tehsil in the district, there were no permanent FPSs. In village Hiraini, the guest register contained a detailed list of the BPL families in the village but these families did not exist in reality. In the villages Rota and Hardaspur, no guest registers were available.

In the Hardaspur village in the Rajpura Development Block, the FPS dealer used to bring all the foodgrains and kerosene oil allotted to him to the village and completed the distribution process in one day. The villagers, however, did not receive any commodity except kerosene for the last five years.

In this village the FPS dealer did not have any records of the commodities distributed, all the records were with the village Pradhan. The Supply Department used to prepare a schedule of the quotas allotted to each FPS dealer in the Tehsil every month but a record of the actual amount collected by them was not maintained at the office. This record was available at the district level supply office.

In the Rajpur development block the staff members, in order to ensure their personal gains and also to protect their jobs, did not oppose any visible irregularities in the PDS. The workers of the Supply Department had connections with the political leaders, the godown-in-charge and the oil depot-in-charge. The PDS was being run under the orders of political leaders and powerful people of the region.

Case Study

Village : Rota
Gram Panchayat: Rota
Development Block: Wazirganj
Tehsil: Bisauli

Fifteen years back a Dalit, Sri Ramlal Jatav, had a quota. At that time the Brahmins, Thakurs and other powerful people had full control over him, but even then the poor people were being given kerosene oil and other commodities. Subsequently, a Thakur, Arvind Pal Singh, was elected as the Pradhan. He guided the people to complain against the FPS dealer and got his licence cancelled. Arvind Pal Singh appointed another Thakur, Devender Singh, as the FPS dealer. All the powerful upper castes started siphoning off the ration items from this Thakur's quota while the poor people started getting only a little oil and small quantities of other items. The village slowly started getting divided into two parts, the main reason for which was the Pradhan's elections. Following the next election, the next Pradhan came to be a Brahmin, who got Devender Singh removed from the job of FPS dealer and merged this village's quota with the Quota of the adjoining village, Dharmapur. The villagers could not get anything from the new ration shop except a little kerosene oil, and that too at intervals of two or three months. The powerful people, however, obtained all the commodities at the quantities required by them. The present Pradhan has sent a fresh proposal for appointing a FPS dealer in the village to the Block Development Officer. The office is, however, reportedly demanding bribe for processing the request. The local people told us that the poor and vulnerable sections are discriminated against because they cannot raise their voice against injustice. The main reason for this was the absence of social security in the villages where the powerful people rule the roost. The powerful people and the FPS dealer prevent any complaints of the people from affecting the running of the shop. According to the local people, the present system is benefiting the FPS dealers, administrative staff and the political parties. In addition, the middlemen are also thriving. The people reported that at the time of issuing the ration cards, the family's economic condition was not verified. Thus, the poor people were issued APL cards while the rich people were issued BPL and ANT cards. Forty one such BPL families, who had been issued APL and ANT cards, visited the BDO and supply office many times to get BPL cards but they did not succeed. When we asked why they were concerned to get their ration cards changed when they did not get any item, they replied the following:

- *They need the card as identification for opening a bank account.*
- *This was the only identification for casting vote.*
- *In the event of any dispute, ration cards were the only identification for filing a legal case.*
- *The hope of getting future benefits from the government based on the BPL card.*
- *Some people believe that the family gets an identity through the card.*

Source: Local people (Interview).

The poor people of the village with no food and wage-employment used to obtain cereals on credit from farmers. In the agricultural season they expected to get wage-work to return the cereals borrowed. Many families in the village used to borrow grain from the big farmers on condition that they would work in their farms for a very low wage rate till their loans were repaid. They were thus bonded to these farmers till they freed themselves of the loan. Some poor families also borrowed money, cereals and essential commodities from the local grocers at a rate of interest 5.0 per cent per month and above. Thus, most of the poor people were forced to work as bonded labourers till their loans were paid back.

6.3 District: Lakhimpur Kheri

The district Lakhimpur Kheri had a large number of migrants from east U.P. who had retained ties with their native villages and regularly brought members of their kith and kin from there to work in a number of villages of the district. Following the break up of the joint family system and the consequent fragmentation of land holdings, many in-migrated people started working as labourers in big farms whose owners entrapped them by lending them money and then exploited their inability to repay the loan by bonding them to their farms and making them work for long hours at a very low wage rate till their loans were repaid. The basic food-*cum*-fuel needs of these bonded families were provided by the owner of the farm. These poor families required only kerosene oil from the Fair Price Shops since they hardly had money for the other essential commodities supplied at these shops. Some temporary labourers were also found to in-migrate to the district during off-agricultural season. The owner of the big farms used to employ these labourers and also provided ration cards to them. However, the cards were utilized by the owners themselves for buying kerosene oil for their machines. These rich landowners had local power because of their connections with the political parties and also with the administration. The patron-client relation thus remained deeply rooted.

Three years back, a scam involving the supply of foodgrains through the PDS was unearthed in the district. Wheat, rice and sugar that were meant for distribution under the BPL and Antyodaya schemes were being siphoned off. The rice was being sold to owners of rice mills and in the open markets in the district and its neighbouring districts while the wheat was being supplied to seven *suji* factories in district Shahjahanpur. Sugar was being sold directly in the open market. It was also alleged that some of these foodgrains were smuggled into the bordering state of Nepal. This scam had been going on for many years and the benefits were being shared by the people at the bottom of the hierarchy of the Supply Department reaching to the top officials and also to some ministers. The staff in-charge of the godowns used to falsely fill up the stock registers of the FPS dealers at the godowns themselves to show that the foodgrains had been supplied. In return the FPS dealers were given some 'consolation money'. The FPS dealers in their turn used to tell the customers that they had not received any supply. All the records at the district office, Tehsil offices, food godowns, oil depots and with the FPS dealers since October 2004 had been sealed by the enquiry committee.

At the district level, no record of BPL families was available for scrutiny. It appeared that the village Panchayat was categorizing families into APL and BPL according to the whims and fancies of the Nagar Panchayat which was based on the influence of the families, their contribution in supplying a vote bank during the elections, their income level and their social status. Thus in the absence of proper identification of genuinely needy families the PDS in the village seemed to be directionless and beyond the reach of poor families.

We found a gross discrepancy in the number of BPL families identified by the village Panchayats and the number of ration cards (BPL + ANT + APL) issued in these villages. The reason for this was that the representatives of the Panchayats followed their own wishes while preparing ration cards for the people of their villages.

A great deal of control was maintained on the PDS at the various levels of the Supply Department like the Tehsil, Godown, FPS dealer, Panchayat etc., but at the level of the beneficiaries there was hardly any control to ensure smooth functioning of the system. The reason was that a large percentage of the target population was poor, vulnerable, illiterate and unaware about their rights as consumers. That is why they unquestioningly accepted whatever the FPS dealer informed in terms of quantity, price, and availability. Neither the FPS dealers nor the card holders had any knowledge about the rights, duties and other relevant information about the PDS that were chalked out in the PDS charter. Not a single FPS dealer was found to have a copy of the charter.

No roster was maintained by any higher official when the allotted quota of essential commodities was collected by FPS dealers from the godowns. Neither was any inspection carried out when the commodities were distributed by them. Only the Gram Panchayats and local bodies at the village level looked after the PDS, resulting in large scale malfunctioning of the system and providing enough space for corruption and black marketeering.

The FPS dealer of village Bahamanpur in the Nidhasan Development Block informed that they were often forced to sell the essential commodities allotted to them in the black market, in order to recover the money spent by them to obtain their quota of commodities every month. He narrated that he had to pay Rs. 10 per quintal as bribe at the godowns for collecting the foodgrains and Rs. 100 per drum of kerosene oil at the oil depots, in addition to Rs. 50 per drum and Rs. 30 per quintal of cereals at the supply office. The FPS dealers were also often given less than the allotted quantity by the godown owners and oil depot owners who often manipulated the weighing machines. Along with this, the dealers had to pay around Rs. 5,000 to Rs. 7,000 every four or five months to the Supply Department to be paid to the SDM and other high level administrative officers. The local level Panchayat workers and the influential people of the village had also to be kept 'happy' from time-to-time.

The demand for allotment of kerosene oil was made by the district office to the Tehsil office and from there it was sent to the oil depot owners. The role of the Supply Department in the distribution system was absent. In practice, the allotment of foodgrains was being done by godown owners. The issuing of ration cards was being done by Gram and Nagar Panchayats. The verification of foodgrains that had been allotted to FPS dealers was being done by Panchayats or state government workers. The verification of the foodgrains distributed by FPS dealers was done by village Panchayats and state government workers.

None of the FPS dealers possessed shop registers, card details, unit details or old distribution registers. The information regarding the number of cards was calculated on the basis of the earlier allotment and the unit detail was calculated by multiplying by four or five.

Many poor families were found to consume '*Atta*' directly rather than buying wheat from the ration shops and then grinding it in mills. These families gave their cards to the mill owner who collected wheat and supplied ground *Atta* to the beneficiaries after keeping a certain portion for himself. Thus the mill owner benefited in two ways—first, they got the grinding charges from the buyers and second they got wheat at a lower price than in the open market.

Most of the poor families in the villages worked as labourers in the farms in that district. These people often did not have money in cash to buy the essential commodities that were usually distributed only on one or two days in the month. These people even could not collect the kerosene oil that they were entitled to since it was distributed at intervals of one to two months and that too, only one or two litres per card was supplied.

After the allotment and distribution of foodgrains every month the FPS dealers had to pay Rs. 1000 to Rs. 2000 to the Gram Pradhan when they received the verification certificate from the Pradhan. If they declined the Pradhans threatened to get their licence cancelled.

In each region of the district the number of ANT, BPL and ANP cards remained constant every year. In the case of ANT and BPL, the names of the families were changed frequently while this was supposed to be done only for the dead beneficiaries in the case of ANP card holders. No record or information about card holders was sent to the FPS office that could be verified with the people actually existing. In urban areas the only basis for issuing new BPL, APL and ANT was the recommendation by the members of the local bodies. The Nagar Panchayat had neither the list of BPL population nor any other basis for issuing cards.

In the Mailani Nagar region, the godowns and oil depots from where the FPS dealers had to collect their allotted supplies were nearly 30 km away from the village. The transportation cost for fetching these supplies had to be borne by the FPS dealers.

We found a large population of poor labourers in Vichitranagar and Ibrahimpur engaged as wage labourers in the farmhouses. The owners often gave them loans which forced many of them to become bonded to the owners. Often their ration cards were mortgaged.

The BPL and ANT card holders had no idea how much foodgrains they were entitled to or who they should complain to in case they did not get their allotted quota.

In case of the rare visit of any government official in village Vichitranagar because of its remoteness, notice was served to the FPS dealers and the block and district offices much in advance. This enabled them to prepare a camouflaging environment in their favour. According to the local people, most of the commodities meant for distribution under PDS went straight from the godowns to the open markets either in the adjoining region or in Nepal. The commissions of the people involved at each step of this transaction were decided in advance and they performed their duties in the process of black marketing very efficiently.

The Supply Department, the in-charge of the godowns, the Gram Pradhan and the FPS dealers were in collusion. On the surface these people appeared to be detached from each other but they were all bonded by ties of corruption.

6.4 District: Lucknow

In Lucknow the wholesale distributors of kerosene oil were very powerful because of their political connections. They used to sell most of the kerosene oil in the black market in collusion with the FPS dealers. The oil siphoned off was usually diverted to petrol pumps, sellers of generators, and agricultural sector. The cardholders were unaware that the FPS dealer was allotted his quota in installments.

The FPS dealers in the district distributed kerosene oil according to their wishes and not according to the quantity the cardholder was entitled to. One major reason for this was that the number of ration cards issued in the villages had been increased but not the amount allotted to the FPS dealers.

The allotment of kerosene oil and foodgrains to the FPS dealers of each block was being done from the district. According to the FPS dealers the allotment used to reach the concerned godowns without any information at the Tehsil level. Thus the Tehsil office got no prior information about the quantity being allotted to the FPS dealers and the quantity that was being actually collected. There was lack of coordination between the Supply Department, the Gram Panchayat and the Block office, each blaming the other for delay.

There was no information in any of the supply departments of the selected Tehsils about ration cards, collection of allotment by FPS dealers, distribution of commodities, categorization of FPS dealers, and information about cancelled cards. Even if they were present in some offices, most of them were obsolete.

In all the selected development blocks, a scrutiny of the records of allotment and collection of commodities by the FPS dealers revealed that in many places there was obvious overwriting. This implied that the quantity had been changed but the overwriting was not attested by the concerned officials. From the selected regions what we observed is presented below:

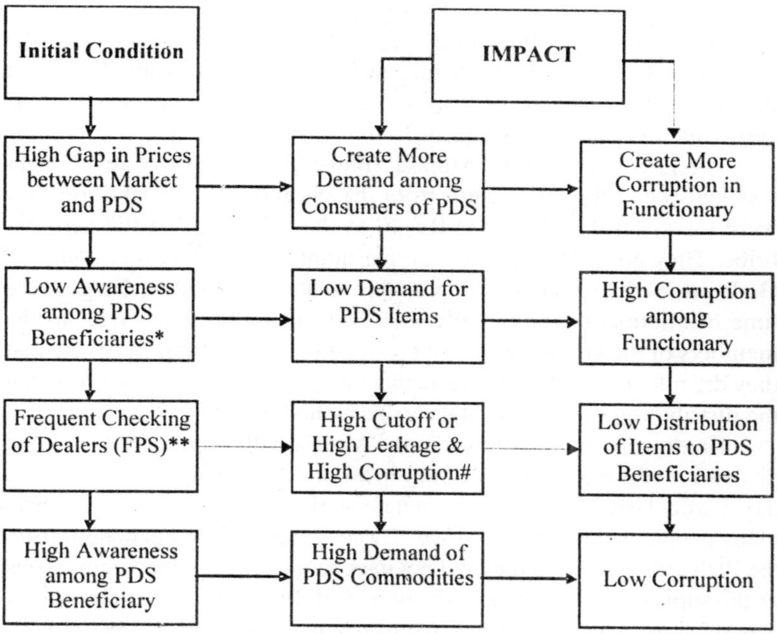

Note: * Awareness of 'Right to Food' etc., ** By Food Inspectors, and # Centered on FPS Dealer.

The high gap in the prices of the commodities distributed through PDS and those sold in the open market, the lack of awareness among the consumers and the multiple check points and frequency of checking in the Supply Department, were affecting the smooth functioning of the PDS.

In the village Ahmadbad Katauni in the Malihabad development block we found that except for a few scheduled castes the distribution of essential commodities under the PDS was running smoothly. Due to the lack of awareness among the scheduled castes they were given only kerosene oil by the FPS dealer.

The Gram Pradhans did not want the distribution system to be smooth and efficient since that would decrease the popularity of the Pradhans and increase the popularity of the FPS dealers. This would affect his chances of winning the next Panchayat elections. In parallel, the money flow from the FPS dealers to the Pradhan every month would stop. Thus the real intention of all the Pradhans was to run the PDS according to their own wishes.

In the Mulama village in the Malihabad development block out of four settled hamlets only that hamlet used to get benefits from PDS where the FPS was located. The motive of the dealer was to ensure good certificate in case of any enquiry.

The FPS dealer of the Mujasa village used to receive seven litres less kerosene oil every month from the oil godowns. In addition they were forced to pay Rs. 30 to Rs. 40 to the 'Munshiji' at the depot as bribe. They also had to pay Rs. 20 per quintal as bribe to the foodgrain Godown-in-charge and Rs. 70 per drum to the oil Depot-in-charge at the time of allotment. Additionally they had to supply items 'free' to the members of the Gram Panchayat and the Pradhan in order to ensure that they did not oppose the certificate that had to be submitted verifying that the distribution system was done as per schedule.

There were many families in the Mujasa village who survived one or two months every year without meal or could take only one meal a day. Particularly in the autumn when no work was available in agriculture, many people in the district starved. These families could not benefit from the PDS either because they did not have money to buy the commodities or the supply was irregular or the period of distribution of commodities was so short that they were unable to reach the ration shops in time.

In almost all the villages the FPS dealers distributed the commodities only for a period of one to seven days. In such a situation most of the very poor families and the ones working in the unorganized sector found it difficult to benefit from the PDS since they often did not have disposable money during that period. If some of them had any savings, they preferred to buy kerosene oil since there was a huge difference between the PDS price and the open market price. Thus, the section of the population that needed PDS the most was deprived of its benefits because of lack of purchasing power and because of the short duration for its distribution.

Almost all the FPS dealers in the villages had no means of influencing the quantity allotted to them at the food godowns and the oil depots. They also opined that running the FPS had become troublesome because first, they had to invest more for collecting their allotted commodities; second, the types of ration cards had increased which entailed more paper work; and third, the expenses for running the ration shop had multiplied.

However, the commission that they were being given 20 years back had not been increased. The large number of formalities and rules at different levels and layers made the implementation of the system difficult.

The PDS in this district was better than in the other districts for the reasons mentioned below:

- Because of its proximity to the headquarters of the state government, the high level officers often conducted random checks to ensure that the system was working well.
- The involvement and cooperation of the political leaders and their pressure on local elected leaders like the Gram Pradhan kept the system running smoothly.
- Because of the physical proximity to the state government offices, the district administration tried hard to keep the machinery run smoothly.
- The early implementation of new rules by the district administration made PDS more efficient.
- The good infrastructural facility in the district made it easy for the officers and inspectors to travel for vigilance.
- Telecommunication network worked well in the district.
- A section of the beneficiaries was aware.

However, a few FPS dealers reported that often the officers of the Supply Department demanded bribe money from FPS dealers and owners/controllers of Godowns and Oil Depots if they came across any irregularity at the time of verification. If they were not given the sum demanded, the FPS dealers and the godown/depot owners were penalized either financially or by imposing sanctions on them. In such situations, the irregularities remained intact.

The FPS dealer in the village Baragaon in the development block Kakori used to distribute 50.0 per cent of his allotted quantity and sell the rest at the godown and depot itself. In many villages people got ration cards made not in the expectation of the commodities that would be supplied to them but as identification for various governmental requirements.

In Mubarakpur village in block Kakori, oil and foodgrains were distributed only one day each month. Most of the people were unable to buy these commodities because of poverty. Many card holders did not even know the process of buying under PDS. People were afraid to complain because of absence of social security. The powerful people of the village used to take away around 10 to 12 litres of kerosene oil each month while the poor people were given according to their family size.

An FPS dealer in the Malihabad Tehsil of the district whose licence had been cancelled for also being a teacher reported the 'real' revenue-expenditure position of a dealer if he ran it properly which is given below:

Table 6.1: Revenue and Expenditure of an FPS Dealer (Per Month)

Revenue from Distribution of Items		*Expenditure*	
Items by Name-cum-price	*Revenue Earned (Rs.)*	*Heads*	*Expenditure*
Sugar 04 Qntl.	5400.00	Sugar 04 Qntl.	5378.80
BPL Wheat 6.10 Qntl.	2826.50	BPL Wheat 6.10 Qntl.	2799.00
BPL Rice 15.25 Qntl.	9378.78	BPL Rice 15.25 Qntl.	9828.25
ANT Wheat 14.0 Qntl.	1120.00	ANT Wheat 5.60 Qntl.	1086.60
ANT Rice 14.0 Qntl.	4200.00	ANT Rice 14.0 Qntl.	4116.00
Kerosene Oil 1600 litre	158400.00	Commission to prepare Bank Draft	51.00
Empty Sack 04 of Sugar	60.00		
Empty Sack 82 of Foodgrains	410.00	Transport costs R. 12.00/ qntl.	540.00
		Weighing Rs. 4 Qntl.	180.00
		Register and Photo copy	30.00
		Kerosene Oil 1600 litre	15,162.58
		Transport Cost for carrying Kerosene/200 litre	400.00
		Labour Cost for Carrying, Weighing etc.	360.00
Total	39,389.25	Total	39,984.00
Net Benefit = Rs. 39,389.25 – 39,384 = Rs. 5.25			

Source: An FPS dealer's report to the Tehsil office of Malihabad.

Case Study

Tehsil - BKT
Kasba - Itoja
Name of FPS dealer - Rani/Ajit Pandey

There were a total of 10 wards in the Itoja Kasba. There was only one ration shop for this whole region run by a lady called Rani Pandey catering to 3000 ration card holders. The shop, *de facto*, was run by her son Ajit Pandey. The allotment given to this shop every month was as follows:

Table 6.2: Allotment of Distributable Items (in Physical quantity) of FPS Dealer

Commodities	*BPL*	*ANT*	*Total*
Wheat	92.70	57.70	150.40
Rice	231.75	144.25	376.00
Sugar	—	—	53.00
Kerosene oil	—	—	10,000

Source: Interview with FPS Dealer.

Ajit Pandey opined that it was very difficult to run a ration shop. No rules and regulations worked and only the power of money helped FPS dealers to run their shops safely. He had to spend huge money the year before as bribe to keep his shop functioning (Table 6.3).

Table 6.3: Corruption/Bribe Money Paid by FPS Dealer for Keeping FPS Functioning

Department	*Designation/ Name of the Person paid*	*Period of payment*	*Bribe Money (Rs.) spent/paid*	*Items given (free of cost)*
Godown Foodgrains	Godown-in-charge	Per month	2,000.00	—
Supply Department	Raman Mishra (Sup. Inspector)	Per month	10,000.00	—
Supply Department	Senior Clerk	Per month	2,000.00	—
Revenue Department	Driver of SDM	Per month	500.00	Sugar 10 kg.
Revenue Department	Lekhpal	Per month	1,000.00	—
Revenue Department	Kanungo	Per month	—	Sugar 10 kg.
Local Panchayat	President, Nagar Panchayat	Per month	—	Sugar 20 kg. Foodgrains 50 kg.
Local Panchayat	All Members(10)	Per month	—	Sugar 2 kg.
Local Panchayat	President, Nagar Panchayat (Donation)	Per Annum	4,000.00	—
Health Department	Food Inspector	Following Inspection once a Year	15,000.00	—
Supply Department	Z.S. Zedi, ARO	Once a Year	8,000.00	—
Supply Department	Supply Inspector and Staff	Following Inspection after every three months	4,000.00	—

Source: Interview with an FPS dealer, 2006.

Even an SDM had to be paid Rs. 6,000 per month. The FPS dealers were involved in transactions (black marketing) worth Rs. 2 to Rs. 3 lakhs regularly in order to save Rs. 10,000 per month. He gave the following description of the black marketing of commodities done by him (Table 6.4).

Table 6.4: Extent of Black Marketing by an FPS Dealer (As Reported by the FPS Dealer)

Items	*Distributable Quantity, Qntl./lt*	*Quantity Black Marketed*	*Profit per Qntl./per Drum*	*Total Profit*	*Venue of Black Marketing*
Wheat	150.40	40.00	150.00	3000.00	FPS
Rice	376.00	100.00	50.00	5000.00	FPS
Sugar	53.00	40.00	200.00	8000.00	FPS
Kerosene Oil	10,000	6,000	250.00	7500.00	Kerosene Depot

Source: Interview with FPS dealer, 2006.

The overall story is shown in Fig. 6.1.

6.5 District: Lalitpur

In this district the poor families also owned one to four acre land and practiced traditional farming. The PDS in this district, including both urban and rural areas, were found to function better as compared to the other selected districts. The existence of cordial relations between all the communities in the village was probably the reason for this. The reason for cordial relations was that most of the people settled in the village were economically homogeneous. Thus the PDS worked better in case of strong social relation based on mutual accommodation, transparency, and hence low corruption.

This can also be put in the following way:

- If there exists low economic gap among the village communities then there is good inter-community relationship, leading to high sympathetic cooperation, low corruption and good distribution.
- High dependency on market for food grains creates more demand for FPS items, leading to high pressure on FPS dealers. This leads to low corruption and good distribution.

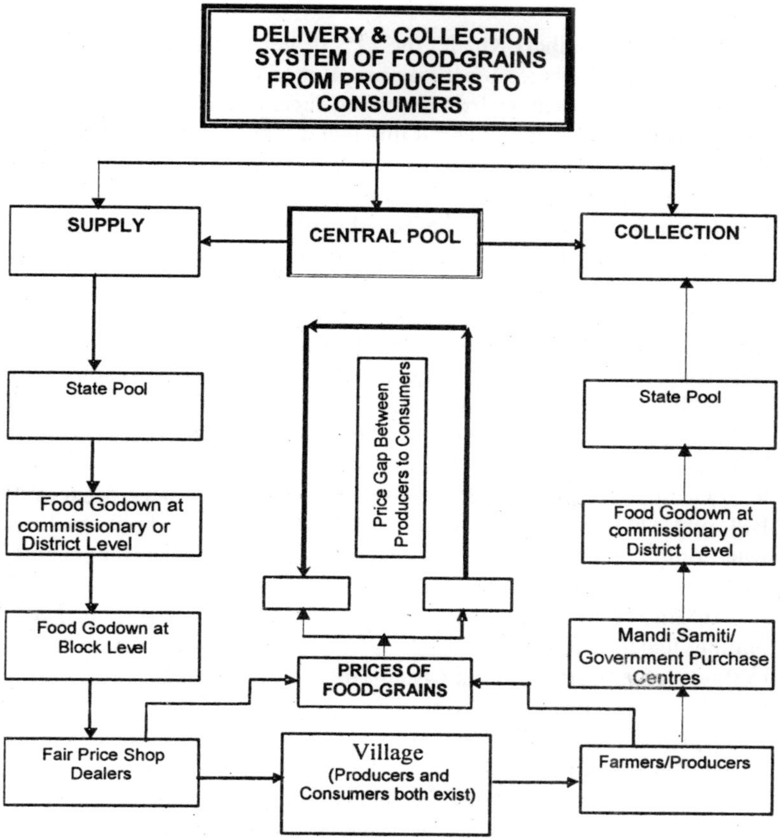

Fig. 6.1: Delivery and Collection System of Foodgrains

The FPS dealer in the village Bamhouri Kharait in the Bar Development Block in the district had to pay Rs. 1,500 to the Supply Inspector and Rs. 4,000 to the Godown-in-charge while collecting his allotment every month. He had paid Rs. 25,000 for getting the shop-licence 16 months earlier. In spite of this he used to earn profit from this system because many families of this village used to migrate out for four to six months every year. Since they did not buy their commodities during their absence, he used to sell the equivalent quantity in the open market. In addition, many poor families could not afford to buy sugar, which he sold in the market. However, his licence was later cancelled because he could not satisfy the new Pradhan.

In village Bamheri Khadet the FPS dealer had to pay a large sum extra as cost on logistics for lifting his allotted quota from the oil depot nearly 37 kilometres away from the village every month. The cardholders of the village who were aware of this fact did not mind paying 30 to 35 paise extra per litre to cover the transportation cost of the FPS dealer.

The village Meguan in the Mehrauni development block was located at a distance of 33 km from the Tehsil office, of which 7 km remained inaccessible for four or five months during and after the rainy season allowing no vehicle to ply excepting tractors. Given the distance of this village from the foodgrains godown (33 km) and the distance to the oil depot (62 km), the FPS dealer had to hire tractors and pay the transport cost from his own pocket for lifting the allotted commodities each month.

In this village Meguan many scheduled caste families used to migrate to Madhya Pradesh for four to eight months a year. The FPS dealer benefited from this situation by selling the commodities they were entitled to in the open market and filling false entries in the registers. Most of the BPL and ANT card holders in the village did not know how much and what commodities they were entitled to. They accepted whatever quantities and whatever goods the FPS dealer gave them as the grace of God.

In almost all the regions in the district the actual BPL and ANT families had little money to buy goods from the FPS. Most of them worked in the unorganized sector as casual labourers. The FPS dealer used to distribute the commodities at most six days a month. Not having disposable money most of the time, these poor families remained deprived of the benefits of the PDS.

The accounts of many FPS dealers in the selected regions showed a lot of discrepancy between the stock and distribution registers. The distribution registers were signed without any goods being distributed. The storage capacity at each godown was much less than the amount meant for allotment. The tank storage capacity for supplying 1.3 lakh litres of oil was only 6 to 20 thousand litres, which was even less than the storage capacity of a tractor which could store 24,000 litres. This implied that if the collection by the FPS dealers was as per schedule then they would not be able to supply more than one tractor per day. In parallel, if the collections did not take place as per schedule then there would remain no capacity for storing the oil at the depots.

Most of the villages were far from the oil depots (between 30 and 65 kms). The FPS dealers thus were attached to far off depots if the depot close by did not have adequate supplies.

Most of the depots had a storage capacity of only 15 to 20 kilolitres while they had to allot nearly 120 litres each month. One tractor can carry a capacity of 120 kilolitres of oil, so that most depots could store only 1 tractor load. If the FPS dealers delayed in picking up their allotted quantity and on the o ıer side the oil companies send a fresh supply, it caused panic in the depot. No roster was prepared in the district for the order in which the FPS dealers should collect their allotted quota. In this situation, each FPS dealer preferred to collect their quota at the end of the month so that he had to invest his money for a short time.

Case Study

Block Bar, Village Bastravan

The majority of the population residing in this village lives below the poverty line. The FPS in the village is a good support system for these people. The primary occupation of the people is farming and the main crops grown are wheat and corn. The ANT card holders undoubtedly benefit from the FPS in the village but we found that the BPL card holders faced a number of irregularities. The people who complained the most against the FPS dealer for cheating them in weighing the goods were the ones living in the Dhadhli Tola. The ANT beneficiaries were given the goods at the right rates but they were grossly underweighed. The FPS dealer, Sri Parvat, though present, did not appear before us. According to the supply inspector, there are many complaints against this dealer. The major problem facing the villagers was that they did not get the wage rate in the village that they were entitled to. This forced many of them to migrate out of the village in search of work for six to eight months in a year to places like Indore, Gwalior, Bhopal etc. in MP to work mainly as labourers in brick kilns.

Many urban scheduled castes in the Vichitranagar village in the Bar block used to leave the village with their families for five to six months a year to work as labourers in brick kilns. The FPS dealers used this opportunity to sell off the quantities meant for them. The FPS dealer was alleged to cheat the card holders while weighing. The FPS dealer defended himself by alleging that he too was given items less in weight than the actual one at the Godown. Post-distribution items were sold in the open market at the market rate.

The FPS dealers of all the selected villages did not have adequate space in their shops to store the foodgrains allotted each month. It was possible that the commodities were stored elsewhere unknown to the consumers. This may be the way the FPS dealers could practice leakage. In this village too, the distribution was done only for one or two days per month.

Case Study

Block Bar, village Bamhauri Khadait

This village is located in a highly remote area in the middle of mountains. The land of this village is very stony and has low water content. Consequently the productivity of this land is very low. Thus most people of this village migrate for seven to eight months to neighbouring places to earn their livelihood. The PDS in the village was found to be comparatively good. The FPS dealer has been running the shop for the last 16 months and all the card holders were found to receive all the goods that they are entitled to 1 kg of sugar was also distributed to each card holder every month.

The FPS dealer in the Bamhauri Khadait village in the Bar block was a supporter of the old Pradhan and an opponent of the new Pradhan. The FPS dealer was illiterate whose work was being carried out by his literate son. We found advance entries in many ration cards. The FPS dealer acknowledged the mistake. Many poor families of the Pali Kasba had been issued APL cards while the well-off families had been issued BPL cards. The charges for issuing ration cards by the Gram Panchayat were the following: ANP Rs. 150 to Rs. 300, BPL Rs. 10 to Rs. 15, ANT Rs. 20 to Rs. 100, and APL Rs. 10 to Rs. 25. The people who could not afford the money were given the cards many months later.

Case Study

Nanhi Bai, Age 26 years, Widow, Caste—Harijan

Non-beneficiary Nanhi Bai's husband died in 2001 after a prolonged illness. She has three children. She works as a daily labourer. Nanhi Bai received a widow's pension for one year which fetched her Rs. 550 per month. Of this she got only Rs. 500 since she had to give the rest as commission. The next year when she went to renew it, she was told that it was cancelled. She alleged that the Pradhan and a few villagers had complained against her. When her widow pension was stopped, she asked the Pradhan to issue her a ration card but he told her that widows were not entitled to ration cards. Nanhi Bai is bringing up her children in extreme poverty and hopes the administration will renew her widow pension and give her a ration card.

The Supply Department in the district told that the amount that was sent to the supply office by the administration was distributed proportionately among the poor families in the district and that the amount of kerosene oil that was being distributed in the district over the last many years was much less than the number of ration cards there. Both these statements were however found to be false when they were cross checked at the village level. We did not find an exact number of poor families in the village. The number of ration cards recorded in the FPS dealer's records, especially the APL cards, was not the same as the number recorded with the Supply Department.

6.6 District: Jhansi

The PDS in the district was highly inefficient. In the Moth Tehsil the distribution of cards was biased in favour of the people who constituted the vote bank of the party. There was a direct link between the leaders of the constituencies and the powerful people who openly influenced the Pradhan and the contractors.

We offer the following observations regarding the condition of the Public Distribution System in this district:

- If there is a narrow economic gap between the various communities living in the village, then the social relations between them are cordial, leading to a smooth functioning of the system.
- If there are an equal number of supporters of two conflicting parties in the village, then the functioning of the PDS is smooth. This is because there is local pressure from the village society, who maintains strict control to ensure smooth functioning of the system. The political presence in the village also leads to more awareness among the villagers regarding their right to obtaining essential commodities regularly.
- If the village is inhabited by people of only one caste or if there is dominance of one particular caste in the village, then the people belonging to the caste constituting the majority remain more privileged so far as obtaining the essential commodities are concerned.
- In a village where the present and past Pradhans are in competition and there is little difference in the number of supporters of each of them, PDS is efficient.

- If a village is divided into a large number of caste-based hamlets located at distances, a few hamlets were deprived from the facility of obtaining essential commodities under PDS.

In Tehsil Moth the officers of the Supply Department on duty were afraid of the powerful political leaders of the region. The power wielded by the leaders compelled the workers of the Department to carry out any imperatives even if that were considered illegal. The Gram Pradhans and the Lekhpals were given the authority at the level of the FPS dealers to verify the honesty of the latter. These people certified only after ensuring rent.

In the district there was no particular day fixed for wholesale dealers of kerosene oil to collect their quota. They could collect it on any day between the 1st and 20th of the month. Most of the FPS dealers preferred to collect their quota at the end of the period since they would then have to block their money for a shorter period of time. Also, there was no verification at the depots when the retail dealers collected their allotted quota of oil. The possibility of the occurrence of irregularities, thus, increased manifold.

According to the instructions of the Regional Food Controller, all the FPS dealers of the region had to deposit money at the food-grain Godown for the next month's allotment of essential commodities for distribution to card holders by the 15th of each month and lift the items allotted to them between the 23rd and 30th as per the roster. The commodities could be verified between 1st and 5th. After getting the verifications done at the village level could the distribution begin. The actual duration for distribution of the essential commodities at the village level was only nine days. Based on one holiday per week, only eight days would be available for distribution. Since all the FPS dealers of a district had only one source of income with which they could run their shops and since they had to deposit the money for the next month's supply by the 14th, they tried to clear their stock within three days out of the eight days available for distribution. Often poor families could not save money needed by them to buy their quota in this short period.

In many godowns the distribution of foodgrains to the FPS dealers by the district administration was not done according to the roster prepared for this purpose because of bad weather condition, lack of transport facilities etc. Very often the FPS dealers used to lift their allotted foodgrains in the absence of any external officer. The verification of all the allotted commodities lifted throughout the day was done in evening when the concerned officer came back to check.

Because of ignorance about entitlement, the cardholders accepted whatever the FPS dealers offered to them as an expression of his benevolence. Many BPL families were familiar with the system but could not complain against any irregularities practiced by the FPS dealers because of the following reasons:

- Many did not know where and to whom they should lodge their complaint.
- In spite of knowing many cardholders could not lodge complaints because of poverty and fear to miss a day's labour.
- Social insecurity and desire to avoid conflict were other reasons cited for not lodging complaints against the corrupt FPS dealers.
- Many people expressed fear, in case they complained against the FPS dealers, of being excluded from even the present entitlement.
- Many complaints made earlier had no outcome since the FPS dealers bribed the enquiry officials to silence the voice of protest or to turn the report in favour of the FPS dealers.
- Very often there was a strong link between the FPS dealers and the village Pradhan. Thus even if the FPS dealers committed irregularities the Pradhan succeeded in influencing the Panchayat and the local leaders in favour of the FPS dealers. The card holders were afraid to complain against the FPS dealers because of this nexus.
- The absence of an objective evaluation system at the village level for ensuring smooth functioning of the PDS was often the reason why unsatisfied customers could not complain.
- According to a recent system, people would receive the reply to their complaints only when it was accompanied by an affidavit. Because of this complex process, many people did not dare to complain.
- The major reason why poor people did not complain against the FPS dealers was the prevailing strong nexus between the FPS dealers and the powerful people of their village.

In the district the godowns were being looked after by the Marketing Department. The in-charge of one of these godowns, a senior Marketing

Officer, informed that each month the high level officers demanded money (bribe). The godown-in-charge was forced to pay the money.

At almost each village there was high demand for kerosene oil during the agricultural season (between October and December and between April and May). This was because there was a large difference in the prices of kerosene oil and diesel, which was used for running pump sets and other machines. Many farmers preferred substituting kerosene oil for diesel since it was cheaper. Also, kerosene oil was needed for cooking. In order to take advantage of this high demand many people sought the help of the administration or political leaders to procure kerosene oil and sell the same at higher price in the open market.

In most of the villages people were not aware of their rights under the charter of PDS. Although many customers, especially the poor and *dalits,* had complaints against the FPS dealers about underweighing the foodgrains supplied, they were unable to protest because of the power wielded by the FPS dealers in collusion with the influential upper castes of the village.

Kerosene Distribution Scheme

In order to ensure distribution of kerosene oil more efficient and to stop black marketing, the government launched a pilot project in 51 development blocks of the state on 2nd October, 2005. Under this scheme, in each identified block a wholesale distributor was to be selected by the oil companies who would own an underground tank that could store 20 kilolitres of oil, adequate number of barrels, and dispensing units to fill these barrels. This distributor would then select 2 to 10 sub-distributors with the advice of the district administration. These sub-distributors would be given a licence during the period of the project and also enough barrels to store 2,500 litres of oil by the oil companies, which would have the names of the people concerned with the project. Based on the number of card holders, the District Supply Department would supply a quota of oil in multiples of 200 litres for each village, 52 kilolitres for each wholesale distributor and 200 litres for each sub-distributor and FPS dealer. Each month the sub-distributor would be given 200 litres of oil as quota for distribution. These would be filled in each barrel having the names of the oil companies. The FPS owners could obtain their allotted share from there each month, according to the specified roster. This system would be supervised at the district level by a six-member committee presided by the District

Panchayat President of which at least three would be women. At the level of the development block a five-member committee would be constituted under the presidentship of the Regional Panchayat President, of which two would be nominated and three would be elected. At the village level, the system would be monitored by a six-member committee under the chairmanship of the village Pradhan.

The system was found to be in operation in the development block of Mausnipur in the Mauranipur Tehsil. We offer the following observations regarding the system:

- The godown of the sub-distributor was nearly 8 kilometres away and the wholesale distributor's godown was nearly 10 kilometres away from the villages. Thus, the locations of these godowns were not proper.
- The FPS dealers informed that each month the sub-distributor supplied kerosene oil less by 8 to 10 litres.
- The wholesale distributor at Mauranipur informed that the administration had told them that they had to pass on their commission to the sub-dealer and also spend their own money to deliver the oil to the sub-distributor in drums. This money would be reimbursed by the oil companies. However, no reimbursement had been received by the dealers. The owners of the oil companies opined that the government seemed to be encouraging black marketeering. The FPS dealers did not receive the amount allotted to them from the sub-dealers.
- The transportation charges for lifting the oil allotted to them had to be borne by the FPS dealers themselves.
- At the level of the development block, the influential leaders and the representatives of the Panchayat pressurized the sub-dealers to supply them 8 to 10 litres of oil at the subsidized rate. Since the sub-dealers could not dare to refuse, they adjusted this amount by giving less oil to each of the FPS dealers. The sub-dealers also benefited economically since they received the full payment (money) from the FPS dealers. The sub-dealer also said that between October and December when there is heavy demand of kerosene oil because of the peak agricultural season, there was great political and administrative pressure on the Supply Department for supplying kerosene oil. The Department passed down this order to the sub-dealers which they had to fulfil.

- Most of the drums in the custody of the sub-dealers and the FPS dealers did not fulfil the standards set by the government in terms of colour and the names of the people that had to be written on them. Additionally all the drums with the sub-dealer belonged to the FPS dealers. The sub-dealers themselves did not have the required number of drums.
- Although all the sub-dealers were supposed to follow an FPS dealer's roster prepared by the District Administration, they rarely did so. Each of them supplied oil to the FPS dealers following their own discretion.
- At the levels of the wholesale dealer, the sub-dealer and the FPS dealers, no fixed system was followed for supplying and carrying away oil. Although the administration had established a definite norm, it was a mere formality. The whole system was efficient in corruption and black marketing.
- The wholesale dealer reported that if the kerosene was distributed by the filler system the leakage of oil would have been higher than if it were distributed by the meter system as done in petrol pumps.

The Supply Department had no provision for the training of the inspectors before they assumed charge and for the FPS dealers after being selected. They started functioning immediately after being appointed, without having any knowledge of the rules, regulations, formalities and the various schemes implemented by the government.

The majority of the people in the Shyavari village informed that they got a regular supply of essential commodities but the quantity given was less by 10.0 per cent to 15.0 per cent. The FPS dealers, however, defended themselves by saying that they had to pay Rs. 1,100 every month to the supply inspector, Rs. 400 to the Godown-in-charge and also frequently pay donations to people at various levels. Thus, they were compelled to distribute the commodities under PDS on only two days and sell the rest in the open market. Unless they did this, they would not recover the extra money they paid.

Some of the economically more weak FPS dealers revealed that the relatives of the Gram Pradhan used to collect the quota allotted for the FPS dealers from the godowns with their own money, and the records of the distribution were maintained by somebody else. The FPS dealers only weighed and measured the quantities for distribution. Only a certain percentage of the profit in the chain of corruption reached them. However, the FPS dealers were held responsible if any irregularity came to light. This situation was found in both Moth and Mauranipur villages.

In almost each village the FPS dealers did not maintain shop registers. This implied that they were unable to determine whether the card brought by a particular customer had been allotted to him or whether he had borrowed it from someone else. They had to simply measure out the quantities of the commodities demanded by him.

In the village Amgaona in the Moth Development Block, the ration cards of all the people had been deposited with the Pradhan two or three months back for renewal. During that period they were only supplied kerosene oil. Only a few selected people were provided the other commodities.

In the same village the upper castes, especially Thakur, constituted the majority while the FPS dealer belonged to the SC community. The local people narrated that as soon as the FPS dealer lifted his quota from the godowns to the FPS each month, the powerful upper caste people would forcibly take possession of it. The FPS dealer could supply only a portion of the left over commodities to the needy eligible people. The FPS dealer alleged that these upper caste people had strong connections with the polity. That is why none of the PDS officials could take them to task although they were aware of their activities. No supply inspectors or other officials ever visited the Moth Tehsil for inspection. We felt that the FPS dealer was only a puppet since he was poor and all his allotted quotas were paid for and collected by the relatives of the upper caste Pradhan.

6.7 District: Gorakhpur

In many shops in this district the registers were not verified by the Supply Department. As reported by some FPS dealers, in case of any problem with the authorities, the Supply Department would be given Rs. 200 to Rs. 500 as bribe to change the registers.

The amount of kerosene oil supplied to the wholesale distributors from the oil companies was not verified. No verification was done even when the wholesale distributors supplied oil to the FPS dealers. Neither did the administration prepare any roster for the FPS dealers to collect oil from the oil depots every month. Many ordinary FPS dealers were used to return empty hand from the oil depots while the powerful FPS dealers were able to collect their quota readily. The drums used by the FPS dealers to carry oil back to the shops from the wholesale distributors were not coloured according to the specifications of the administration and neither were their names written on them. It was, thus, not known what the drums were for, where they were going and whose drums they were.

In most villages the number of BPL households fixed by the Gram Panchayat was not an authentic figure. The Gram Panchayat, however, passed on the responsibility for issuing wrong ration cards to the Village Secretary and Lekhpal while the latter two passed it on to the Panchayat and Supply Department.

Instead of taking the actual number of BPL households in the village into consideration, the district administration had fixed a target number of BPL households which the block and village administration had to fulfil. The Panchayat members used this opportunity to distribute BPL cards to their caste members, to supporters and sympathizers and to people whom they wanted to appease. The actually needy BPL families remained deprived of the PDS facility.

The transportation of foodgrains from the wholesale godowns in the districts to the block godowns was done by contractors who had powerful political connections. The in-charge of the godowns often demanded Rs. 30 per quintal as transportation charges for the BPL cereals failing which they did not release them the allotment.

The FPS dealer got a commission of only Rs. 6 per quintal for food-grains and Rs. 30 per drum of kerosene oil that contained 200 litres that continued for last 30 years since its fixation.

The distribution of kerosene oil in all the selected villages was almost regular but the quantity distributed was less than that decided upon by the administration. The reasons for this were the following:

- The quantity of kerosene oil allotted to the FPS dealer had not been increased in proportion to the increase in the number of APL cards in the villages.
- Many cardless families were given kerosene oil under the instructions of the Gram Panchayat.
- The influential people of the village appropriated oil.
- The FPS dealers were given five to ten litres oil less per drum than the allotted quantity.
- The representatives and staff of the Panchayat demanded more oil per month.

Even the kerosene oil continued to be distributed regularly as opposed to failure in distribution of foodgrains. The main reasons for this were:

- In rural areas, there was no alternative to kerosene oil for lighting up at night in the absence of electricity.
- There persisted high difference in prices between the kerosene oil sold through PDS and that sold in the open market.
- Kerosene oil was not available in the market.
- Kerosene oil was used for other purposes like for irrigation.
- The price of diesel was higher than kerosene oil so that the latter could be substituted for the former.

If the people were not given kerosene oil, there might be chaos in villages and the FPS dealers would find it difficult to run their shops. Distribution of kerosene oil, thus, showed the bottom most layer of functioning of PDS.

The FPS dealers belonging to the scheduled castes were not well-off economically. Such FPS dealers were also found to be close to the Pradhans since they often had to borrow money from them to lift their quota every month. This helped the Pradhans to use the FPS dealers to their benefits.

In almost all the villages the FPS dealer was allegedly charging the BPL and ANT card holders 30 paisa to Rs. 1.50 extra per kg for food grains and 50 paisa to Re 1.00 extra per litre for kerosene oil. They were also not being given the amount entitled to them. The FPS dealer of Vishnupur defended him by saying that if he had charged the price fixed by the government, then he would not be able to earn any surplus.

In the village Vishnupur many BPL and ANT card holders knew the irregularities but were unable to protest. The reasons were the following:

- The FPS dealer had strong links with the rich and powerful people of the village whom the ordinary people fear or respect. The latter also used to work in the fields of the former and often used to borrow money from the former.
- Most people were convinced that even if they complained, no action would be taken since the FPS dealer would be able to bribe his way out. Later on, the complainants would be penalized by 'imposed deprivation' of any commodity.
- The majority of the poor, weak and vulnerable BPL and ANT

card holders had no energy and time to complain.

- Most of these cardholders did not even know where and to whom they should complain.
- Most of these cardholders believed that no action would be taken after complaining since there was no vigilance committee to monitor the activities of the FPS dealer.

The FPS dealer of the Pali village was found to bribe the in-charge of the godowns while lifting his goods every month but concealed the fact. The FPS dealer mentioned that every month he got kerosene oil less by 10 litres per drum at the depot but there was no way to stop this practice. The reason for this was that the owner of the oil depot was a 'Raja' of the region and had a lot of political and administrative connections.

The FPS dealer of the Baragadahi village lifted less quantity because in his view local self-production mostly met self-consumption of rice and wheat. The ration card holders, however, reported that there was adequate demand for wheat, rice and sugar in the village. Many BPL card holders had not received wheat, sugar or rice since the last many years. Many APL families in the village did not even know what commodities they were entitled to. The FPS dealer's shop was located inside his house right next to a grocer's shop. The FPS dealer was alleged to sell the remaining quantities in black from that shop. The FPS dealer reported that he had to pay bribe at the godown and to the Supply Department which he compensated by selling the items in black.

According to some FPS dealers, no verification was carried out at any FPS dealer's shop in any village. The supply inspector and other officials visiting the shop for verification were given money (bribe) to complete the formalities. The FPS dealer had maintained a stock register but there was no record of who was given what item and by what quantities.

In the village Golriha in Bhathat block, the Gram Panchayat had issued 60.0 per cent of the BPL cards and 40.0 per cent of the ANT cards to the well-off people of the village. Thus, many needy people of the village had been deprived of the facilities of PDS.

The people of the village reported that the FPS dealer and the Godown-in-charge were in collusion under which the FPS dealer deliberately did not lift the entire quota that he was entrusted with.

Flow Chart

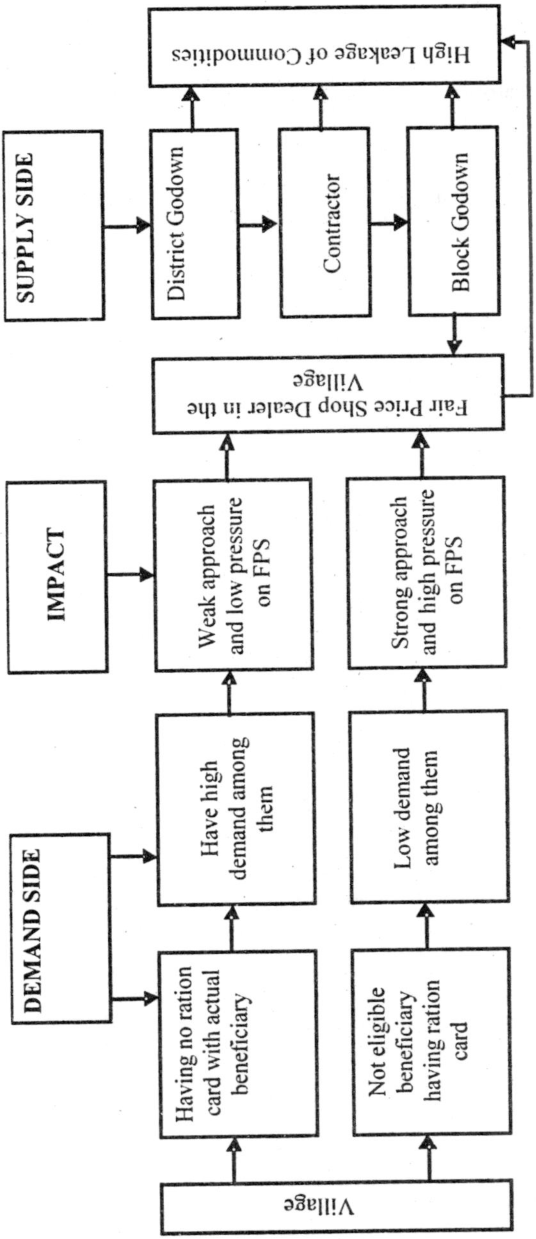
DEMAND SIDE
IMPACT
SUPPLY SIDE
Village
Having no ration card with actual beneficiary
Not eligible beneficiary having ration card
Have high demand among them
Low demand among them
Weak approach and low pressure on FPS
Strong approach and high pressure on FPS
Fair Price Shop Dealer in the Village
Block Godown
Contractor
District Godown
High Leakage of Commodities

6.8 District: Varanasi

The foodgrain godowns in the district were monitored by the Marketing Department. However, because of shortage of staff, the responsibility for management of most of the godowns was entrusted with the Supply Department as an additional charge. The supply inspectors had to allot the monthly quota to the FPS dealers from the godowns and also ensure proper supply of the commodities to the godowns. We found the distribution of food grains to the FPS dealers in district Varanasi better relative to that in other districts.

The district supply officer (DSO) had organized awareness camps in all the villages in the district where the consumers learnt what commodities they were entitled to, the quantities and the prices, the process of lodging complaints against irregularities in distribution. These camps, thus, helped to raise awareness of the consumers for efficient functioning of PDS.

In the villages under the Pindara block, the Jan Kerosene Scheme was underway. Under this scheme ten sub-dealers had been appointed in the entire district through whom the FPS dealers had to be allotted kerosene oil every month. We observed the following in this regard:

- The appointment of sub-dealers and their location was not within the perimeter of the village.
- Almost all the sub-dealers were agents of the wholesale dealer who had no objections to irregularities carried out by them.
- The drums were not coloured as specified.
- The FPS dealers had to deposit their money with the wholesale dealer.
- The oil did not reach the wholesale dealer's godown from the oil company within the stipulated period since the oil company had only one vehicle.
- In most villages the wholesale dealer supplied oil to the FPS dealers directly in the oil company's tanker with a capacity of 220 litres. The wholesale dealer informed that he supplied oil directly to the FPS dealers to avoid the excessive formalities, and financial losses.
- The FPS dealers were supplied oil twice in a month.

The owner of the Pindara oil depot had to pay a bribe of Rs. 85,000 to the Supply Department every month and other wholesale dealers had to pay similar money depending on the quantity allotted to them. In return, no checking was carried out by the Supply Department implying that they were free to sell 15 to 20 per cent oil in black.

There was collusion between the FPS dealers and the Gram Panchayats for making a large number of false ration cards. It was alleged that the Gram Panchayats committed great irregularities while issuing ration cards. Usually the cards were issued to the people close to the Panchayat members like their supporters, relatives, friends, and caste members. Many needy people were, thus, denied this facility.

No vigilance committees, consumer committees or monitoring committees were found to be in existence in either the urban or rural areas of this district. In the non-Jan Kerosene project regions in the district we found that the dealer of kerosene oil did not supply oil to the FPS dealers from the filler point according to the directive of the administration although fillers were installed in oil depots in 2004.

In the villages many ration cards did not have the dates when they were issued and also the registration numbers were missing. The Panchayat members deliberately delayed in issuing new cards since the ration would be supplied only on production of the ration cards and the intervening period would be used for selling the goods in the open market.

The commodities supplied to the FPS dealers by the godowns were never weighed but they were strictly told to say that the commodities are properly weighed. The responsibility for transportation of foodgrains from the FCI and UPSFI godowns to the regional godowns was given to contractors. The truck owners/operators gave one quintal less of each commodity with the logic that they had to bear the carrying cost. The godown-in-charge reported that the transport contractors were criminal type having strong connections with political leaders. They deliberately offered low tenders which were even lower than the actual cost incurred for transportation. After getting the tender they diverted a few truckloads of food-grains to cover their loss. The godown-in-charge was not given a detailed description of the quantities of food-grains supplied by FCI and UPFCI. The tendency for misappropriation by the godown in-charge thus increased. The supply of commodities to the regional godowns and to the FPS dealers was taken to be 100 per cent but the distribution by the FPS dealers was not 100 per cent. The information about the actual distribution of food-grains by the FPS dealers was not maintained at any level. There was a definite date for FPS dealers to collect their quota specified in the roster but if he was unable to collect it by that date, he was charged extra by the godown in-charge. Most FPS dealers used to pay Rs. 5 to Rs. 10 per quintal as bribe to the godown-in-charge while collecting their quota but were forced to keep quiet out of fear of closure of shop or delay in supply of commodities by them.

The PDS as it operates in UP was *de jure* targeted to the poor but *de facto* served the local elite and the political patrons of the local elite. The administrative set up seemed outwardly dysfunctional in rectifying the corrupt-*cum*-inefficient system but was involved in the collusion that camouflages deprivation of the poor by 'kerosene factor'. Availability of kerosene showed the bottommost layer of a 'sick' system. The central persons in maintaining the system are the FPS dealer and the supply inspector, one paying bribe and the other receiving bribe, where bribe was received not only for self but also for concerned administrative hierarchy in ascending order. The households as consumers have remained demobilized and never knew their entitlement to essential commodities as a matter of 'right'. For rice and wheat, self-production to some extent satisfies for some seasons the minimum consumption requirements of the poor. In case of a narrow economic gap between sections in the local society, 'uniform deprivation' was well accepted across the sections. There existed inclusion by deprivation at the lowest level of the economy and this might be read as localized social inclusion even with economic general exclusion. Exclusion was reported in PDS when it occurred with acute inequality at a relatively higher level of economic well-being. The system in U.P. survived well even after leakage and food scam because of the absence of voice of the deprived and the absence of an aware civil society. In this situation the system remained cornered by the privileged.

7

Political Economy of Public Distribution System: Policy Recommendations

In this book we tried to examine the extent to which the Public Distribution System (PDS) in India has succeeded in providing essential commodities to the people living below poverty line (BPL). The book examined the functioning of the delivery system beginning from the procurement of foodgrains by the government till their distribution to the beneficiaries of the PDS. For empirical basis, we examined the PDS in Uttar Pradesh. Through an in-depth study of 960 households, including both beneficiary and non-beneficiary, in eight districts covering all the four regions of UP we tried to unearth the problem sites in the functioning of the PDS in this state which has one of the largest population of poor people in the country and who remain deprived of their right to food security because of the various vested interest groups operating at each level of the system.

We tried to find answers to questions like whether factors like absence of purchasing power, non-information about distribution of items, absence of the household while items are distributed, short period of distribution, long distance of the shop from the residence and cardlessness explain the deprivation, or is it ignorance of the poor that obstructs them from having access to the system. In addition to the deprived households, the book also looked into the reasons for exclusion of the eligible non-beneficiaries. In addition we tried to examine whether the Panchayats and Government machinery worked for the success of the system and suggest for its rectification as and when warranted. Since the FPS dealers, the polity and the local administration in the shape of the Gram Pradhan are the bottommost rung of the PDS, the local power structure in the context of PDS is often explained by the relations between them. In the book we examined the kind of relationship existing between these three vertices of the triangle. Some other allegations regarding the system like leakage of foodgrains from godowns, purchase of foodgrains from open market, subsidy grabbed by the non-poor, purchase of foodgrains by private corporate firms from the field, bribing and other types of corruption in the system emanate from the weaknesses built-in and/ or inserted in the system were also examined in this book and their answers were sought within the political economy frame of food security in India.

Problems Perceived by Beneficiary Households

In U.P. excepting kerosene, the fulfilment of requirement of all the other essential items like rice, wheat and sugar were mostly met from the market in spite of the provision for supply of these commodities through the PDS at subsidized rates for the poor. Self-production was a major source for both rice and wheat in meeting the requirement. Since there is no self-production of kerosene and generally market response to supply of kerosene was rare in rural areas, so the role of FPSs was most prominent in case of this commodity. Self-production determined to some extent the fulfilment of total consumption requirements in case of rice and wheat, which was more so in case of APL. Consumption requirements of rice, wheat and sugar were found to be met more by self-production in rural region than in urban region. Most of the requirements of commodities excepting kerosene were met by market in each of rural and urban regions and in each district. Self-production, even when positive, was not at all a significant factor in explaining fulfilment of consumption requirements excepting rice to some extent (Table 7.1).

Table 7.1: Consumption Gap in Essential Commodities

(Per Household per month in kg.)

Commodities	*Requirement (Total in kg.)*	*Fulfilled through PDS (%)*	*Gap (%)*
Wheat	52.1	11.5	88.5
Rice	25.3	33.2	66.8
Sugar	3.3	18.6	81.4
Kerosene (lt.)	3.5	82.6	17.4

Note: Gap = Requirement – Fulfilment through PDS.

Source: Field Survey, 2006.

The fulfilment of per capita annual average requirement of essential commodities from alternative routes showed both surplus and deficit relative to consumption requirement by items. The supply points covered self-production, market supply (including wage labour and kind payment) and supply by FPSs.

The balance equation is:

$$\text{Supply} \geq \text{Demand (Requirement)},$$

where $\text{Supply} = \text{Self-Production} + \text{Market Supply} + \text{FPSs Supply}.$

There was general deficit (requirement > supply) for kerosene, but for all households across income brackets, requirement of kerosene was met mostly by FPSs. We found increasing requirement of kerosene per annum for higher income brackets and increasing quantity requirement met by FPSs. The contribution (supply) of FPSs in fulfilment of consumption requirements of essential commodities of the beneficiary households was more in lower income brackets relative to what it was in higher income brackets. While the contribution of FPSs in fulfilment of requirement of all the essential items excepting kerosene was very low, its support role was beyond doubt. Most of the beneficiary households across cardholding and by regions reported adequacy of quantity of kerosene oil that they received from FPSs. However, the households paid more when they bought kerosene from other FPS dealer(s) relative to what they paid when they bought from the dealer their cards were attached to. Ignorance of the beneficiary households was the most important factor when the question centred on their rights as consumers to check the records of FPS dealers.

Most of the beneficiary households reported the collusive alliance of the FPS dealers with Panchayats. The households' report pointed at the FPS dealers who kept government officials in favour, manipulated in measurement of items for distribution and involved in black marketing. Thus, the factors that were visible and that affected the beneficiary households directly had been reported most.

Most of the beneficiary households did not perceive any weakness in the system. The rural BPL households mostly perceived weaknesses in the PDS, most of whom perceived it at the level of the FPS dealers. The perceived weaknesses also centred on higher officials, Gram Pradhan, Panchayat Secretary, MLA, DM, Lekhpal and Supply Department. Of those who perceived weaknesses in PDS, the most important reason cited was corruption in issuing ration cards and sharing bribe. The other reasons cited by the households were non-distribution of items through FPSs, marketing in the open/black (market), cheating in weight, non-checking, poor quality, higher price charged than what was fixed and irregular distribution.

Problems Reported by FPS Dealers

The problems reported by FPS dealers focused on getting dealership which depended on political support and connections, payment of bribe to the Supply Department for preparation of documents/file, payment of bribe to other officials, and frequent visit of Government officials at different levels. Most of the FPS dealers reportedly did not pay bribe (money) to the Supply Department to continue dealership in future. The average bribe paid by an FPS dealer was Rs. 1,422. The person identified by the dealers who received the most bribe money was the Supply Inspector. The major difficulties faced by the FPS dealers in running their shops included the incompatibility between high demand and low allotment, illegal demand by political party leaders, low commission fixed for the dealers, cardless customers' pressure and 'loot' by officials in the name of vigilance.

Coordination among Supply Department, FPS Dealers and Godown/Depot-in-Charge

Three-fourths of the depots-in-charge opined that the coordination among the Supply Department, FPS dealers and depot-in-charge was good, while the rest argued for the necessity for improvement. Four-fifths of the Godown-in-charge opined that the coordination among the Supply Department, FPS dealers and Godown-in-charge was good, while the rest argued for the necessity for improvement.

The major problems reported in case of oil depots included pressures and responsibilities imposed by government functionaries, higher officials in the government suspecting the depot staff of corruption, short duration fixed for distribution of oil, and high price gap between kerosene oil and diesel leading to black marketing of kerosene.

The major problems reported by the Godown-in-charge included high-level government officials suspecting the Godowns staff, and inadequate capacity of Godown.

Monitoring Methods Adopted by the Government Functionaries for Betterment of PDS

The methods adopted by government functionaries for betterment of PDS included control covering consumers, FPS dealers, regional offices and regional Godown/Depot. Most of the functionaries followed a three-tier checking and monitoring system at all the levels mentioned. It was also reported that the SDM, BDOs and tehsildars regularly monitored at all the levels under their respective jurisdictions. Excepting at the level of the consumers, the supply inspectors, ARO, and DSO performed physical verification of items.

Administrative Set Up, Local Power Structure and the Delivery System

The facts that we collected through interviews, conversations and group discussions were perception-based and hence subjective. Since most of these centred on the administrative set up that was meant to manage the system and the local power/polity structure that affected the system, we offer here the observations centred on administrative set up and local power structure:

- The number of BPL families at the village level was found to change often, the reason being that the Pradhan kept adding people of his own choice to the list.
- The economic/family register of the BPL families was never found to be updated.
- The basis of selection of BPL families and the duration of time for their remaining BPL was unclear.
- In some villages many lists of BPL families were found.
- The educational level of most of the FPS dealers was very low, which prevented them from maintaining correct accounts.
- Most FPS dealers did not have adequate space in their shops to store the allotted kerosene oil and the foodgrains.
- The records of the quantity allotted to the FPS dealers and collected by them from the godowns and oil depots every month were not maintained properly.
- No vigilance committee had been constituted by the Gram Panchayats in many villages to ensure proper functioning of the PDS.

- BPL and ANT cards were issued arbitrarily in many villages with the connivance of the Panchayats.
- The Panchayats had been given the authority by the district level office to verify the distribution of commodities by the FPS dealers every month. The Panchayats often misused power to extract money or favour from the FPS dealers and gave false verification certificates.
- The Panchayats have the power to recommend the cancellation of the ration shops under special circumstances. This is the reason why the FPS dealers could not oppose the 'bribe benefits' demanded by the Panchayats. If the FPS dealer was not in the same group maintained by the Pradhan, the latter often got the licence of the FPS cancelled and attached cardholders with another ration shop. In return, the Pradhan got between Rs. 2,000 and Rs. 4,000 from the newly selected FPS dealer.
- The departments of the PDS and the MPs and MLAs considered the distributable commodities to be their own resources and used to manoeuvre with the supplies and allotment, which prevented the Supply Department from taking independent decisions.
- The Supply Department did not have a master list of BPL families per village, which made it difficult to judge the accuracy of ration cards by number by types.
- The state had given a target of BPL, ANT and ANP cards to each district, which was proportionately distributed among the villages in the districts. The grassroots implementing bodies did not like to surrender the cards allotted in their villages even when these did not have eligible BPL households.
- In the absence of magisterial power, the District supply officer had to remain dependent on the District Magistrate or the Tehsildars for action if he came across any incident of irregularity. In such an event he had to forward it to the administrative officers for necessary action. Often political pressure or bribery at the administrative level helped the culprits to get away.
- Often the FPS dealers provided no information to the consumers regarding the arrival of essential commodities in his shop.
- On arrival the consumers generally found the shop closed or that the commodities were not available.
- In many places BPL households were issued APL cards.
- In many places the old description of families were retained in the new ration cards.

- There was lack of coordination between the Supply Department, the Gram Panchayat and the Block Office, each blaming the other for delay.
- There was no information in any of the supply departments of the selected Tehsils about ration cards, collection of allotment by FPS dealers, distribution of commodities, categorization of FPS dealers, and information about cancelled cards. The information available in some offices was obsolete.

Local Power Structure and PDS

The following qualitative observations regarding the local power structure may reveal the current condition of the Public Distribution System in U.P.:

FPS Dealers, Local Polity and Consumers: Relations in PDS

- Very often there was a strong link between the FPS dealers and the village Pradhan. Thus, even if the FPS dealers committed irregularities, the Pradhan succeeded in influencing the Panchayat and the local leaders in favour of the FPS dealers.
- The major reason why poor people did not complain against the FPS dealers was the prevailing strong nexus between the FPS dealers and the powerful people of their village. The card holders were afraid to complain against the FPS dealers because of this nexus.
- Many households did not know where and to whom to lodge their complaint.
- In spite of knowing some people could not lodge complaints because of 'voicelessness' of the poor and fear to miss a day's labour.
- Social insecurity at the local level and desire to avoid conflict were other reasons for not lodging complaints against the FPS dealers.
- Many people expressed fear that if they complained against the FPS dealers they would be excluded from the existing entitlement.
- Many earlier complaints had no outcome since the FPS dealers bribed the enquiry officials to silence the voice of protest or to turn the report in favour of the FPS dealers.
- According to a system implemented recently, people would receive the reply to their complaints only when it was

accompanied by an affidavit. Because of this complex formality, many people did not like to complain.

Relations between FPS Dealers, Sub-dealers of Kerosene, Wholesale Dealer, Oil Depots

- The FPS dealers reported that the transportation charges for lifting the oil allotted to them had to be borne by them themselves whereas this charge was adjusted per drum in the cost to the sub-dealer. This did not happen when they used to collect the oil from the wholesale oil depot.
- There was no verification of the oil supplied or distributed at the level of both the wholesale dealer and the sub-dealer.
- Most of the drums in the custody of the sub-dealers and the FPS dealers did not fulfil the standards set by the government in terms of size of drums and the names of the people that had to be written on them. Additionally, all the drums with the sub-dealer belonged to the FPS dealers. The sub-dealers themselves did not have the required number of drums.
- Although all the sub-dealers were supposed to follow an FPS dealer's roster prepared by the District Administration, they rarely did so. Each of them supplied oil to the FPS dealers following their own discretion.
- At the levels of the wholesale dealer, the sub-dealer and the FPS dealers, no fixed system was followed for supplying and carrying away oil. Although the administration had established a definite norm, it was a mere formality. The whole system efficient in corruption and black marketeering in the absence of strict vigilance and control.
- In view of many wholesale dealers, if the kerosene oil was distributed by the filler system then the leakage of oil would be higher than if it were distributed by the meter system as done in petrol pumps.

Distribution of Kerosene Oil

Distribution of kerosene oil was almost regular but the quantity distributed was less than what the cardholders were entitled to. The reasons for this were the following:

- The quantity of kerosene oil allotted to the FPS dealer had not been increased in proportion to the increase in the number of APL cards in the villages.
- Many cardless families were given kerosene oil under the instructions of the Gram Panchayat.
- The influential people of the village appropriated oil.
- The FPS dealers were given five to ten litres oil less per drum than the allotted quantity.
- The representatives and staff of the Panchayat demanded more oil per month.

Under these circumstances, the question centred on why kerosene oil was still being distributed regularly as opposed to non-distribution of foodgrains. The main reasons for this were the following:

- In rural region, there was no alternative to kerosene oil for lighting up at night in the absence of electricity.
- A high difference in prices between the kerosene oil sold through PDS and that sold in the open market existed.
- Kerosene oil was generally not available in the open market.
- Kerosene oil was used for other purposes like agriculture, irrigation.
- The price of diesel was higher compared to kerosene oil.
- Since demand for kerosene oil was much in rural region, there would be chaos in villages if the people were not given kerosene oil.

This is why the FPS dealers took care to ensure that the distribution of kerosene oil did not halt under any circumstances. Distribution of kerosene oil, thus, showed the bottommost layer of functioning of PDS.

Jan Kerosene Scheme

Under the Jan Kerosene Scheme, ten sub-dealers had been appointed in the selected districts through whom the FPS dealers had to be allotted kerosene every month. We observed the following in this regard:

- The appointment of sub-dealers and their location was not within the perimeter of the village.
- Almost all the sub-dealers were agents of the wholesale dealer who had no objection to irregularities carried out by them.

- The drums were not coloured as specified.
- The oil did not reach the wholesale dealer's godown from the oil company within the stipulated period since the oil company had only one vehicle.
- In many villages the wholesale dealer supplied oil to the FPS dealers directly in the oil company's tanker with a capacity of 220 litres.

Contradictions and Accommodation in PDS

- If there was a narrow economic gap between the various communities living in the village, then the social relations between them were cordial, leading to a smooth functioning of the system.
- If the number of supporters of two conflicting parties in the village was equal then the functioning of the PDS was smooth. This was because there was local pressure from the village society, who maintained strict control to ensure smooth functioning of the system.
- If the village was inhabited by people of only one caste or if there was dominance of one particular caste in the village, then the people belonging to the caste constituting the majority remain more privileged so far as obtaining the essential commodities were concerned.
- In a village where the present and past Pradhans were in competition and there was little difference in the number of supporters of each of them, PDS remained efficient.

Suggestions for Improved Performance of FPS Dealers

- The existing rate of commission is 0.06 paise per kg. of rice and wheat and 0.15 paise per litre of kerosene sold by FPS dealer. The former rate should be raised to 20 paise per kg while the latter rate should be raised to 25 paise per lt. This may reduce malpractices at the level of the FPS dealers.
- The FPS dealers were not entitled to get any support for logistics for the items they used to draw from generally a long distance for distribution. This support has to be provided.
- The willing FPS dealers should be given the additional responsibility to sell at market prices additional items like salt, edible oil, janata (cheap) saree, pencil and notebooks. This will

ensure livelihood security of the vulnerable households as well as add to the incentives of the FPS dealers.

- The FPS dealer has to be educated at least up to tenth standard to realize the duties and responsibilities and maintain records, must be a local resident with no criminal record, must have support saving in his bank account and completed 21 years of age.
- To the extent possible, the FPS dealer with support from the supply inspector has to ensure supply of items to the kitchen of the poor. The delivery has to be authenticated by a representative of the PRI. The supply has to be made in presence of the representative of the PRI.
- Village-level FPSs has to be in public building like community hall/Panchayat Ghar etc. If this Hall/Ghar is not there they must be constructed under NREGA/Rural Housing Scheme.
- There has to be training of FPS dealers for at least one week just after his selection. The training has to cover the rules and regulations in PDS, the responsibilities of the dealer, the economics and ethics in distribution.
- Transportation facility and field allowance for FPS dealers have to be ensured.
- An FPS in rural area should serve no more than 200 households or 1000 population as opposed is 2000 as per National target. In the urban region, this may vary depending on the urban concentration.

Suggestions for Improved Performance of Supply Inspectors

- Appointment of supply inspectors should be based on the number of FPS dealers in a development block.
- There has to be time-*cum*-merit bound promotion of supply inspectors.
- The supply inspectors must verify the distribution system by taking the beneficiaries into confidence and report the same to the higher authority immediately. The verification report must be displayed at the level of consumers in village and block.

Suggestions for Execution by Godown-in-Charge and Depot-in-Charge

- Improve the transportation services and control the contractors involved in carrying the commodities.

- Period of lifting items by FPS dealers should be decided in advance and informed.
- Transportation cost of the dealer must be compensated in case the items are not sent by the Godowns to the doorsteps of the FPS dealers.

Steps to be Executed by Panchayats

The local Panchayat has to listen to the voice of the poor by pursuing the following:

- Ensure regular meeting of Gram Sabha,
- Assist in BPL survey, identify the needy and poor,
- Protect local Food Bank,
- Assist in estimating household income,
- Control local mafia,
- Avoid discriminatory protection of the non-poor, and
- represent the absentee/migrant household, the widow and the physically/mentally challenged while making cards.

The Panchayat has to play a positive role supported by immediate formation of functioning vigilance committee and that should be monitored by local NGOs or higher level officials. Monthly and quarterly meetings should be held where NGOs and government officials must participate.

Recommendations

While at the delivery points, FCI Godown to FPSs, we found responses that show a well functioning PDS, at the final consumption point we found less than a happy scenario. The final consumption point covered both the beneficiary (by BPL, APL, Antyodaya and Annapurna) and the non-beneficiary households. The centre of the PDS was the FPS dealer who linked the remote delivery point and the local receiving point. Leakage of foodgrains from Godowns, purchase of foodgrains from open market, migration of people and hence their absence, subsidy grabbed by the non-poor, private purchase of foodgrains by corporate firms from the field and hence competition-*cum*-low price, bribe and other types of corruption in PDS emanated from the weaknesses built-in and/or inserted in the system that needed to be eliminated rather than eliminating the system. Self-production, even when it is positive, cannot be considered as an alternative to supply of essential commodities distributed through the FPSs. Providing pension should not be seen as an alternative to providing subsidized food.

In the light of the above, we offer suggestions for improvement of the system:

Suggestions for Implementation by State Level Functionaries

- Allotment of kerosene oil should be increased per card/unit.
- Identify local need and supply/distribute items accordingly.
- Every household should have a ration card not only to get items but also as an identity.
- A single window (Department) at the level of the state must be assigned the responsibility for the execution of the delivery mechanism, right from FCI Godown to FPSs. This is to be a Government Department as different from the autonomous Food Rights Commission.
- Each Block should have at least one foodgrain Godown and at least one oil depot.
- Kerosene oil depot owners may be allowed to distribute LPG also.
- Household expenditure per annum on basic needs for livelihood support should be followed for being listed as BPL.
- Occupations of members in the household should be in the unorganized/informal sector to be eligible for BPL card.
- The state government has to supply items at the supply point in the village, rather than the FPS dealer going a long way with cash to carry back distributable items. This will save FPS dealer's cost on transport-*cum*-transactions and time.
- BPL and Antyodaya categories should be clubbed as BPL; these households should be issued identical cards to avoid grassroots level discrimination and distributional inefficiency. In the same way, the subsidy-related extra cost on Antyodaya cards may be eliminated.
- Distribution of items to households once a month is based on households having accumulated money (saving or disposable money revealed in purchasing power) to buy those items. If available items are lifted by FPS dealers for distribution to target households, it must be available with the FPS holding and

carrying forward a stock and hence the households must be allowed to draw items any time (on any day) of their choice.

- Items are distributed based on cards irrespective of family size. In reality, the family size varies over a wide range. Hence, items should be distributed based on units in the family. This will reduce the actual/fake division of family. This will also lead to enhanced per capita availability of foodgrains.
- There being no self-production of kerosene and no open market for kerosene, households feel compelled to buy from black-market at a much higher price. Hence, a second local source has to be there for availability of kerosene for households.
- There has to remain an emergency stock of foodgrains at the FPS level to counter calamities and hunger. The 'zero balance' reported by the FPS dealers thus may be converted into accumulated positive balance.
- Any failure in supply/distribution of items at grassroots level is an institutional failure and hence an institution has to be marked responsible for this failure.
- The Jan Kerosene programme should be stopped.
- There has to be flexibility in FPS price as a reflection of prevailing market price. A high gap between the two prices may lead to non-functioning PDS and/or corrupt PDS. Hence, the gap between the two prices has to be minimized.
- Temporary ration cards should be provided for in-migration households as workers in construction work, rituals and religious festivals etc.
- There has to be at least one-day campaign initiated by Government functionaries in the village about awareness/rights of consumers in PDS every month.
- There has to be transparency in the system. The availability, allocation, lifting and distribution of items per period per FPS should be on display. For this, the block office and the local school building may be the site.
- The reservation category for FPS dealers often creates problems. The person in reservation category by being poor borrows initial working capital and gets trapped. Hence, either the reservation category has to be abolished or working capital has to be provided to the FPS dealer under reservation category through bank loan.

- Selection/appointment of FPS dealer has to be through a single authority, either local Panchayat or Government administration, not both. This will ensure accountability of the FPS dealer.
- The State Food Corporations (SFCs) in U.P. in poor condition by lack of staff, storage capacity, rented godown, poor documentation, high corruption, non-owning responsibility need reorganization.
- The fixed target has to be flexible for distribution of cards by categories among the eligible non-beneficiaries.
- Identify at the level of village/block/district the food insecure households by indicators which are observable and quantifiable like land ownership, residential house, and number of days employed in wage-work in the past one year. Involve the PRIs in the selection of such households through open meeting and declaration of the list in public and maintenance of the list in Panchayat Bhawan. The list has to be flexible for inclusion of representatives of households absent in the meeting(s) and marginalized people who may slip into the category of BPL anytime for many reasons.
- Launch a BPL survey with immediate effect for the whole state by an autonomous institution with uninterrupted support from the state. The same institution will be responsible for assessment and monitoring of steps initiated and implemented by the state to ensure freedom from hunger and food security of people at the bottom of social and economic ladder. This institution may be called 'Food Rights Commission' in the line of Human Rights Commission.
- Cancel false cards (APL households having BPL cards) and delink cardholding from political affiliation.
- Ensure state vigilance over stocks and release by FCI, *Kothedars* etc. A double check/lock on food store may be executed, for example, one lock used by FPS dealer and the other lock by Gram Panchayat when it is FPS. To check collusion of both, the FPS dealer and the entrusted Panchayat representative, a 'food custodian' from the locality may be appointed to ensure checks and balances.
- Annapurna card holders need to be ensured foodgrains at the lowest price.
- There should be no limit on the number of distributable cards. If BPL cards cannot be distributed (because of low price of

items and hence subsidy burden), at least APL card has to be ensured for all, so that there is no case of cardlessness in the state. To assess the households for selection in the BPL and Antyodaya category, the basis has to be 'Arthik Register' and 'Revenue Register'.

- The Gram Pradhans have to be trained about their duties and responsibilities once every year in the line of the 73rd and 74th Amendments of the Constitution.
- There has to be a Food Bank at the level of the village (Panchayat) so that no news of death from hunger comes. For this, a community hall has to be constructed, if it is not there already, in each village having at least 50 households covering all hamlets. If the villages are small by number of households, a cluster of neighbouring villages should be covered for having such a community hall. The maintenance of the community hall will be the responsibility of the PRIs.
- The households must be allowed to draw quota/items in installments, and hence pay in installments. In case these poor households cannot pay for the time being, food coupon has to be given to the households so that they can buy at their time.

The book takes the basic assumption that national food self-sufficiency by production and presence of food in the economy or in the market does not automatically ensure food security. Even the ability to buy may not guarantee food security of the poor unless it is accompanied by a functioning distribution system. The public distribution system as a social safety net can be appreciated by the fact that aggregate availability of foodgrains *per se* is not enough to ensure the ability of people at the bottom to buy foodgrains. The book concludes that the state intervention through public distribution of essential commodities for direct consumption particularly aimed at the poor will expectedly ensure the access of the poor to these commodities. While we accept in principle universalization of access to essential commodities through state support, for a number of reasons in a large populated country like India it may not be feasible. Thus, we argued in favour of implementation of targeted PDS by exclusion of the non-poor from the social safety net. It remains ultimately doubtful if at all the targeting in principle and actual listing in the villages in India serve the same vulnerable sections. This is where the continuous re-evaluation of the TPDS as a programme is needed.

Bibliography

Ahluwalia, M.S. (1996). 'New Economic Policy and Agriculture: Some Reflections', *Indian Journal of Agricultural Economics*, Vol. 51, No. 3, July-September.

Balakrishnan, P. (1999). 'Agricultural Growth and Economic Welfare since 1991,' Paper presented in the Foundation Day Seminar on 'Rural Prosperity and Agriculture: Strategies and Policies for the Next Millennium', November 4-5, National Institute of Rural Development, Hyderabad, India.

Balakrishnan, P. and Ramaswami, B. (2000). 'Analysing Public Intervention in the Foodgrains Markets', Krishnaji, N. and Krishnan, T.N. (ed), Public Support for Food Security, *The Public Distribution System in India*, Sage Publications, New Delhi.

Chatterjee, P.K. (1995). 'Emerging Perspectives of Agricultural Development in India', *Indian Journal of Agricultural Economics*, Vol. 50, No. 3, July-September.

Claffey, Barbara A. and Stucker, Thomas A. (1982). 'The Food Stamp Program', in Hadwiger Don, F. and Talbot Ross, B. *Food Policy and Farm Programs*, New York.

Clay, Edward (1981). 'Food Policy Issues in Low-Income Countries', *World Bank Staff Working Paper No. 473*, Washington D.C.

Dandekar, V.M. (1994). *The Indian Economy, 1947-92*, Vol. I, (Agriculture). Sage Publications, New Delhi.

Dantwala, M.L. (1993). 'Agricultural Policy: Prices and Public Distribution System', *Indian Journal of Agricultural Economics*, Vol. 48, No. 2, April-June.

Dev, S. Mahendra (2000). 'Food Security with Emphasis on PDS vs EGS: A Tale of Two States', in Krishnaji, N. and Krishnan, T.N.(ed), *Public Support for Food Security, The Public Distribution System in India*, Sage Publications, New Delhi.

Dev, S. Mahendra and Ranade, Ajit (1997). 'Poverty and Public Policy, A Mixed Record', Parikh, Kirit S. (Ed), *India Development Report, 1997*, Oxford University Press, Delhi.

Dreze, J. (1990). 'Famine Prevention in India', in Dreze, J. and Sen, A. (ed), *The Political Economy of Hunger,* Vol. 2, Clarendon Press, Oxford.

Dreze, J. and Sen, A. (1989) *Hunger and Public Action*, Clarendon Press, Oxford.

Food and Agriculture Organization of the United Nations (1987). *Agricultural Price Policies: Issues and Proposals*, Rome.

Ghose, Ajit Kumar (1999). 'Food Supply and Starvation: A Study of Famines with Reference to the Indian Sub-Continent', in Dreze, Jean (ed), *The Economics of Famine*, Edward Elgar Pub. Ltd., U.K.

Government of India, Ministry of Agriculture and Irrigation (1976). *Report of the National Commission on Agriculture, Part I and Part II*, New Delhi.

Government of India, Ministry of Finance, (1991-08), *Economic Survey*, New Delhi.

Hopkins, Raymond F., (1982) 'Food Policymaking', in Hadwiger Don, F. and Talbot, Ross B., *Food Policy and Farm Programs*, New York.

Institute of Social Sciences, (2000). *Status of Panchayati Raj in the States and Union Territories of India*, Concept Publishing Co., New Delhi.

International Labour Office (ILO), (2000). *World Labour Report*, Geneva.

Janvry, Alain De and Subbarao, K. (1986). *Agricultural Price Policy and Income Distribution in India*, Oxford University Press, Delhi.

Johl, S.S. (1995). 'Agriculture Sector and NEP', *Indian Journal of Agricultural Economics,* Vol. 50, No. 3, July-September.

Kashyap, S.P. 2002, 'Food and Livelihood Security Concerns for Rural India', in Acharya, S.S. *et al.* (ed), *Sustainable Agriculture, Poverty and Food Security*, Vol. 2, Rawat Publication, Jaipur.

Khusro, A.M. (1973). *Buffer Stocks and Storage of Foodgrains in India*, Tata McGraw-Hill Pub. Co., Bombay-New Delhi.

Lappe, F.M. and Collins, J. (1977). *Food First, The Myth of Scarcity*, Souvenir Press (E&A) Ltd., London.

Majumder, Bhaskar (1998). 'Commodity Production and Command Differential: Implications for Economic Development', *Productivity*, Vol. 38, No. 4, January-March.

———— (1999). 'Liberalization of Indian Agriculture: Implications for the Home Market for Foodgrains', in Roychoudhury, K.C., and Singh, R.P. (ed), *Rural Prosperity and Agriculture: Policies and Strategies*, National Institute of Rural Development, Hyderabad, India.

———— (1999). 'Liberalization of Indian Agriculture: The Relevance of Public Intervention in the Market for Foodgrains', *IASSI Quarterly*, Vol. 17, No. 4 April-June.

———— (2004). *Poverty, Food Security and Sustainability*, Rawat Publications, Jaipur.

Meenakshi, J.V. (2000). 'Food Consumption Trends in India: A Regional Analysis', in Krishnaji, N. and Krishnan, T.N. (ed.), *Public Support for*

Food Security, The Public Distribution System in India, Sage Publication, New Delhi.

Mellor, John W. and Desai, Gunvant M. ((1986). 'Agricultural Change and Rural Poverty: A Synthesis', in Mellor, John W. and Desai, Gunvant M. (ed), *Agricultural Change and Rural Poverty*, Oxford University Press, Delhi.

Mooij, Jos, 1999, *Food Policy and the Indian State, The Public Distribution System in South India'*, Oxford University Press, Delhi.

Narayana, N.S.S., Parikh, Kirit S., Srinivasan, T.N. (1991). *Agriculture, Growth and Redistribution of Income*, North-Holland in Association with Allied Publishers Ltd., New Delhi.

Pearse, Andrew (1980) *Seeds of Plenty, Seeds of Want, Social and Economic Implications of the Green Revolution*, Clarendon Press, Oxford.

Planning Commission, GOI, *Tenth Five Year Plan,* 2002-07, Vol. II.

Platteau, Jean-Philippe (1990). 'The Food Crisis in Africa: A Comparative Structural Analysis', in Dreze, J. and Sen, A (ed), *The Political Economy of Hunger*, Vol. 2, Clarendon Press, Oxford.

Rajiv Gandhi Foundation (2000). *Panchayati Raj in India, Status Report* 1999, March, New Delhi.

Rangarajan, L.N., (ed) (1992). *Kautilya, The Arthashastra*, Penguin Books.

Rao, V.M. (1996). 'Policy Research for Liberalized Agriculture: Some Illustrated Research Areas', *Indian Journal of Agricultural Economics*, Vol. 51, Nos. 1&2, January-June.

Savy, Robert (1972). *Social Security in Agriculture and Rural Areas*, International Labour Office, Geneva.

Storm, Servass (1997). 'Trade Liberalization, the Terms of Trade and Agricultural Growth: The example of India', in Bhaduri, A. and Skartein, R. (ed), *Economic Development and Agricultural Productivity*, Edward Elgar, U.K.

Suryanarayana, M.H. (1999). 'Poverty, Food Insecurity and Levels of Living: Maharashtra', *Journal of Indian School of Political Economy*, Vol. XI, No. 1, January-March.

Suryanarayana, M.H. (2000) 'Food Security and Calorie Adequacy Across States: Implications for Reform', in Krishnaji, N., and Krishnan, T.N. (ed), *Public Support for Food Security, The Public Distribution System in India*, Sage Publication, New Delhi.

The Hindu, 2000, October. 1, Sunday.

Zhang-Yue Zhou and Gandhi Vasant P. (2002). 'The Role of Public Food Distribution System in the Strategy for Food Security of the Poor: A Comparison of Indian and Chinese Experiences', in Acharya, S.S., Singh, Surjit and Sagar, Vidya (ed), *Sustainable Agriculture, Poverty and Food Security*, Vol. 2, Rawat Publications, Jaipur and New Delhi.

Index